Globalization and Language Teaching

'This book represents a major theoretical and empirical statement on the impact of globalization on language policies and practice around the world. It addresses diverse and complex questions on the subject from a variety of perspectives, and in a broad and richly comprehensive manner . . . An invaluable resource.'

David Nunan, University of Hong Kong

Language is a vital commodity in the globalized world. The services- and information-based economy makes increasing demands on workers' language skills; new technologies and media change the cultural landscape; migration produces more linguistically diverse populations worldwide.

These developments change the conditions in which languages are learned and taught. *Globalization and Language Teaching* considers the issues globalization raises for second language learning and teaching. Drawing together various strands in the globalization debate, this rich collection combines theory with case studies, exploring concerns that range from literacy to bilingualism and from identity to the internet.

This is an invaluable resource for anyone involved in language teaching or with an interest in the effects of globalization.

Contributors: David Block, Deborah Cameron, A. Suresh Canagarajah, John Gray, Roxy Harris, Monica Heller, Claire Kramsch, Ryuko Kubota, Constant Leung, Ben Rampton, Steven L. Thorne, Catherine Wallace.

David Block is Lecturer in Languages in Education at the Institute of Education, University of London. **Deborah Cameron** is Professor of Languages in Education at the Institute of Education, University of London.

Globalization and Language Teaching

Edited by David Block
and Deborah Cameron

London and New York

First published 2002
by Routledge
2 Park Square, Milton Park, Abingdon, Oxon, OX14 4RN

Simultaneously published in the USA and Canada
by Routledge
270 Madison Ave, New York NY 10016

Reprinted 2008

Routledge is an imprint of the Taylor & Francis Group, an informa business

Transferred to Digital Printing 2005

Typeset in Perpetua by M Rules
Printed and bound in Great Britain by MPG Books Ltd, Bodmin

British Library Cataloguing in Publication Data
A catalogue record for this book is available from the British Library

Library of Congress Cataloging in Publication Data
Globalization and language teaching/edited by David Block and Deborah
Cameron.
    p.   cm.
Includes bibliographical references (p.) and index.
Contents: The impact of globalization on language teaching in Japan/Ryuko
Kubota – Globalization, diaspora, and language education in England/Roxy
Harris, Constant Leung, and Ben Rampton – Globalization and the
commodification of bilingualism in Canada/Monica Heller – Globalization
and the teaching of 'communication skills'/Deborah Cameron – Foreign
language learning as global communicative practice/Claire Kramsch and
Steven L. Thorne – Local literacies and global literacy/Catherine Wallace –
'McCommunication': a problem in the frame for SLA/David Block –
Globalization, methods, and practices in periphery classrooms/
A. Suresh Canagarajah – The global coursebook in English Language
Teaching/John Gray.
    1. Language and languages – Study and teaching – Economic aspects. 2.
Language teachers – Training of. 3. Second language acquisition.
I. Block, David, 1956– II. Cameron, Deborah, 1958–

PR53.G545   2001
418'.0071–dc21   2001040367

ISBN 10: 0–415–24275–4 (hbk)
ISBN 10: 0–415–24276–2 (pbk)
ISBN 13: 978–0–415–24275–2 (hbk)
ISBN 13: 978–0–415–24276–9 (pbk)

Contents

PART III   **115**
Methods and materials

Tables

Contributors

David Block is Lecturer in Languages in Education at the Institute of Education, University of London.

Deborah Cameron is Professor of Languages in Education at the Institute of Education, University of London.

A. Suresh Canagarajah is Associate Professor in the Department of English, Baruch College of the City University of New York.

John Gray is Lecturer in TEFL at Queen's University Belfast.

Roxy Harris is Lecturer in the School of Education, King's College, London.

Monica Heller is Professor in the Centre de récherches en education franco-ontarienne, Ontario Institute for Studies in Education, University of Toronto.

Claire Kramsch is Professor of German and Foreign Language Acquisition at the University of California at Berkeley.

Ryuko Kubota is Associate Professor in the School of Education, University of North Carolina at Chapel Hill.

Constant Leung is Senior Lecturer in the School of Education, King's College, London.

Ben Rampton is Reader in the School of Education, King's College, London.

Steven L. Thorne is Associate Director of the Center for Language Acquisition, Pennsylvania State University.

Catherine Wallace is Senior Lecturer in Languages in Education at the Institute of Education, University of London.

Acknowledgements

We wish to thank all the contributors to this book, not only for the high quality of their contributions but also for their efficiency, their promptness and their patience. We would also like to thank our colleagues and students, past and present, at the Institute of Education. We are particularly indebted to those who participated in a day conference held in 1999, organized by Catherine Wallace, to mark the fiftieth anniversary of the MA TESOL; this book is not a record of the conference, but it does explore many of its themes. Finally, we are grateful to Lorna Carsley for assistance in producing the typescript, and to the editorial staff at Routledge for their support throughout this project.

Introduction

David Block and Deborah Cameron

Globalization is nothing if not a fashionable term – it pervades contemporary polit-ical rhetoric and is a keyword of both academic and popular discourse on economy, society, technology and culture. In languages as diverse as Japanese and Spanish, the word exists in cognate form – as *gurôbarizêshon* and *globalización*, respectively – and where it does not (e.g. the French term *mondialisation*), it is still understood, in Giddens's (1990: 64) terms, as 'the intensification of worldwide social relations which link distant localities in such a way that local happenings are shaped by events occurring many miles away and vice versa'; or in Malcolm Waters's terms as '*a social process in which the constraints of geography on social and cultural arrangements recede and in which people become increasingly aware that they are receding*' (1995: 3, emphasis in original).

Any invocation of 'worldwide social relations' unfettered by 'the constraints of geography' must immediately raise questions about *language*. Language is the pri-mary medium of human social interaction, and interaction is the means through which social relations are constructed and maintained. While much everyday inter-action still occurs, as it has throughout human history, within local networks, large numbers of people all over the world now also participate in networks which go beyond the local. New communication technologies enable individuals to have reg-ular exchanges with distant others whom they have never met face-to-face. Even more people participate vicariously in the social and cultural arrangements of remote others through their consumption of new media such as satellite television. Members of international political and business elites spend an increasing propor-tion of their time interacting with one another at gatherings whose physical location in Rome, Seattle or Tokyo is largely irrelevant to the way transactions are conducted.

Distance is not an issue for these non-local networks, but language remains an issue of some practical importance: global communication requires not only a shared channel (like the internet or video conferencing) but also a shared *linguistic* code. For many participants in global exchanges, the relevant code(s) will have been learned rather than natively acquired. In many contexts, then, the 'intensification of worldwide social relations' also intensifies the need for members of global networks to develop competence in one or more additional languages, and/or to master new ways of using languages they know already. At the same time, globalization changes the conditions in which language learning and language teaching take place.

These observations provide the starting point for this book. Below, we will examine the implications of globalization for language learning and teaching in more detail. First, though, we must look more closely at what globalization means in general terms, and explore some of the debates that surround it – for in addition to being a fashionable term, *globalization* is a highly contested one.

Globalization: a brief survey

Although there seems to be a consensus that we are living in an increasingly globalized world, it is not clear exactly when globalization, as it is presently understood, actually started. While Kilminster (1997: 257) maintains that the word first appeared in Webster's Dictionary in 1961, Roland Robertson (1992), considered by many to be the originator of the term, argues that globalization is in fact a pre-modern phenomenon. He traces its beginnings to fifteenth century Europe when the nation-state was born, the Catholic Church began to spread worldwide and explorers began to map the planet and colonize the world. Elsewhere, Anthony Giddens (1990) suggests origins in the seventeenth century, while Robert Cox (1996) argues that globalization effectively began after the first major fuel crisis of 1973. In Cox's view, it was at this time that the developed capitalist states began to abandon

> . . . the Fordist mode of production . . . which had been based on a well-paid labor force able to buy its own products and protected by institutionalized collective bargaining and by redistributive state policies acting as an economic stabilizer . . . [in favor of] strategies [which] emphasized a weakening of trade union power, cutting of state budgets (especially for social policy), deregulation, privatization, and priority to international competitiveness
>
> (Cox 1996: 22)

Apart from the debate on whether globalization has been going on for thirty years or 500, there is debate on how far it represents an achieved reality. For some commentators it is essentially a 'done deal'; for others an exaggerated or even fabricated phenomenon. As Anthony Giddens (2000) points out, these polarized views are generally held by authors who place economics at the heart of their analysis. Thus, while Kenichi Ohmae (1990, 1995) argues that global market forces and transnational corporations run the world today, and that the nation-state and labour unions have become obsolete as structures of social organization, Paul Hirst and Grahame Thompson (1996/9) adopt what they call an attitude of 'moderate scepticism', arguing that it is too early to write off such structures and that globalization is not as developed or extended as writers like Ohmae would have us think. More overt sceptics, such as Paul Smith (1997) and Eric Hobsbaum (1994) argue that capitalism has always been globally oriented. The significant change that has occurred in recent years is that the diffusion of capitalism has accelerated, because of the fall of communism and because of technological advances enabling faster and more efficient communication.

Most sociologists and social theorists take a view that falls between the two extremes described above. They accept that 'globalization' names a real phenomenon, something which differentiates the present from the more distant past, but they also recognize that the process is not complete and has not been experienced in the same way everywhere (see e.g. Albrow 1996; Beck 1992, 2000; Giddens 1990, 2000; Held *et al.* 1999; Nash 2000; Robertson 1992; Tomlinson 1999).

Another area of debate and disagreement concerns the extent to which globalization should be regarded as a homogenizing process. While some commentators view it as promoting an extreme of standardization and uniformity (Gray 1998; Ritzer 1998), others introduce into the discussion concepts such as *hybridization* (Pieterse 1995) and *glocalization* (Robertson 1995) to make the point that globalization entails a synergetic relationship between the global and the local as opposed to the dominance of the former over the latter. Connected to the issue of homogenization is the issue of the geopolitical origins of globalizing forces. While some see globalization as hegemonically Western, and above all as an extension of American imperialism (e.g. Ritzer 1998; Schiller 1985), others make the point that the process is more dispersed than this argument implies (Friedman 1994; Robertson, 1992) and that it is unhelpful to frame the discussion in terms of Western dominance over 'the rest'.

Arising from such debates about Western hegemony and the relative strength of the local is the question of whether globalization is on balance a 'positive' or a 'negative' phenomenon. Gray (1998) sees the new globalized economy in the form of the Washington Consensus (i.e. the post-Fordist scenario described by Cox, quoted above) as fundamentally destructive, leading above all to the dismantling of the welfare state characteristic of the world's most advanced industrial countries in the second half of the twentieth century. Ritzer's account (1996, 1998) is equally dystopic: he paints a picture of a homogenized global culture of consumption, leading to a soulless and 'disenchanted' existence where commodified experiences replace authentic experience. Similarly, Benjamin Barber argues that we are heading towards a single global culture, which he calls 'McWorld', defined as 'an entertainment shopping experience that brings together malls, multiplex movie theatres, theme parks, spectator sports arenas, fast food chains (with their endless movie tie-ins) and television (with its burgeoning shopping networks) into a single vast enterprise' (Barber 1995: 97). Latouche (1996: 3) writes about the 'westernization of the world' and the progressive 'worldwide standardization of lifestyles'. For Latouche, a fundamentally Western ideology and culture, best exemplified by the modern United States, is becoming the norm around the world. There is a creeping uniformity in all aspects of our lives, from how we dress to how we eat, from our entertainment preferences to our work habits and from the design of our buildings to our attitudes towards personal freedom.

On the positive side, we find economists such as Ohmae (1990, 1995), as well as social theorists such as Beck (1992, 2000) and Giddens (1990, 2000). These authors seem to revel in the excitement and challenge of life in what Giddens calls the 'runaway world' of late modern times. For Beck and Giddens, globalization does bring with it some negative consequences such as increasing economic inequality and the growing possibility of environmental disaster; at the same time, where there is risk there is opportunity. Individuals are not the dupes of overpowering social structures and events, but active, reflective agents in the ongoing construction of social reality. As Giddens (2000: 19) expresses it:

> Many of us feel in the grip of forces over which we have no power. Can we reimpose our will upon them? I believe we can. The powerlessness we experience is not a sign of personal failings, but reflects the incapacities of our institutions. We need to reconstruct those we have, or create new ones. For globalization is not incidental to our lives today. It is a shift in our very life circumstances. It is the way we now live.

For Giddens and others who share his views, globalization is a fact of life which we cannot ignore. Rather than dreaming of a return to the past, we should engage with the new, post-traditional order, forging new identities, institutions and ways of life.

Globalization is seen by some authors as coterminous with postmodernism, while others reject this equation. This debate is particularly salient for those social theorists who examine questions of cultural identity – what it means to be of a particular nationality, ethnic group, religious tradition or sexual preference. One example of a postmodern approach to identity is to be found in the work of Mathews (2000). While acknowledging that 'nationally shaped cultures of societies such as Japan, China and the USA do indeed exist' (Mathews, 2000: 4), he suggests that there is a sense in which the most affluent 10 or 15 per cent of the world's population wander through a 'cultural supermarket', choosing, albeit in a highly conditioned way, the identities they perform within their social worlds (2000: 5–6). Elsewhere, Giddens, who rejects the term 'postmodernity', preferring instead 'late modernity', extends the notion of choice in identity construction beyond the elites cited by Mathews. For Giddens, the breakdown of tradition in many parts of the world along with increasing access to information has made it possible for those at the bottom of the social ladder to reflexively construct their own identities. The poor and dispossessed may lack access to the range of possibilities on display in the cultural supermarket, but for them, too, identity construction is a reflexive process drawing on whatever resources are available.

In the foregoing discussion we have drawn attention to a set of debates about globalization, and to the interrelated themes – economics, culture, identity, politics and technology – around which debates are commonly organized. At this point, we turn to consider in more detail how the arguments discussed above relate to the subject of this book, namely the implications of globalization for language learning and teaching.

Globalization and language teaching

We noted above that globalization changes the conditions under which language learning takes place. In this sphere as in others, some of the most significant changes are economic. People have always learned languages for economic reasons, but in a post-industrial economy it has been argued that the linguistic skills of workers at all levels take on new importance (Cameron 2000; Cope and Kalantzis 2000; Gee *et al.* 1996). 'Communication skills' and the new literacies demanded by new technologies, as well as competence in one or more second/foreign languages, all represent valuable 'linguistic capital', to use Pierre Bourdieu's (1991) term. Some commentators have suggested (e.g. Heller 1999a) that languages are coming to be treated more and more as economic commodities, and that this view is displacing traditional ideologies in which languages were primarily symbols of ethnic or national identity. The commodification of language affects both people's motivations for learning languages and their choices about which languages to learn. It also affects the choices made by institutions (local and national, public and private) as they allocate resources for language education.

Technological change is connected to economic change, since the operation of global markets depends on the rapid information flows made possible by new information and communication technologies. But the effects of technological change are not confined to the economic sphere: they are also seen in the development of new cultural forms and the popularity of new leisure activities (e.g. visiting on-line 'chat rooms'). Education, too, is increasingly affected by the advent of new technologies and media. These are having a significant impact on second language teaching (Warschauer and Kern 2000), and in the process raising questions about the potential of technology to radically change the experience of learning languages.

Finally, changing political conditions raise important questions for language teaching professionals. Since the early 1990s issues of linguistic imperialism have been much debated, especially in relation to English language teaching (Canagarajah 1999a; Holborow 1999; Pennycook 1994, 1998; Phillipson 1992). As we noted above, though, there are conflicting views among analysts as to whether globalization represents an extension of Western, and particularly USA, geopolitical dominance, or whether it destabilizes the old order, opening up new possibilities for local resistance on the part of subaltern groups. This general question can also be posed more specifically in relation to the politics of language: how far does globalization change the terms in which we debate issues of language and power?

It is evident that the questions raised by globalization for language teaching are both diverse and complex. No single volume can cover the whole terrain, but in this collection we have tried to avoid too narrow a focus. We have included contributions dealing with the teaching of languages other than English; those that do deal with English language teaching locate it in a variety of social and cultural contexts (though of course, these represent only a small part of a much larger and more varied picture). We have not excluded discussions of the way globalization is affecting the kinds of instruction given to *first* language users. And we have made no attempt to limit the diversity of viewpoints represented by contributors. Our aim is not to advance a single thesis, but to show how broader debates on the meaning and significance of globalization are taken up and carried forward in the field of applied linguistics.

The nine chapters that follow are organized thematically, in three parts. The chapters in the first part, 'The global and the local', examine the implications of globalization for language teaching in three different national contexts – Japan, England and Canada. Ryuko Kubota (Chapter 1) discusses the teaching of both English and Japanese in Japan's schools, and also touches on the teaching of Japanese as a second language. Roxy Harris, Constant Leung and Ben Rampton (Chapter 2) focus on the teaching of English as an additional language to members of bilingual diasporic communities in England. Monica Heller (Chapter 3), writing about Canada – the only officially bilingual nation among the three – is particularly concerned with the role and the teaching of French.

Why begin with these national case-studies? It is often claimed that globalization, as a *trans*national phenomenon, tends to weaken the nation-state as an economic and political entity, yet the nation-state clearly continues to exert significant influence in many areas of its inhabitants' experience, including their experience as users and learners of languages. Although the nature and extent of state involvement varies considerably between nations, both language and education are areas where, in modern times, agents of the nation-state have typically played a major role in planning and policy. Globalization does not make that role superfluous. On the contrary, global developments, particularly in the economic sphere, are still perceived as putting *national* interests at stake, and therefore as demanding a coordinated national response. But any such response must inevitably be affected by the particularities of history, culture and politics; the interplay between 'global' and 'local' considerations produces different outcomes in different places. By examining three contrasting cases in detail, contributors to this section collectively illustrate the important point that national differences, the histories they arise from and the conflicts they engender are not rendered insignificant by globalization. At the same time, all three chapters suggest that globalization does shift the terms in which we conceptualize 'the nation' and the role of language in defining it.

Globalization leads to patterns of movement across national borders that produce increasingly diverse populations within them, and this may put in question traditional representations of the 'imagined community' of the nation (Anderson 1983). Historically, for example in both Japan and francophone Canada, discourses of nationhood and national identity have relied heavily (though differently) on the idea of a distinctive ethnic 'Japanese-ness' or 'French Canadian-ness'. But this version of nationhood becomes problematic when there are significant numbers of French-speaking Canadians with roots in the Caribbean or francophone Africa, or when Japan's population includes a rising proportion of people of non-Japanese origin. Migration, though in itself hardly a novelty, is – for some communities at least – a rather different experience today than it was a century ago. In England, the continuing and relatively intense interaction between diasporic communities and ancestral communities elsewhere in the world – made easier by the communication technologies that accompany globalization – makes possible plural or hybrid identities, challenging the assumption that people must identify with a single imagined community.

In England and Japan, national education systems have responded to new conditions for the most part by ignoring them. Provision for the teaching of English as an additional language in England continues to be based on simplistic and conservative assumptions about the nature and meaning of bilingualism in contemporary societies. The Japanese discourse of *kokusaika* – 'internationalization' – looks outward to the West rather than inward to the growing social and linguistic diversity of Japan itself. 'If you dream in English, you are an international person', says the graffito in the Tokyo subway. Dreaming in Korean or Portuguese, languages spoken by significant minorities in Japan, does not have the same meaning.

This is related to another consequence of globalization, the tendency to treat languages as economic commodities. In the linguistic commodity market, English has higher value than Korean or Portuguese: Kubota observes that in Japan, the phrase 'foreign language' is frequently used as if it *meant* 'English'. Monica Heller reminds us, however, that English is not the only linguistic commodity with an exchange value on the global market. French is also an international language, and in the context of linguistic commodification this has implications for the meaning and status of French–English bilingualism in Canada. Bilingualism itself becomes a commodity: individuals who command two languages are attractive to businesses competing in multiple, or multilingual, markets. But the bilingualism such businesses value is not the kind traditionally observed in francophone communities – rather it is effectively 'double monolingualism'. The French that is cultivated for its economic advantages is not the same (local vernacular) French that was and is a marker of ethnicity and community.

As Heller points out, language issues do not become less political because they are discussed in terms of economics. Struggles between ethnolinguistic groups in Canada always were ultimately about economic resources. As bilingualism becomes a more valued economic commodity, access to French and education in French becomes another resource for which groups compete. At the same time, older nationalist discourses have not simply disappeared. Ryuko Kubota, too, shows that in Japan, the ideology of *kokusaika* coexists with an overtly nationalist and essentialist discourse on Japanese language and culture. English is seen, among other things, as a vehicle through which the uniqueness of Japan and its people may be explained to the rest of the world.

The three national case-studies illustrate something of the complexity of the relationship between 'global' and 'local', and the varying impact globalization may have on language and language education in different local conditions. The second part, 'Zones of contact', also examines the global/local dichotomy, but from a different angle. Its three chapters examine sites or domains where language users and language learners attempt to communicate *across* national and other borders, inspired often by the rhetoric according to which globalization and the associated communication technologies make possible a new kind of more direct and more equal exchange between individuals who are both different and distant from one another. The focus in this part is less on language as code (English, French, Japanese, etc.) than on issues of medium, genre and style. Contributors show that these are in fact key issues for language teaching in an age of global communication.

Deborah Cameron (Chapter 4) examines the discourse on 'communication skills' which increasingly informs the teaching of spoken language to both first and second language users. She argues that what is emerging is a global ideology of 'effective communication', instantiated not in the use of any particular language, but rather in particular genres and styles of speaking. The favoured genres and styles may be adopted without adopting the code they are, in fact, associated with (a particular kind of American English). This, Cameron suggests, is not unlike the kind of liberal multiculturalism (much in vogue among new global capitalists) which holds that 'we're all the same under the skin'. On the surface there are (still) many different languages, but under the banner of 'effective communication', all become vehicles for the expression of similar values and the enactment of similar subjectivities.

Cyberspace is frequently invoked as a 'zone of contact' where distant/different individuals may 'meet' on equal terms, and language teachers are increasingly exploiting the opportunities it seems to offer for real and meaningful interaction between learners and native speakers. In a close analysis of some computer-mediated exchanges between USA college students and their peers in France, however, Claire Kramsch and Steven Thorne (Chapter 5) show that this kind of communication is rendered problematic by differences which manifest themselves not at the surface level of the linguistic code, but at the deeper level of genre. What causes difficulty in an exchange about social conditions in the suburbs of French cities is not the inability of the USA students to express themselves intelligibly in French (or of the French students to do likewise in English), so much as their different but unnoticed assumptions about the kind of exchange they are having, and the social roles and relationships entailed by such an exchange. In their attempts to find common ground with distant others, the Americans do not recognize the cultural specificity of the very assumption that 'finding common ground' is the overriding goal of interaction with people different from oneself. Nor does either party fully recognize the specific effects and demands of the medium they are using.

For Catherine Wallace (Chapter 6), the idea of finding common ground on which to conduct global exchanges is less problematic. Her chapter presents a critical view of the tendency for politically committed researchers and teachers of language and literacy to respond to what are seen as the oppressive and dehumanizing effects of globalization by valorizing the local – community languages, vernacular literacies, personal modes of speech – over supralocal, schooled and public forms of speech and writing. Wallace does not question the intrinsic value of the local, but she suggests that if there is to be effective resistance to new, globally organized forms of domination, language users and language learners must also have access to a 'syncretic' language capable of facilitating critical, public exchange across widely dispersed communities. She proposes 'literate English', a way of using English which is rooted in the conventions of educated writing, though it may also be deployed in speech, as a good candidate for this role. In a world where a majority of users of English are not native speakers, and where most learners are not motivated by the need to get things done in face-to-face encounters with native speakers, Wallace argues that English language teaching should be less preoccupied with learners' ability to engage in informal spoken interaction and more interested in developing 'literate English'.

Wallace is more optimistic than either Cameron or Kramsch and Thorne about the potential for global interaction to be conducted on terms of linguistic and cultural equality. For Cameron, the norms which are held to define 'effective communication' are covertly those of a specific, Anglophone sociocultural milieu – a point that remains salient even if the relevant norms are being taught in Japanese. Kramsch and Thorne's analysis focuses primarily on national *differences*, but one might well think that the conflicting assumptions of the USA and the French students are not just 'different but equal': the USA ones are likely to have wider currency and legitimacy, given the massive global diffusion of USA cultural products.

An analogous debate is carried on in the last part, 'Methods and materials', which deals more directly with questions of language pedagogy. David Block (Chapter 7) and A. Suresh Canagarajah (Chapter 8) are both concerned with the issue of method, but their arguments are in sharp contrast. Block observes that the rapid information flows which are characteristic of global formations create favourable conditions for the wide dissemination, not just of information but of 'frames' for conceptualizing complex phenomena. One such frame, he suggests, is the notion of communication as information exchange that underpins currently influential theories in SLA, and the associated method, task based language teaching. The consequence of framing communication in this way, Block argues, is that language teaching becomes part of the rationalizing and standardizing tendency

George Ritzer (1996) has dubbed 'McDonaldization'. Concepts such as 'task' and 'negotiation for meaning', which originate in a US-dominated international community of expert SLA researchers, form the basis for recommendations on method which are taken to have universal applicability. In Block's view, however, the notion of communication that underlies them is both culturally specific and insufficiently complex to capture important aspects of language learning.

'McDonaldization' is presented by Ritzer as carrying the rational technicist logic of modernity to new extremes; adherents of the 'McDonaldization' thesis dispute that globalization implies a shift towards a 'postmodern condition' in opposition to that logic. Canagarajah inclines more to the alternative view. In the domain of language teaching, the postmodern condition is also the 'post-method' condition, in which the adoption of a particular method has ceased to be regarded as the solution to all problems, and there is no longer a one-way flow of expertise from centre to periphery. This opens up new opportunities for the expertise of language teachers in periphery contexts to be recognized and valued. The demise of 'method' also makes it more feasible for teachers to acknowledge and work with the diversity of the learners in their classrooms, guided by local assessments of students' strategies for learning rather than by global directives from remote authorities.

It is often observed that discussions of method have an 'academic' quality, not only because they are conducted among academics, but also because, in the real world of the classroom, teachers' decisions are influenced by multiple factors: their practice seldom exemplifies a specific method in its pure or paradigmatic form. One real-world constraint on teachers is the kind of teaching materials available to them, and this is the topic addressed by John Gray (Chapter 9). Gray investigates the 'global coursebook', a kind of text designed to be used in English language teaching worldwide. Drawing on research with producers as well as users, Gray explores the peculiar worldview presented in many best-selling ELT coursebooks, and explains the contradictory pressures that give rise to it. He also suggests that in this case, the imperatives of the market combined with the capabilities of new technology seem more likely to increase diversity than homogeneity. Coursebooks could become 'glocal', with a generic formula being customized for different local or regional markets. Such a development would not displease the EFL teachers Gray interviewed in Catalonia, who spoke of their desire to 'build bridges' between the world of English and the world their students live in. Is 'glocalization' an opportunity for the local empowerment of teachers and students? Or is it merely an instance of contemporary capitalism's surrogate for power, namely increased consumer choice?

As we have already observed, this volume offers no single, simple thesis concerning the effects of globalization on language teaching. What we are dealing with is not an achieved state but an ongoing process of change, whose effects are complex and locally variable, and whose consequences continue to be debated. The analyses that follow are intended above all to inform future debate among scholars and practitioners by reflecting this complexity.

Part I
The global and the local

1 The impact of globalization on language teaching in Japan

Ryuko Kubota

Globalization implies increased local diversity influenced by human contact across cultural boundaries as well as speedy exchange of commodities and information. Japan is no exception to this trend: in 1999, over sixteen million Japanese people travelled out of Japan and close to five million non-Japanese people entered Japan (Ministry of Justice 2000a). The number of non-Japanese residents in Japan is larger than ever before. Reflecting an ethnic boom, a variety of ethnic foods is readily available at restaurants in Japanese cities.

While globalization projects the image of diversity, it also implies cultural homogenization influenced by global standardization of economic activities and a flow of cultural goods from the centre to the periphery. This tendency is related to Americanization, or 'the diffusion of American values, consumer goods and lifestyles' (Friedman 1994: 195). Cities in Japan have many American franchise stores and fast-food restaurants. These commodities could also arouse people's desire to identify themselves with Americans (particularly with whites). This desire is manifested in a statement made by Den Fujita, President and Chief Executive of McDonald's Japan, in the 1970s. He told reporters, 'If we eat McDonald's hamburgers and potatoes for a thousand years, we will become taller, our skin will become white, and our hair blonde' (Love 1986: 426). Furthermore, Americanization has been promoted by the discourse of *kokusaika* or 'internationalization'. Fujita stated in the mid-1980s that hamburgers were the 'international commodity' and that the Japanese could initiate internationalization by eating hamburgers (McDonald's Japan 2000). The transformation of skin and hair colours by eating hamburgers sounds quite absurd, but in fact, one can easily find blonde Japanese young men and women in the street at the turn of the century.[1]

The other side of globalization is increased nationalism. More and more Japanese flags are displayed in public spaces. A 1998 bestseller, Yoshinori Kobayashi's comic book, *Sensôron* (Theory of wars), justified Japanese military aggression in Asia during Japanese imperialism. The paradoxical nature of globalization is indeed recognized by globalization theorists. Appadurai (1990: 295) notes that '[t]he central problem of today's global interactions is the tension between cultural homogenization and cultural heterogenization'. Similarly, Friedman (1994: 102) states, 'Ethnic and cultural fragmentation and modernist homogenization are ... two constitutive trends of global reality'.

This chapter conceptualizes the tension of globalization in language learning and teaching in Japan as constituting three corners of a triangle: (1) ethnic, linguistic, and cultural diversity in the local communities; (2) the prevalence of English; and (3) nationalism endorsed by linguistic and cultural essentialism. These three elements can be conceptualized in different ways. The first and second dimensions tend to threaten national identity and stimulate the third dimension, nationalism, as resistance to Anglicization and diversity. The second and third dimensions represent a form of convergence to a certain norm, while the first dimension represents divergence from the existing norm. These three dimensions also present contradictions. For instance, the increased local diversity, which requires people to affirm pluralism, is not compatible with convergence to the American norm. Also, as discussed later, nationalistic views are sometimes promoted by using a Western mode of communication in the classroom. These contradictions, however, are resolved in a discourse of *kokusaika* (internationalization), which has become a popular economic, political and cultural slogan and has influenced education reforms since the 1980s. *Kokusaika* essentially blends Westernization with nationalism, failing to promote cosmopolitan pluralism. In other words, *kokusaika* tends to promote convergence to predetermined norms rather than divergence towards cultural and linguistic multiplicity.

This chapter will focus on language teaching in Japan and explore the three-dimensional tension in relation to the discourse of *kokusaika*. First presented is demographic data that demonstrate growing ethnic and linguistic diversity in Japan. Then an outline of the discourse of *kokusaika* and education reforms is provided, followed by a critical examination of teaching English as a foreign language and teaching Japanese to speakers of other languages. Finally, the chapter outlines resistance to and criticisms of Anglicization.

Ethnic and linguistic diversity in Japan

Contrary to the stereotype, Japan is not an ethnically and linguistically homogeneous nation (see Noguchi and Fotos 2001). Whereas the population in Japan has always included ethnic minorities such as Ainu and Okinawans, Japanese imperialism from the late nineteenth century to the end of World War II brought Koreans and Chinese to Japan, many of whom had no choice but to stay after the war. Globalization, particularly since the late 1980s, has attracted a large number of foreign workers and students to Japan. Indeed, the data compiled by the Ministry of Justice (2000b) demonstrate that the increase in registered non-Japanese residents in Japan has been continuous since the 1970s. According to the Ministry of Justice, the total number of registered non-Japanese residents in Japan in 1999 was 1,556,113, or 1.2 per cent of Japan's total population. This population increased at a rate of 58.1 per cent between 1989 and 1999. Tables 1.1 and 1.2 show these residents' places of origin. The data indicate that Asians and South Americans constitute the majority of this population with Korean residents constituting the largest group, although a majority of Koreans are permanent residents and linguistically assimilated (cf. Ministry of Justice 2000b).

Table 1.1 Non-Japanese residents' region of origin in 1999

Region	1999	Percentage
Asia	1,160,643	74.6
South America	278,209	17.9
North America	54,882	3.5
Europe	41,659	2.7
Oceania	11,159	0.7
Africa	7,458	0.5
Other (no citizenship)	2,103	0.1
Total	1,556,113	100.0

Source: Ministry of Justice 2000b

Table 1.2 Non-Japanese residents by citizenship (country of origin) in 1999

Country	Number	Percentage
South and North Korea	636,548	40.9
China	294,201	18.9
Brazil	224,299	14.4
Philippines	115,685	7.4
USA	42,802	2.8
Peru	42,773	2.7
Other	199,805	12.9
Total	1,556,113	100.0

Source: Ministry of Justice 2000b

These numbers, of course, represent only a part of diversity in Japan. As mentioned, Ainu and Okinawans have long been ethnic minorities in Japan. Other ethnic minorities, mostly Koreans, who have been naturalized are not included in the data either.

Table 1.3 illustrates the increasing ethnic and linguistic diversity in the nation's schools. Between 1995 and 1997, the number of non-Japanese students in need of Japanese language support increased by 46.5 per cent. Again, these students are mainly from Asia and South America, as shown in Table 1.4.

As these figures demonstrate, ethnic and linguistic diversity within Japan certainly exists and is growing. Unfortunately, as discussed later, these diversities are not sufficiently reflected in language education.

Table 1.3 Number of non-Japanese students in need of Japanese language support and the number of schools these students attend in 1997

	Elementary		Junior High		Senior School		Total	
	Students	Schools	Students	Schools	Students	Schools	Students	Schools
1997	12,302	3,402	4,533	1,659	461	148	17,296	5,209
Increase rate from 1995	50.2%	30.3%	35.3%	34.1%	74.6%	102.7%	46.5%	32.8%

Source: Shimuzu 1999

Table 1.4 Number of non-Japanese students in elementary, junior high, and senior high schools in need of Japanese language support in 1997 by native language

Language	Number of students	Percentage
Portuguese	7,462	43.1
Chinese	5,333	30.8
Spanish	1,749	10.1
Filipino	618	3.6
Korean	482	3.1
Vietnamese	475	2.8
English	443	2.6
Other 46 languages	734	4.2
Total: 53 languages	17,296	100.0

Source: Shimuzu 1999

The discourse of *kokusaika*

The discourse of *kokusaika* (internationalization) became prominent as Japan expanded its economic power in the 1980s. As implied by the term, *kokusaika* aims to understand people and cultures in the international communities through various social, cultural and educational opportunities. It also aims to transform social and institutional conventions to adapt to the international demands. In the 1990s, the term *kokusaika* began to be replaced by *gurôbarizêshon* or 'globalization', which implies a borderless society in the age of the global economy and information technology (Nakamura 1999). Nonetheless, terms that include *kokusai-* (international) are still widely used. Despite its ideal, one notable aspect of *kokusaika* is its preoccupation with Western nations, particularly the USA, and its promotion of nationalistic values in educational contexts (cf. Kubota 1998a, 1999, in press). *Kokysaika* also parallels the discourse that regards English as the international language, influencing foreign language education. What political and economic circumstances generated *kokusaika*?

As Japan's economic development peaked in the 1980s, trade imbalances between

Japan and Western nations prompted criticism of Japan. Japan's government and large corporations needed to avoid further economic conflict and possible world isolation, while continuing to develop economic strengths through international investment. The strategy adopted in order to contest the Western demand was to seek membership in the Western industrialized community rather than establish its own hegemony in isolation. This accommodation strategy was inevitable given the post-World War II military subordination of Japan to the USA and its allies.

The accommodation, however, does not imply total assimilation to the West. Juxtaposed to joining the Western community is an attempt to maintain Japanese identity and to communicate distinct Japanese perspectives to the rest of the world. This attempt to protect Japan's identity while investing in the international market is demonstrated in a number of 'cross-cultural manuals' for Japanese expatriates and travellers (Yoshino 1992, 1997). These manuals, written in both Japanese and English, feature sociocultural characteristics that are perceived as uniquely Japanese *vis-à-vis* the West, mirroring and reinforcing *nihonjinron* – a discourse that celebrates the uniqueness of Japanese culture and people (cf. Dale 1986; Sugimoto 1997).

In sum, *kokusaika* reflects Japan's struggle to claim its power in the international community through Westernization (Anglicization in particular) and to affirm Japanese distinct identity rather than local ethnic and linguistic diversity. To put *kokusaika* in the three-dimensional tension mentioned earlier, it balances a tension between the promotion of English and nationalism. However, *kokusaika*'s preoccupation with Anglicization and nationalism tends to neglect the domestic diversity which is constituted mainly by Asian and South American residents. Insufficient attention to domestic diversity is reflected in language education policies and practices as discussed below.

Kokusaika and education reform in the 1980s and 1990s

The impact of the discourse of *kokusaika* was particularly prominent in the education reform in the 1980s prompted by *Rinji Kyôiku Shingikai*, the Ad Hoc Committee for Education Reform, which compiled four reports on education reform between 1985 and 1987. In short, the committee's reports promoted the acquisition of the communication mode of the West, especially English, to express and explain unambiguously Japanese points of view in the world while maintaining Japanese identity (Morita 1988; also see Kubota 1998a, 1999, in press). This trend has continued throughout the 1990s and into the present.

The education reforms influenced by *kokusaika* have envisioned the development of self-expression fostered through learning English for communicative purposes as well as focusing on the 'expressive' rather than 'receptive' mode in learning Japanese as L1. Also regarded as important is logical thinking, which is supposedly necessary in international communication. In learning Japanese as L1, logical thinking in speaking and writing is to be developed by learning the logical organization of paragraphs and arguments, as specified in the *Course of Study,* the national curriculum guidelines. In teaching English, logical thinking is to be developed through writing and cross-cultural understanding. Wada (1999) shows the diagram presented by Kaplan (1966) and states that English demonstrates a linear logic whereas Japanese has a circular logic and that Japanese students need to learn to think according to the English logic, despite recent criticisms of this view (e.g. Kubota 1997, 1998b; Pennycook 1998). Teaching English also affects the development of logical thinking in Japanese as seen in a suggestion that the principles of English writing be applied to Japanese L1 writing (Watanabe 1995). Furthermore, self-expression and logical thinking are combined into a pedagogical approach using 'debate', adopted from Western education, in various academic subjects.

Unambiguous self-expression and logical thinking, however, have not been emphasized at the cost of Japanese identity. The education reform promoted the acquisition of an English-based communication mode for the purpose of conveying Japan's unique traditions and way of life to other people in the world. Thus, juxtaposed to the focus on self-expression and logical thinking is an emphasis on nationalistic values. The education reform stressed fostering love of nation and awareness of Japanese identity in the international community. The 1989 *Course of Study* mandated the use of the national flag and anthem in school ceremonies, despite oppositions to these nationalistic icons symbolizing Japanese imperialism.

The education reform in the 1990s followed a similar path. The most recently revised *Course of Study* (Ministry of Education 1998) continues to emphasize expressing one's opinion logically in Japanese. Also emphasized is teaching and learning a foreign language, especially English. For the first time in the post-World War II curriculum, foreign language became an officially required subject in junior high and senior high schools. For junior high school, the *Course of Study* specifies English as the foreign language to be taught. Furthermore, the new *Course of Study* offers an option for offering foreign language (i.e. English) conversation in the elementary school, as discussed in the next section. Nationalism was intensified in the 1990s as seen in the establishment of the legal status of the national flag and anthem.

Nationalism is also seen in a reform movement in history education. Some scholars and critics formed a group called the Japanese Society of History Textbook Reform to advocate a 'liberal' view of Japanese history that legitimates Japanese military domination of Asia and the Pacific in the past (Japanese Society for History Textbook Reform 1998). However, a paradox of nationalism in globalization is demonstrated in their promotion of 'debate', a Western communication mode, to instil nationalistic viewpoints (see Kubota in press).

The above overview indicates that *kokusaika* has played the role of resolving the tension between Westernization and nationalism in education reform. However, the third corner of the triangle – increased domestic diversity – was not a major impetus in education reform. Although concepts of multicultural education were introduced to Japanese educational research in the mid-1980s (Fujiwara 1995), the push for self-expression, logical thinking, and learning English does not stem from the need to interact with an ethnically diverse population in Japan and the rest of the world. The following sections will further examine recent trends in foreign language education in Japan.

Foreign language education in Japanese schools

The discourse of *kokusaika* has emphasized teaching and learning a foreign language, particularly English, with a vision of fostering the ability to unambiguously and logically express oneself in the imagined international community. In this community, it is assumed that communication takes place mainly with people from the economic and military powers of the West, particularly the USA. Consequently, English, typically regarded as *the* international language,[2] has become the focus of teaching and learning. *Kokusaika* has produced the following premises in foreign language education: (1) 'foreign language' is 'English'; (2) the model for 'English' should be standard North American or British varieties; (3) learning English leads to 'international/intercultural understanding'; and (4) national identity is fostered through learning English. These premises demonstrate convergence towards English, so-called standard English, and Anglophone cultures as well as maintenance of national identity, while failing to promote linguistic and cultural pluralism.

'Foreign language' is 'English'

Influenced by *kokusaika,* the Internet, and the discourse of English as the international language, 'English' has become synonymous with 'the foreign language' (Oishi 1990). Although there has been an increased attention to teaching languages other than English, the emphasis on teaching English has been intensified. The emphasis on English is observed in: (1) foreign language offerings in high schools; (2) the new initiative at the elementary school; and (3) the number of Assistant Language Teachers.

First, the *Course of Study*, except for the most recent junior high schools version, does not specify which 'foreign language' should be taught. However, English is *de facto* the only option in many secondary schools, although the number of high schools that offer languages other than English has increased significantly recently as shown in Table 1.5 (Ministry of Education 1999a; Shimizu 1999). Given that the total high school enrolment in 1999 was 4,211,826 (Ministry of Education, Culture, Sports, Science and Technology 2001), high school students learning languages other than English account for less than 1 per cent of the enrolment. It will be interesting to see if local and global linguistic diversity will be more reflected in the future foreign language curriculum. A promising development is the plan to add Korean to the currently offered tests in English, French, German and Chinese in the national entrance examinations for universities (*Asahi Shinbun,* 24 September 2000).

Table 1.5 Number of senior high schools that offered languages other than English in 1999 (numbers in parentheses show the 1995 data)

Language	Public School		Private School		Total	
	School	Enrolment	School	Enrolment	School	Enrolment
Chinese	251 (124)	9,684	121 (68)	8,757	372 (192)	18,441
French	113 (74)	3,942	93 (73)	5,982	206 (147)	9,923
Korean	84 (47)	2,361	47 (26)	1,611	131 (73)	3,972
German	60 (43)	1,515	49 (32)	2,931	109 (75)	4,446
Spanish	55 (27)	1,383	21 (16)	942	76 (43)	2,325
Russian	15 (11)	414	8 (9)	294	23 (20)	708
Italian	1 (0)	21	6 (5)	137	7 (5)	158
Portuguese	4 (0)	52	2 (2)	37	6 (2)	89

Source: Ministry of Education 1999a

Second, the equation of 'foreign language' with 'English' is clearly observed in the discussions of teaching a foreign language in the new elementary school curriculum to be put into effect in 2002. The *Course of Study* lists 'foreign language conversation' merely as an option for teaching 'international understanding (*kokusai rikai*)', which is itself one of the options for a newly created curricular area called 'comprehensive study'. Nowhere in the curriculum is there a mention of teaching 'English conversation'. However, 'foreign language' is usually interpreted as 'English' as seen in a teachers' guide for teaching 'English' conversation prepared by the Ministry of Education. The public also interprets this development as introducing English, rather than a foreign language, into the elementary school (cf. Higuchi 1997).

Third, in 1987, the Japanese government initiated the JET (Japan Exchange and Teaching) Program and recruited young people from abroad to assist foreign language teachers in public schools. During the first year, all of the 848 Assistant English Teachers (AETs) were from the USA, UK, Australia or New Zealand. The title AET was later changed to ALT (Assistant Language Teachers) in order to lower the 'English fellow' status (McConnell 2000). However, about 98 per cent of the 5,096 ALTs in 1998 were still English teachers (Shimizu 1999).

The equation between 'foreign language' and 'English' is influenced by the conception that English is the international language and that the acquisition of English is useful for international communication. Many high school textbooks include a topic on English as a useful tool for international communication. This reflects a discourse that legitimates the global spread of English as natural, neutral and beneficial (Pennycook 1994) and a discourse of colonialism that elevates English to the status of 'marvelous tongue' (Pennycook 1998).

The symbolic power attached to English as the international language reinforces the perceived superiority of English over other languages. This is reflected in an observation that a bilingual child in Japanese and English is enthusiastically praised, whereas a child who is bilingual in Japanese and Portuguese is paid no special attention (Parmenter and Tomita 2000a). Also, an ethnographic study by Matsuda (2000) demonstrated that Japanese high school students most often described English as 'cool' or 'fashionable' with their overwhelmingly positive impression of the English language. For many of her interviewees, 'foreign countries' meant the West – i.e. North America and Europe – with the most frequent reference made to the USA. This, in part, seems to reflect the conception that equates foreign language with English and indicates that foreign language teaching in Japan distances itself from the rich linguistic and cultural diversity existing in schools and local communities.

The model for 'English' should be standard North American or British varieties

Similar to the converging tendency towards English in foreign language education, the model of English to emulate tends to be only the Inner Circle varieties of Anglo-English, particularly North American and British, rather than diverse varieties of World Englishes. This tendency is apparent in the makeup of ALTs referred to above. Of the 5,096 ALTs in 1998, about 48.8 per cent were from the USA, 21.1 per cent from the UK, and 16.2 per cent from Canada, counting for a total of 86.1 per cent. Among other Inner Circle countries, 5.8 per cent were from Australia, 4.4 per cent from New Zealand, and 1.6 per cent from Ireland (Shimizu 1999). Although the door to ALT positions recently opened to eight participants from Singapore who could become instrumental in raising awareness of World Englishes (*Asahi Shinbun,* 5 July 2000), these percentages indicate a heavy focus on Inner Circle, particularly North American and British, Englishes. Despite the rhetoric of learning English for international/intercultural communication, opportunities for students to interact with the Outer and Expanding Circle English speakers are scarce.

These observations manifest the 'native speaker myth' – the idealization of a native speaker as someone who has perfect, innate knowledge of the language and culture and thus is the best teacher of English (cf. Amin 1999; Auerbach 1993; Canagarajah 1999b; Phillipson 1992; Rampton 1990). The native speaker myth also entails a perceived superiority of the Inner Circle, particularly North American and British, varieties of English. Matsuda (2000) documented high school students' perceptions that American English is 'pure' and 'authentic', in contrast to their lack of interest in and knowledge of the Outer Circle varieties of English. This tendency also parallels what Kachru (1997) found in the English language curriculum of fifteen universities in Japan – a heavy focus on American and British white middle class literary canons compared with a scarcity of works by ethnic minority writers in these and other countries.

Added to these biases is prejudice towards certain geographical and ethnic varieties of the Inner Circle English. ALTs from countries other than North America and the UK often face linguistic biases. Some Australian participants, for instance, were told by Japanese teachers to reduce their accent by listening to tapes (Juppé 1995) or to use only American English while teaching (McConnell 2000). Furthermore, a 'white bias' exists in the JET Program. Some non-white participants of the JET Program experienced racial prejudices, particularly during its initial years. An African American ALT was frequently asked by Japanese teachers, 'Can you speak standard English?' (McConnell 2000: 80). The white bias in teaching English in Japan has been pointed out since the 1970s; Lummis (1976) criticized the racist practices in hiring, paying and advertising in private English conversation schools for adults. Other critics also criticized the notion that native English teachers ought to be white Americans or British (Tsuda 1990; Oishi 1990, 1993).

In sum, the English model tends to be viewed as the Inner Circle, particularly North American and British, varieties spoken by white people. Here, despite local and global linguistic diversity and the rhetoric of *kokusaika*, the linguistic model tends to be narrowly restricted to certain geographic and racial varieties.

Learning English leads to 'international/intercultural understanding'

Another reductionist equation often made is between 'learning English' and 'international understanding (*kokusai rikai*)' or 'intercultural understanding (*ibunka rikai*)'. There is indeed a widespread conception that because English is the international language that bridges multiple cultures, learning English enables understanding of the world and cultural diversity (Horibe 1998), despite its odd fallacy that any English speaker has international understanding (Oishi 1993; Tsuda 1990).

However, learning English, particularly with an emphasis on the Inner Circle white middle class varieties, does not lead to international understanding. Rather, it is likely to promote a narrow view of world cultures and, furthermore, produce essentialized images of both Inner Circle countries and Japan. Stemming from the assumption that Inner Circle varieties of English are 'authentic' English, international/intercultural understanding in English language teaching is often focused on cultural differences only between Anglophone countries and Japan. Some educators try to reconcile this limitation by arguing that, although learning about various cultures is important, it is impossible to learn about them all. Therefore, the goal of international understanding through learning English is to develop nonbiased attitudes and cross-cultural communication skills rather than knowledge about world cultures (Wada 1999). Thus, actual examples are drawn mostly from Inner Circle Anglophone culture, which are diametrically contrasted with stereotypical images of Japanese culture found in *nihonjinron*.

A good example is a booklet on teaching international understanding in English classrooms (Wada 1999). Cultural dichotomies such as an emphasis on social hierarchy versus egalitarianism, collectivism versus individualism, and high context versus low context cultures are presented as differences between Japanese and Anglophone cultures and incorporated into communicative activities and assessment. For instance, the text presents a dialogue between characters called Hanako and Betty. Betty bought a new stereo and thinks that her Japanese neighbour upstairs likes it because the neighbour said she enjoyed the music the previous night. But Hanako tells Betty that Betty misunderstands her neighbour. The dialogue ends with Hanako's line, 'Well, if you live in Japan, you should be careful about *this*'. The subsequent communicative activity engages students in the continuation of this dialogue. The evaluation criteria suggest that Betty should ask Hanako what 'this' means, and that Hanako should explain to Betty that indirect expressions are preferred in Japan (therefore, Betty's neighbour was indirectly complaining). Here, cultural difference is treated as an objective fact providing a correct answer.

The cultural dichotomies are further reinforced in testing situations. Wada (1999) stresses the need for cross-cultural knowledge in university entrance examinations, stating that about 50 per cent of national universities and 45 per cent of private universities included English reading comprehension passages on culture in their 1998 examinations. Reflecting this trend is a study guide that aims to provide basic knowledge on cultures to students preparing for university entrance examinations (Kotoh 1992). The guide includes chapters on British, American and Japanese cultures, and presents common beliefs as if they were facts that these students need to know in order to pass the test.

The above observations indicate that learning English leads not so much to 'international understanding' in a sense of cosmopolitan pluralism or critical multiculturalism (cf. Kincheloe and Steinberg 1997) but to cultural essentialization and dichotomization between Japanese and Anglophone cultures. As McConnell (2000) argues in the context of the JET Program, 'international understanding' does not imply diminishing national boundaries between individuals but improving understanding between groups who would always be fundamentally different. While the discourse of *kokusaika* promotes Anglicization, it also reinforces cultural nationalism through constructing a rigid cultural boundary between Us and Them.

National identity ought to be fostered through learning English

Essentialized Japaneseness constructed through teaching 'international understanding' is related to the premise that national identity should be fostered through learning English. This premise is clearly demonstrated in the *Course of Study*, which stipulates that teaching materials for junior and senior high school English courses should enhance a student's awareness as a Japanese person in the international community (Ministry of Education 1999b). The thinking behind this appears in the final report of the National Curriculum Committee (Ministry of Education 1998). According to the report, education for the age of internationalization aims to develop the ability to coexist and interact without prejudice among people who have different cultures and customs. But the first step to achieve this goal is to foster pride, love and understanding of the history, culture and traditions of one's own country. The emphasis on national identity echoes *kokusaika* which aims to disseminate Japanese ways of thinking to the world. Here we see adherence to a single national identity rather than exploration of multiple identities incorporating Asian and global perspectives (Parmenter and Tomita 2000b).

In sum, *kokusaika* discourse that combines Anglicization and nationalism is reflected in foreign language education in Japan. Anglicization is demonstrated in the emphasis on teaching English over other languages and the preference of white middle-class North American and British varieties of English and culture over other varieties and cultures, while nationalism is promoted as seen in the adherence to a monolithic Japanese identity in international understanding. Foreign language teaching thus exhibits a converging trend into the legitimation of certain linguistic and cultural norms and a monolithic national identity, failing to give a serious consideration to multiculturalism, multilingualism, and multiethnic populations that currently exist in Japan as well as in global communities.

The JET Program, as mentioned several times in this chapter, was created to promote *kokusaika* in schools by providing students with opportunities for intercultural communication and understanding. Intercultural communication and understanding, however, should be a two-way process in which ALTs also develop their intercultural understanding. The title of the JET Program, Japan Exchange and Teaching, implies that some type of 'exchange' takes place. Nonetheless, the program provided ALTs with little opportunity to learn the Japanese language during its first five years. While Japanese language instruction was eventually introduced – mainly for the purpose of training the participants who want to become future Japanese language teachers after returning home, serious work on offering conversational Japanese courses began only in 1999 (McConnell 2000). This symbolizes a complex desire of the Japanese to preserve these native English speakers' pure Anglophone identity, which the Japanese worship (Nakamura 1989; Tsuda 1990; Oishi 1990 1993), while protecting the pure Japaneseness from being contaminated by the white Anglophone Other. The containment of Japaneseness is indeed manifested in teaching Japanese as an additional language, which I discuss in the next section.

Japanese culture and language in teaching Japanese to speakers of other languages

Japan's economic strength in the 1980s and the promotion of *kokusaika* increased the popularity of teaching and learning Japanese as L2. Although the globalization of Japanese language implies linguistic creolization and hybridity similar to the situation of English, teaching Japanese as L2 has tended to focus on the essentialized forms of Japanese language and culture, trying to converge learners' behaviours towards an ideal norm. This tendency is observed in how Japanese culture is presented in classrooms and teacher training. In fact, the conception of culture in teaching Japanese as L2 tends to mirror *nihonjinron* discourse which accentuates the uniqueness of essentialized Japanese culture.

Yoshino (1998), in critiquing cultural nationalism promoted by the popularity of cross-cultural communication, summarizes five premises in *nihonjinron*: collectivism, non-verbal and non-logical communication, social homogeneity, innate cultural competency, and the uniqueness of geographic attributes and rice production influencing other aspects of Japanese uniqueness. These premises indeed appear in materials for teaching and learning Japanese as L2. According to Yoshino (1997, 1998), advanced Japanese reading and writing classes at a university in Tokyo required students to read such typical *nihonjinron* texts as Nakane (1967) and Doi (1971).

There are also texts on Japanese culture for Japanese language teachers. Matsui (1991) presents a history of *nihonron* (synonymous with *nihonjinron),* some popular publications in this genre, and explanations of often-cited notions that are believe to be unique to the Japanese: social harmony, preference for ambiguity, etc. One text published for Japanese language teacher training (Matsui *et al.* 1994) is interesting in that it acknowledges the danger of stereotyping cultural and national characteristics. Nonetheless, the text argues that knowledge of these characteristics is necessary for passing the Japanese Teaching Competency Test and is useful for getting students interested in Japanese language and culture. One of the practice books for this examination published in 1997 also contains a brief chapter on Japanese culture, which includes sample questions that require knowledge about such notions as high context versus low context culture, collectivism, and popular publications on *nihonjinron*. Here, Japanese culture is presented uncritically as consisting of predetermined facts that are imagined rather than lived (Kawakami 1999) and reproduced in textbooks, teaching, and teacher training.

Not only is Japanese culture essentialized but also Japanese language. For instance, the taken-for-granted view that the Japanese are conscious about social hierarchy and gender roles endorses the pedagogical practice that presents the normative use of honorifics (polite registers) and gendered language (seen in sentence-ending particles). However, through observations of actual language use among Japanese men and women with different social status and occupations, Okamoto (1997, 1999) found many instances of honorifics and gendered language usage deviated from the textbook case. Okamoto argues that the use of honorifics and gendered language is not solely determined by status or gender difference but is strategically based on the multiple social aspects of the context and beliefs or attitudes that the speakers have concerning language use (Okamoto 1997). Nevertheless, Siegal and Okamoto (1996) found that all of the five Japanese textbooks examined generally prescribe the use of honorifics and gendered language, presenting the language according to fixed social status and gender roles.

As in teaching a foreign language to Japanese students, teaching Japanese to speakers of other languages tends to converge towards cultural and linguistic norms that highlight distinct Japaneseness while failing to recognize the diversity and dynamic nature of language and culture. It is interesting to note that these converging tendencies simultaneously alienate learners from discovering how to function effectively in real social contexts. In other words, while the fixed norm expects learners to assimilate into an imagined, ideal Japanese society, it also prevents them from becoming accepted members of the mainstream Japanese society. This paradox parallels Japan's colonial education policy as detailed by Tai (1999), indicating the past–present continuity of colonialism.

As already mentioned, there are some critical voices raised against the reductionist views of Japanese language and culture (see Siegal and Okamoto 1996). Kawakami (1999), in introducing postmodern paradigms such as hybridity and creolization of culture, advocates a new possibility for teaching Japanese culture that is based on a dynamic, rather than static, view of culture. Nonetheless, the static normative view of culture and language overwhelms these minority voices. The next section will focus on the other side of Japanese essentialism – i.e. Anglicism – and discuss resistance and criticisms in foreign language education.

Resistance and criticisms against Anglicism

Although Anglicization prevails in foreign language education in Japan, it has met with some resistance and criticisms. In the nation's secondary schools, not all Japanese teachers of English welcome native English-speaking teachers. Some conservative teachers view the status quo as superior and perceive ALTs and their communicative teaching methods as a virus that could potentially harm the intellectual development of students and traditional cultural virtues (McConnell 2000).

From theoretical perspectives, the linguistic imperialism of English in Japan has been critiqued in many publications since the 1990s (for a summary, see Kubota 1998a; Tsuda 1998). Echoing and influenced by the same kind of critique raised by Anglophone scholars such as Phillipson (1992) and Pennycook (1994), these Japanese critics problematize the prevalent view that English is a useful and beneficial language. They critique inequality in communication, the influence of English on Japanese people's identity and their view of the Other, and the idealization of native speakers. Unequal relations of power between native and non-native teachers of English in a professional organization in Japan have also been criticized (Oda 1999).

An interesting political development in early 2000 was seen in a proposal made by a private advisory council to the Prime Minister for setting concrete goals to enable every Japanese to communicate in English and for discussing the future possibility of making English the second official language of Japan. This initiated heated debates among educators and the general public. For instance, *Mainich Shinbun,* one of the nationally circulated newspapers, featured on-line debates on giving English an official status. The nearly 400 e-mail messages demonstrated opinions varying from one extreme – that English should become the sole official language of Japan – to the other – that Japanese should become a common language in Asia and the world. While some agreed with the proposal on the ground that English is *de facto* the international language and being able to use it is politically and economically beneficial, others criticized the proposal, arguing that it would undermine the Japanese language and cultural identity. Some critics also argued that English is merely one of the world languages and making it an official language is practically and ideologically problematic.

One vocal critic of language education and policy is Takao Suzuki (1999). Suzuki explains that the Japanese attitude towards learning foreign languages has been influenced by an inferiority complex towards foreign cultures, which promoted self-colonization or self-Americanization. In order to transform this attitude, Suzuki suggests learning English in order to express oneself and explain Japanese culture to the rest of the world, rather than learning about the cultures of Anglophone nations, which could be done more effectively in social studies classes. To this end, he proposes using teaching materials only on Japan and divorcing 'international understanding' from English language teaching. Suzuki's arguments appear to be a liberal criticism against self-colonization that tends to regard American sociocultural protocols as universal. His views also recognize the creolized nature of English and the importance of learning languages other than English. However, his suggestion about explaining 'Japanese culture' to the rest of the world in English (and other languages) echoes the nationalistic profile of *kokusaika* discourse. Horibe (1995) argues that the opposition to linguistic imperialism of English should advocate linguistic and cultural pluralism rather than nationalism. This comment indicates the two possible directions in which resistance to Anglicism could go: nationalism and cosmopolitan pluralism. These two directions will further make the triangular tension unstable and unpredictable.

Conclusion

Language learning and teaching in Japan in the age of globalization has been influenced by *kokusaika* discourse that blends both Anglicization and nationalism. The Anglicization aspect of *kokusaika* indicates that the development of international understanding and intercultural communication skills is heavily focused on the white middle class English and essentialized Anglo culture rather than on other languages and cultures that constitute the linguistic and ethnic diversity of Japan as well as the world. Conversely, cultural nationalism in *kokusaiaka* is manifested in the emphasis on national identity and in the construction of essentialized images of Japanese language and culture contrasted with English and Anglophone culture. Oseki (1999) rightly points out that no matter how much the rhetoric of intercultural coexistence or multiculturalism is advocated, *kokusaika* always parallels the promotion of Japanese tradition, essentialized culture, and national identity. It seems that the triangular tension – i.e. Anglicization, nationalism, and diversity – actually represents an isosceles triangle with two angles pulling the other angle with a strong force. Despite cultural linguistic diversity conjured up by *kokusaika* and globalization, it is Anglicization and nationalism, the two strong corners of the triangle, that converge towards essentialized norms. In contrast, language education pays insufficient attention to the increased ethnic and linguistic diversity at the local and global levels and to the need for democratic coexistence among the mainstream Japanese population, the ethnic and linguistic minority groups in Japan, and people of many different backgrounds around the world. With that said, there is some optimism in the increased number of secondary schools offering languages other than English. This trend will perhaps continue and potentially could become a counter force against nationalism and Anglicization.

Notes

1 The process of cultural transformation, however, is not a complete conversion to the American or White norm – it involves local adaptation and hybridization. As Ritzer (1998) notes, McDonald's varies its product and atmosphere to local conditions. Furthermore, some argue that the recent popularity of body aesthetics in Japan, including the fad with brown and blonde hair and the removal of men's body hair, may not necessarily reflect a desire to become Caucasian (e.g. Miller forthcoming). While these social phenomena cannot be interpreted from a single perspective, I argue that Americanization certainly influences them.
2 Although English as *an* International Language (EIL) might be a more accepted term (see Pennycook 1994; 1998), English as *the* International Language seems to more accurately describe the adherence to English in Japan.

2 Globalization, diaspora and language education in England

Roxy Harris, Constant Leung and Ben Rampton

This chapter[1] seeks to:

- outline the ways in which notions of 'globalization' and 'diaspora' have changed the ways we can conceptualize language, ethnicity and the nation-state;
- describe how education policy has responded to these changes, referring in particular to the language education of newcomers and pupils with diaspora connections;
- illustrate something of the reality of life in schools, and of the failure of current policy to engage with this.

England provides the frame for our discussion, and some of the processes we describe are specific to the local English historical context. English education policy is not alone, however, in its failure to engage adequately with multi-lingualism in a globalized era; people in other places are just as ill-served by analytical vocabularies that take notions like 'community' and 'native-speaker' for granted; and indeed, the argument we develop in the chapter is well-summarized in Cameron McCarthy's comments on North America (1998: 154–5):

> The . . . proposition that culture is radically hybrid has sharp implications for the dominant curriculum and the . . . discourses of multicultural[ism] that continue to represent culture and identity in static and a-theoretic terms. . . . [P]roponents [of multicultural education] must address the contemporary reality of students' lives in a post-colonial, globalized, market-driven world in which schooling is only one of numerous spaces available for the negotiation of both identity and culture.

To provide a historical baseline for our discussion, the first part of the chapter looks back at educational responses to ethno-linguistic diversity in the mid to late 1980s, before globalization became such an issue in academic and everyday discourse. We then consider some of the ways in which our understanding of the relations between language, ethnicity and the nation-state has been challenged by globalization over the last ten to fifteen years. The impact on education policy in general, and language education in particular, provides the focus for the subsequent two sections. Then in the final section, we present two vignettes, illustrations of the gap between what students need and what policy has to offer.

Education, language and ethnicity *c.* 1970–1985: The 'Swann Report'

Published in 1985, *Education for All: The Report of the Committee of Inquiry into the Education of Children from Ethnic Minority Groups* – 'the Swann Report' – was the last major government report on linguistic and ethnic diversity in education, and it provides a useful illustration of the discourses and political arrangements that up until then had been central to education policy in England.

Power in educational policy making was distributed very differently from how it is today. Central government had no direct powers over the curriculum, and curriculum decision-making lay in the hands of teachers and individual schools, who were usually provided with strong guidance by their Local Education Authorities (LEAs). Central government provided specific funds for the substantial numbers of English as a second language (ESL) teachers and multicultural curriculum advisers who either worked peripatetically from an LEA base or were stationed in particular schools, but for the most part control over education spending was delegated from central government to LEAs. LEA services came under the auspices of local government – the metropolitan, county and borough councils – and accountability to the local electorate encouraged dialogue about education with the representatives of ethnic minorities in areas where they constituted a significant proportion of the local vote. These groups were themselves often vocal in the expression of their educational concerns and expectations: many were relatively well-established in the industrial workforce, were sympathetic to the labour movement, and could draw on discourses of equality and rights that had been successful in relatively recent struggles for colonial independence. Political arrangements such as these made education policy development a matter of persuasion and dispute, and spurred on by the urban riots of 1981, one of the Swann Report's central objectives was to generate a view of ethnic pluralism with which central and local government, teaching unions and minority communities could all concur.

What kind of view was this? Swann offered a vision of nested communities within the framework of the nation-state: Britain as a community of communities,[2] engaged in the process of reconciling itself to the legacy of its imperial past. For the most part, the Report conceptualized its ethnic minorities as well-known, well-defined, settled, and stable, and it made light of any connections that they might seek to maintain with other parts of the world. It focused primarily on people of Caribbean and South Asian descent (DES 1985: 649), drawing on the reviews it had commissioned of the substantial research on these groups (Taylor 1981; Taylor and

Hegarty 1985). It dismissed a European Directive on the teaching of minority languages on the grounds that these groups were British and here-to-stay;[3] it described their thoughts of living in other countries as the '*myth* of an alternative' and the '*myth* of return' (DES 1985: 20–1); and it was in local social services rather than in world markets that minority language proficiency was envisaged as being useful (DES 1985: 409–10). Similarly, the Report's discussion of the mass media, TV and press looked no further than the British nation-state (DES 1985: 16ff. and 38–44).

The educational strategy that the Committee proposed consisted of three basic elements. First, any linguistic and cultural disadvantage that minorities were suffering should be overcome, e.g. through the teaching of English as a second language. Second, *all* children, minority *and* majority, should be encouraged to respect the richness of minority cultures. Third, there should be no ethnic segregation within the public schooling system: ESL teaching should take place in the mainstream, instruction in minority languages should be open to all, bilingual support staff should help everyone (DES 1985: ch. 7). The role of state schools was to eliminate segregation and disadvantage, and to ensure that everyone shared in whatever benefits minority students brought with them: rather than cultivating any specialized cultural or linguistic resources that ethnic minorities might have, the Swann Report sought in effect to *nationalize* them ('Education for *All*').

The Swann Report was written against a background of considerable contestation over ethnicity and race, and published during the ascendance of Thatcherism, not long after the war in the Falklands/Malvinas and a landslide Conservative general election victory in 1983. In certain respects – the frontal engagement with racism and the insistence that minorities belonged – it stands out as important liberal text. In other respects, it said much less than it might, and the refusal to countenance any sustained state-funded bilingual education was widely criticized by those involved in the teaching of ethnic minority languages (NCMTT 1985). Here, however, we are less concerned with its strengths and weaknesses than with the glimpse it gives of the educational and political landscape just prior to the transformation brought about by what is generally considered to be the central force within globalization, neo-liberal market capitalism. It is this transformation that we discuss next.

Globalization

Globalization is an ongoing rather than completed process, but it is inextricably linked with the developments and demands of free-market capitalism:

> Huge flows of money move between foreign exchange markets in different countries (much greater than the amounts necessary for world trade); companies pursuing a global strategy have developed with an annual turnover greater than that of whole national economies (such as Microsoft, Nike, Virgin, Sony,

McDonalds); and a wide array of products from many different countries is readily available worldwide. . . . Local factories and offices can be opened and closed seemingly at will, while individual states . . . are often unable to determine their own national economic policies.

(Abercrombie and Warde *et al.* 2000: 12–13)

Appadurai (1990) characterizes globalization as a dense and fluid network of global flows, and from among its many dimensions (Jameson 2000), he identifies 'ethnoscapes', referring to flows of people (tourists, immigrants, refugees, exiles and guest workers); 'technoscapes', involving the rapid movement of high and low technologies between multinational, national, and government organizations; 'finanscapes', denoting flows of money through currency markets and stock exchanges; 'mediascapes', referring both to information technologies (including newspapers, TV and film) and to the images of the world they create; and 'ideoscapes', ideological discourses concerning freedom, democracy and so forth.

Globalization has major consequences for the nation-state. With flows and scapes criss-crossing national borders, it is increasingly hard for the state to exercise effective authority within its traditional territory (Abercrombie and Warde et al 2000: 15), and rather than aspiring to command empires, the state is under increasing pressure to act as the hopeful host to transnational business, seeking to attract inward investment by offering a secure and stable environment, limited state regulation and an abundance of skilled low-wage labour (Bauman 1998; CBI 2000).

These changes are having a major effect on the character of migrant labour. Particularly in the 1950s, 1960s and 1970s, Britain encouraged the inward flow and settlement of new peoples who were needed to work in the manufacturing, transport and health sectors where the recruitment of indigenous labour was proving difficult (Rose *et al.* 1969). This led to the emergence of the relatively stable working class ethnic communities that Swann was primarily concerned with: the jobs might be low paid, but initially anyway, they were reasonably secure, and the prohibitive costs of international travel encouraged people to build a congenial milieu in their local vicinities. In recent years, however, global market capitalism has reversed this balance of opportunities and constraints, and this has facilitated different kinds of arrangement:

[b]etween 1995 and 2005, travel and tourism within Europe are expected to increase by 78% (OECD 1996a: 30). Significantly – and in contrast with earlier times – after transferring location, people are able to maintain instantaneous links with their point of origin through media and communications systems, strengthening the capacity of migrants to manage their own diasporic identities while resisting full assimilation into the new nation (Marginson 1999: 2).

These new developments have permitted the growth of 'transnational communities',

> characterized by dense networks across space and by an increasing number of people who lead dual lives. Members are at least bilingual, move easily between different cultures, frequently maintain homes in two countries, and pursue economic, political, and cultural interests that require a simultaneous presence in both.
>
> (Portes 1997: 16)

According to Portes, three features distinguish contemporary transnational communities from earlier periods of migration: 'First, the near-instantaneous character of communication across national borders and long distances. Second, the numbers involved in these activities; and third, the fact that, after a critical mass is reached, the[se activities] tend to become "normative".' (1997: 18). In this context, social identity is increasingly 'deterritorialized':

> the scope for multiple affiliations and associations that has been opened up outside and beyond the nation-state has allowed a diasporic allegiance to become both more open and more acceptable . There is no longer any stability in the points of origin, no finality in the points of destination and no necessary coincidence between social and national identities . . . What nineteenth-century nationalists wanted was a 'space' for each 'race', a territorializing of each social identity. What they have got instead is a chain of cosmopolitan cities and an increasing proliferation of subnational and transnational identities that cannot easily be contained in the nation-state system.
>
> (Cohen 1997: 175)

The cosmopolitan or 'global' cities that Cohen refers to serve as centres of finance, transport and communications, and as such, they are inhabited by populations that are both highly diverse and highly stratified, as can be seen in major regional variations in England. Just 2.6 per cent of pupils in maintained primary schools in the North East and 2.7 per cent in the South West are described as belonging to ethnic minorities, while comparable figures for Inner London are 56.5 per cent, Outer London 31.2 per cent, and West Midlands 15.9 per cent.[4] The linguistic consequences for schools are shown in a recent survey of the languages of London's schoolchildren (Baker and Eversley 2000: 5), which states that in Greater London the range of home languages spans more than 350 language names, with English dominant amongst 67.86 per cent of the 850,000 schoolchildren surveyed. At the same time, wealth and income differentials are also sharper in London than anywhere else in the UK (Abercrombie and Warde et al. 2000: 126). On the one hand, it is a home for cosmopolitan elites, professionals and business people, while on the other, there are large numbers of people working in low-skilled, low paid jobs, often in a substantial hidden economy[5] (see also Hannerz 1996: 129–31; Cohen 1997: 167–9).

World cities of this kind aren't merely 'nodes in networks' however. They are also places in themselves, settings for the juxtaposition and mixing of different cultural traditions in a range of different and distinctive combinations. Ethnic and cultural difference are highly salient, and subculturally specific resources – food, dress, music, speech – can be aestheticized and/or commodified, used in artistic production or sold commercially to a wide range of different consumers and not just to tourists and the transnational elite. As a point where a plurality of different transnational and diaspora flows intersect, this is an environment that generates high levels of local meta-cultural learning and awareness (cf. Hannerz 1996: 135–7; Portes 1997), and although there will be different combinations and different processes in different locations, Hall's discussion of black experience in the UK resonates with the cultural dynamics of world cities more generally (1990: 235–6):

> [t]he diaspora experience is defined, not by essence or purity, but by the recognition of a necessary heterogeneity and diversity; by a conception of 'identity' which lives with and through, not despite, difference; by *hybridity*. Diaspora identities are those which are constantly producing and reproducing themselves anew, through transformation and difference. . . . Young black cultural practitioners and critics in Britain are increasingly coming to acknowledge and explore in their work this 'diaspora aesthetic' and its formations in the postcolonial experience.

Hall goes on to quote Mercer:

> Across a whole range of cultural forms there is a powerfully 'syncretic' dynamic which critically appropriates elements from the master-codes of the dominant culture and 'creolizes' them, disarticulating given signs and rearticulating their symbolic meaning otherwise. The subversive force of this hybridizing tendency is most apparent at the level of language itself where creoles, patois and Black English decenter, destabilize and carnivalize the linguistic domination of 'English' – the nation-language of master-discourse – through strategic inflections, reaccentuations and other performative moves in semantic, syntactic and lexical codes.
>
> (Mercer, 1988: 57)

We will return to the linguistic dimension of these processes in subsequent sections, together with the ways in which education policy has responded. Before that, however, it is worth briefly casting a comparative glance back at the conceptualization of ethnic relations offered in the Swann Report.

The Swann Report offered a view of well-defined and often vocal minority communities ensconced within Britain, the old centre of Empire, and it addressed itself to the ways in which 'minority' status was equated with disadvantage, either in actuality or in public perception (see DES 1985: 212). Stereotyping was seen to be prevalent in national press and broadcasting, and the inner city had often been conceptualized as the site of deprivation (DES 1985: 213). It is certainly not our purpose to contradict every aspect of this view, and experiences of racism and disadvantage are still intense for many people with minority ethnic backgrounds. Globalization, however, presents a fundamental challenge to the terms in which these processes are understood.

The descendants of the immigrants in the 1950s, 1960s and 1970s now have affiliations and expectations that often differ from those of their parents' and grandparents' expectations (see below) while massive recent political upheavals, including the collapse of the Soviet Union and the 'Eastern Bloc', have produced a dramatic growth of illegal immigration in the 1990s, both in Britain and across Europe and Asia (Papastergiadis 2000: 48). In the UK there has been a very large increase in people seeking asylum,[6] and there are also very substantial numbers without work and residence permits: 'in practice, such people either exist in limbo, outside state benefits and employment, or else are eventually granted some status due to the passage of time' (Fiddick 1999: 13). They also tend to be politically voiceless: 'there is a strong incentive for those who are here illegally to keep as low a profile as possible, and avoid unnecessary contact with Government agencies' (Grabiner 2000: 17).

At the same time, however, there can also be distinct advantages to diaspora membership in an age of global flows:

> Members of diaspora are almost by definition more mobile than people who are rooted in national spaces. They are certainly more prone to international mobility and change their places of work and residence more frequently. In previous eras and still in some places, when periods of febrile nation-building take place, their cosmopolitanism was a distinct disadvantage and a source of suspicion. In the age of globalization, their language skills, familiarity with other cultures and contacts in other countries make many members of diasporas highly competitive in the international labour, service and capital markets.
>
> (Cohen 1997: 168–9; Bauman 1998: 2)

The global city is a site of cultural creativity and commercial opportunity, and where national/terrestrial communication channels carry tedious or offensive material, people can simply retune to cable and satellite media where programming is more congenial or relevant (see Morley and Robins 1995). For some, the inclusion and hospitality advocated by Swann may start to feel more like a parochial restriction, as when, for example, linguistic resources with massive transnational scope are described as 'local community languages'.[7] Indeed, it is no longer safe to assume that Britain is attractive as a permanent primary residence base, as Cohen's discussion of 'sojourning' makes clear:

> new classes of people educated in a whole range of modern skills are now pre-
> pared to migrate or re-migrate and respond to the pull of centres of power and
> wealth and the new opportunities in trade and industry . . . these people are
> articulate, politically sensitive and choose their new homes carefully. . . .
> Sojourners to the new destinations [Canada, the USA and Australia] are helped
> by the global communications and transport revolutions, by the need for states
> to attract foreign investment through the multinationals, by the stronger legal
> protection accorded to minorities in the receiving countries and by the adapt-
> able tradition of sojourning itself.
>
> (Cohen 1997: 164–5)

That, then, is an indication of how globalization encourages a reconceptualization of ethnic relations, both in England and elsewhere. What of education in England in general, and language education in particular? How have they figured in the shifts that have taken place since 1985?

Education and language 1988–1997

Three years after the publication of Swann, the Conservative Government embarked on a major programme of educational reform, bringing in the Education Reform Act (ERA) in 1988. The policy that this initiated can be summarized as one of neo-liberal market economics combined with cultural authoritarianism.

'LMS' – the 'Local Management of Schools' policy that was one of the corner-stones of ERA – paved the way for a major shift of power away from Local Education Authorities to individual schools, with the result that by the year 2000, 82 per cent of the money spent on school was controlled by headteachers and school governors compared with around 5 per cent in 1990 (Audit Commission 2000). As part of this process, the responsibility for spending money on pupils in need of support with ESL shifted from LEAs to local schools, so that rather than being able to call on an LEA service that was provided free-of-charge, schools had to plan for ESL support in their own budgets and to pay the LEA to provide them with specialist teachers. ESL provision wasn't mandatory, and with a lot of other competing financial priorities, the pressures on schools to reduce ESL expenditure were inevitable.

At the same time as market principles like this were introduced to the way specialist resources were distributed, creating a competitive 'internal market' among schools and LEAs within state education, responsibility for the design and specifi-cation of the curriculum for 5 to 16-year-olds was centralized. Individual teachers and schools were no longer the principal curriculum decision-makers, and the processes of persuasion and debate that the Swann Report had been tuned to were replaced by legislative coercion. A series of national working parties were set up for the 'core' curriculum areas of English, Maths and Science, as well as for a range of other subjects (though not ESL), and by the mid 1990s, a legally binding National Curriculum for 80 per cent or more of the school day had been established, together with a system of national tests for 7, 11 and 14 year olds. These tests meant that the performance of children at different schools could be compared, and their publication in league tables was initiated and justified on the grounds that this was essential 'consumer information' for another new element in education policy, 'parental choice'. Prior to the 1988 ERA, children in the public education system had been allocated to a particular school by their LEA, but parental choice now gave parents the right to choose which school their child went to, with state funding following the child. In this way, a complex combination of marketization and central control was developed – in order to survive, schools needed to attract parents, and they could vary their spending priorities in order to increase their competitiveness, while at the same time, central government dictated curriculum input and standardized the measurement of output (see Heller *et al.* 1999: 89; Bernstein 1999: 252).

These processes had an inevitable effect on schools' attitudes to pupils who were learning English as a second language. The league tables on school performance published raw data, and made no allowance for major differences between schools in their student intake. In this context, pupils from non-English speaking homes were increasingly seen as a threat to a school's public performance profile, depressing its published test scores, undermining its appeal to parents, and ultimately endangering its funding base. Whereas the Swann Report had called for inclusiveness, with the new market principles it was no longer in a school's interest to welcome refugee children and other newcomers to England.

These structural changes undermining Swann's position were accompanied by a number of major changes in the terms of debate. One of the factors widely judged to have helped the Conservatives win the 1987 general election was the so-called 'loony London effect', a perception that the Labour Party was dominated by London-based radicals who were committed to dogmatic multiculturalism and antipathetic to the traditional values of Englishness. In other words (what others later came to call) the 'global city' was deemed a political liability, and in its place, the hearts and minds of 'Middle England' became the main target of competition between the major political parties. At the same, as the replacement of the phrase 'middle class' with 'Middle England' itself reflects, social class also became less and less of a reference point in public discourse.

This decline in the usability and salience of traditional notions of social class was partly the product of the economic restructuring attendant on globalization (the decline of area-based manufacturing industries like mining, steel and shipbuilding, the growth of the services sector, and with women and black people almost 50 per cent of all manual labour, a major shift in the demographic composition of the workforce (Abercrombie and Warde *et al.* 2000: 167; Gilroy 1987: 19; Reay 1998)). But the disappearance of class from public discourse also fitted with the ascendance of two newer ideologies. On the one hand, the traditional association of class with collective solidarity, worker identities and the critique of capitalism was ill-suited to the new emphasis on individualism, consumption and the market. On the other, notions of long-standing class conflict and division were at odds with a growing emphasis being given to (high) national culture as a central unifying element in the new national curriculum (e.g. Tate 1996). In practical terms, this meant that when particular groups continued to underachieve at school, the blame was shifted from political economy — in which everyone was implicated, including the government — to culture, which laid responsibility with the underachievers themselves. In this way, the relatively poor performance of working-class boys became a problem of masculinity, while the disaffection of working-class boys of Caribbean descent was put down to ethnicity.[8] Whereas the Swann Report made an effort to address the ways in which school achievement was influenced by both class and ethnicity together (DES 1985: 71–6), Gillborn and Gipps' major review acknowledges that although social class and gender are important variables, 'data on social class is often absent from research . . . [and] it is exceptional to find studies of achievement by ethnic minority pupils that give full attention to *both* these factors' (1996: 16; see also Gillborn 1997: 377–80).

So much, then, for shifts in education generally. What of language education in particular? There have been a number of fairly detailed accounts of change in language education policy from the late 1980s to the mid-1990s (e.g. Stubbs 1991; Cox 1995; Brumfit 1995; Cameron 1995: ch. 3; Rampton *et al.* 1997), but for our purposes here, it will be sufficient to make two points.

First, language and language education were major political issues during this period, and the intense focus of dispute between on the one hand, a broadly liberal coalition of teachers, local government, teaching unions, researchers and academics committed to the relatively child-centred, pluralist legacy exemplified in Swann, and on the other, back-to-basics conservatives calling for grammar, standards, and a return to traditional teaching methods (central government, its policy advisers, and much of the national media). With legislative force in the new centralized education system at their disposal, conservatives had the resources to push the curriculum in the direction they preferred, and over time, opposition was gradually marginalized. In the process, concern for linguistic diversity became increasingly peripheral. Second, standard English served as a potent, condensed and multivalent symbol in this process, commanding the respect of both conservatives and liberals, either as the unifying core of national identity, as the carrier of a great national tradition, as the prerequisite for national economic efficiency, or as the starting base for social mobility, equality of opportunity and democratic participation. Over time, however, educational discourse shifted towards the conceptualization of

English as an autonomous code, as something that could be identified, described, broken down into parts and taught like a foreign language. In consequence, the acquisition of standard English was increasingly seen as a matter of individual choice and ability, rather than as a process that was deeply connected to pupils' social identities, to their collective affiliations and to their sense of possible futures.

Broadly speaking, then, there were a number of significant ways in which education policy moved in step with the economic dimensions of globalization, dancing to the neo-liberal market philosophy that has been so influential in global 'ideoscapes' from the 1980s onwards. Market principles were introduced into the relations between LEAs, schools and parents; standard English was pushed to the fore as a common currency, accessible to all; and antipathetic discourses of class were eroded. But at the same time, education policy also turned its face away from the human and cultural dynamics associated with the new 'ethnoscapes' and diasporas. A national curriculum dictated cultural values from the centre, issues of linguistic diversity were gradually marginalized, and provision for newcomers to English became increasingly precarious. Earlier on, we argued that there was a substantial gap between the contemporary realities of globalization and the image of society guiding the 1985 Swann Report. Even so, ill-adapted though it now might seem, it offered more educational purchase on the language and ethnicity in a global era than any of the policy initiatives that followed it.

What happened, though, when in 1997, after a 17-year programme in which free market economics had been extended progressively further into the public sector, the Conservative Government finally lost power? What has happened since the 'New' Labour Party took power?

Language education 1997–

The new government came into power determined to tackle social exclusion, and in language education in 1998, it instituted a major 'National Literacy Strategy' (NLS) designed to eradicate the 'long "tail" of underachievement in Britain, and [the] relatively poor performance from lower ability students' (Barber 1997: 10). Government has claimed that the NLS has achieved success in this, though there are complex issues of assessment validity involved that fall outside our current concerns. Here, though, it is worth noting that from the outset, the NLS also took globalization within its sights, arguing that in the society of the twenty-first century, knowledge and information would be keys to success or failure: 'Only if everyone is well-educated and able to learn continuously will we be able to reap the benefits of this emerging society and ensure that they are fairly distributed' (Barber 1997: 6). And indeed, as part of the attempt to build a 'knowledge-driven society . . . to succeed in this digital age' (Gordon Brown, Chancellor of the Exchequer 16.2.00), it began to invest £1 billion over three years up to 2002 in the 'National Grid for Learning', a programme to equip every school with computer technology connected to the web.

The concern with social exclusion was not, however, a return to class analysis. 'Most are agreed', argued Barber, 'that the educational system bears the main responsibility' for poor British performance (1997: 10), and elsewhere it was said that state education had much to learn from private schools. The 'discipline of the market' continued to play a major part in the relationship between LEAs, schools and parents, and indeed schools and LEAs deemed 'failing' (such as the London boroughs of Hackney and Islington) were privatized and taken over by educational and other management companies.

Nor was the National Literacy Strategy designed to equip children with skills in the new information and communications technologies. The 'basics' of reading and writing were targeted (Barber 1997: 6), and New Labour's programme in fact seemed to intensify their predecessors' rejection of the cultural dynamics of globalization.

The new digital communications systems embrace a huge plurality of expressive forms, values, interests and imaginings, and this new power presents a considerable challenge to traditional patterns of authority. According to Castells,

> [increasingly] *electronically-based communication (typographic, audio-visual, or computer-mediated) is communication.* . . . Only presence in this integrated system permits communicability and socialization of the message. All other messages are reduced to individual imagination or to increasingly marginalized face-to-face subcultures. . . . [This] weakens considerably the symbolic power of traditional senders external to the system, transmitting through historically encoded social habits: religion, morality, authority, traditional values, political ideology.
>
> (Castells 1996: 374–5; also Sefton-Green 1998: 12)

Teachers and parents figure among these 'traditional senders', and young people's greater ease and interest in the new media often makes such 'senders' insecure (Richards 1998; Holmes and Russell 1999). The NLS, however, looks designed to reassert the kinds of authority that now feel threatened. The centrepiece of the NLS is the 'Literacy Hour' – an hour a day that all primary schools in England are legally compelled to dedicate to reading and writing (DfEE 1998). The Literacy Hour assumes native-speaker knowledge of spoken English and cultural meaning, and in it, pupils' attention is focused on the basics of print literacy and standard English grammar, overwhelmingly ignoring both the multi-modality of integrated communications systems and the heteroglossia and multi-lingualism of the global city. Indeed, the NLS not only dictates what to teach, but now also *how:* in its concern to 'train teachers in using the most effective ways of teaching literacy' (Secretary of State David Blunkett DfEE 1998: Foreword; Barber 1997: 13), a minute-by-minute programme for the Literacy Hour has been established, and in it, whole class teaching, with pupils' eyes and ears tuned to the teacher, forms the main part (two-thirds).

More detailed discussion of the educational response over the last 10–15 years to new arrivals in England, and to pupils with diaspora connections, can be found elsewhere, addressing, among other things, the confident government assertion that the NLS is well-tailored to the needs of ESL learners, the superficially liberal assumption that a supportive social environment and exposure to the target language are sufficient for L2 development, and the absence of any robust research evidence to justify these views (Leung *et al.* 1997; Rampton *et al.* 1997; Tosi and Leung 1999; Leung and Cable 1997; Mohan *et al.* 2001). At this point, however, two things are in order.

First, it needs to be emphasized that England is not alone in its inability/reluctance/failure to engage constructively with the effects of globalization, with the realities of the global city and new diaspora relations. A broadly comparable pattern of education policy reactions can be found in the USA, Canada and Australia, as the comparative research of Mohan *et al.* (2001) makes plain.

Second, to give a clearer idea of the disjunction between the policies we have described and the contemporary realities of multilingualism at school, as well as to restore some of the '"noise" of multidimensionality, historical variability, and subjectivity' that are so often eliminated in 'both mainstream and radical conceptualizations of racial inequality' (McCarthy 1998: 52), we would like to present two vignettes, one profiling an individual student, the other describing the kind of dilemma in which ESL teachers and students now find themselves.

Two vignettes

The first case, drawing on interviews and classroom work, comes from Harris' ongoing research on representations of ethnicity and language among a class of 31 14- and 15-year-olds in a multilingual high school in the suburbs of London.[9] It focuses on the linguistic and ethnic affiliations of one of these students, T.

Case One: T.

T. is 15 years old and born in the UK. His mother, a Sikh, was born in India but has spent most of her life in Britain. 'When I was born my father left me and my mum', and now his father, a Muslim, lives in the United States, though he often stays with the family in the UK. T. has relatives in India and he has visited there twice.

   T. has strong Sikh affiliations, but doesn't display any visible signs of this. He is, however, a leading member of a Punjabi dhol[10] drumming band, and often performs in school. Three of the seven band members wear Sikh turbans, but when asked if they ever wear traditional Punjabi dress, he is emphatic that for them this denotes the practices of an older generation: '. . . [the] older time ones, yeh, they wear their Indian clothes,

yeh? the proper bhangra so like . . . we're the Dholis of the new generation yeh? so we wear Ralph Lauren clothes and all that we like we got our
Ralph Lauren suits . . . stripey trousers with blue shirts . . . we wear um
black Kickers [shoes].' T. and the band have played alongside well-known
bhangra artists and film stars from India at major shows in London.

T. takes great pride in the Punjabi language – 'my language is very
important to me' – and insists that before he first attended school, he
mainly spoke Punjabi, with little exposure to English. To develop his
Punjabi and to teach him more about Sikh religion, history, culture and
traditions, his family sent him to a voluntary community school on
Saturdays between the ages of 7 to 9, but he didn't continue with this
because: 'I didn't like the writing part . . . I thought my mum can't write it,
so my grandparents can't write it. My grandad can but my grandmother
can't so I thought it isn't really important.'

He also finds it difficult to read Punjabi in the Gurmukhi script at the
Gurdwara, though he can improvise written representations of Punjabi
speech in the Roman alphabet. At Blackhill School, he has been learning to speak, read and write German for almost four years, and so
now, although his written standard English is modest-to-weak, his literacy competence is strongest in English, with German next and Punjabi
third.

In terms of spoken language, T. is very aware of variation in Punjabi:
'When I am with my friends I speak slang Punjabi. When I am with my
family I speak standard casual Punjabi. But when I go to India I get very
weird Punjabi. In India they pronounce words differently.'

He also affiliates to Jamaican language ('rasta talk') – 'we don't say
hello . . . we say 'wha gwan' and all that, we say it like that . . . we don't talk
English' – although not as strongly as some of his peers: 'They've got into
the rasta man talk and all that – they can't come back to Punjabi, like I
know V___ in our year, he's Punjabi but he speaks rasta and all that . . .
I don't think he knows a lot about his religion'.

Beyond its general currency, T. also picks up Jamaican language from
inter-ethnic friendships outside school, and he also loves Reggae music:
'White mans ain't composed it . . . it's the black people they composed
it . . . we like their music . . . I'm not interested in anything the songs that
English people sing, the ones I like Bob Marley and all that, we used to
listen to that . . .'

The second case comes from Leung's work with ESL professionals, and describes some work done to support an early learner of English in the Literacy Hour.[11]

Case Two: Mrs Roberts, Meryem and the Literacy Hour

'South Town' is a small inner London primary school with 200 pupils, a quarter of whom have a home language other than English. The teacher, Mrs Roberts, is a peripatetic ESL teacher[12] who comes to the school for 1½ days a week. Together with the class teacher for 10 year olds ('Year 5'), she was concerned that Meryem wasn't in a position to benefit from next week's scheduled work in the Literacy Hour. Meryem was literate in Turkish, but she was a non-speaker of English when she had arrived at the school just two months ago. For the class as a whole, next week's Literacy Hour objectives were:

- to identify the point of view from which a story is told and how this affects a reader's response;
- to change the point of view, e.g. tell an incident or describe a situation from the point of view of another character or perspective;
- to write from another character's point of view;
- to investigate clauses by identifying the main clause in a long sentence, by investigating sentences which contain more than one clause, and by understanding how clauses are connected (see DfEE 1998: 48)

The text chosen for the week by the class teacher included the following:

'Amanda said bye from both of us and we went back to class. I felt a bit guilty not telling her what Dad had said about her dad, but at that time I still thought she was my friend and I wanted to protect her feelings.

I did have a few doubts about Amanda's dad during the rest of the afternoon. What if he flew into a rage when I walked through the door and said something hurtful about Dad?

Or mum?

And my head erupted again?

And he was cleaning out a goldfish bowl . . .

I told myself to stop being silly.' (Gleitzman 1992: 40)

There was no ESL support available during the Literacy Hour, and so both teachers decided that Meryem should have some focused language tuition in a one-to-one withdrawal session the week before.

Mrs Roberts decided to teach Meryem to use point-of-view constructions such as '*I think Salil is nice*', leading into constructions such as

'I think Salil is nice because . . .'. In their session together, they used a bi-lingual dictionary to read some of the 'Happy Families' books, written by Allan Ahlberg for 6- to 8-year-old monolingual English speakers, and Mrs Roberts introduced character drawings and speech bubbles. During the daily literacy hour the following week, Meryem used these when the class wrote about the different viewpoints, and they also helped her to make an oral contribution to one of the whole class feedback sessions at the end.

Mrs Roberts' written reflections on this episode included the following:

'It was very obvious that M would have no understanding of a text as dense and lacking in supporting visuals . . . I was aware that I wouldn't necessarily have targeted these [sentence] structures pre-literacy hour days. Then it tended to be more child's needs led, married with the demands of the lessons. I think probably the balance has now swung to literacy hour demands, adjusted where possible to meet needs of child'.

Although the language learning needs of T. and Meryem are obviously very different, they are neither exceptional, nor do they exhaust the considerable diversity of ESL learning needs in English schools today. According to DfEE 1997: 34, 'children from ethnic minority backgrounds now form a tenth of the pupil population', and within this, we suggest that there are at least three very broad types of bilingual student (Harris 1999; Mohan *et al.* 2001: 200–1). First, there are 'new' arrivals like Meryem, then there are 'low key' British bilinguals, such as T., and last, there are high-achieving multilinguals. But none of these categories are straightforward, and even within the apparently simple 'newcomer' category, there is enormous variation in the previous educational experience, as well as major differences in wealth and income (with some belonging to cosmopolitan elites). At the same time, students in both the newcomer and the low-key bilingual categories are likely to be short-changed by current language education policy. Meryem needs much more sustained language teaching and a more flexible curriculum than the system allows her, and in spite of Mrs Roberts' valiant and resourceful efforts on her behalf, the conditions for language learning experienced by Meryem can be politely described as sub-optimal. T. needs assistance with standard English academic writing, though this should be set within a rather more subtle understanding of his sociolinguistic situation than is allowed in the description of students like him as 'EAL learners' (e.g. QCA 2000: 23; Rampton 1988). Like a very great many young people in England and elsewhere, T.'s vernacular speech reflects his participation in the complex urban dynamics of class, ethnicity and gender, and as his profile implies, language for him, as for others, is suffused by issues of politics and identity (cf. Hewitt 1986; Rampton 1995, 2001; Back 1996: 123; Brah 1996: 209; Harris 1997: 25). These issues need to be explicitly addressed if pupils like T. are to develop proficiency in class-marked, 'posh' varieties like standard English. In contrast, if policy

on standard English continues to embrace a primarily negative response to vernacular Englishes, treating them as phenomena to be eradicated and avoided (DFE
1995), it looks destined for (continued) resistance and failure.

Education policy also offers relatively little in support of other languages in
Meryem and T.'s repertoire. If Meryem is lucky enough to go to a secondary school
which offers GCSE-exam track courses for 13-year-olds in a range of languages, or
where there are a lot of Turkish-speaking children, in three or so years' time she might
be able to study Turkish at school for several hours a week. It's more likely, though,
that if she wants to develop her first language, she'll have to look for support in community classes outside the state school sector. As for T., Blackhill School recently
introduced a two-year GCSE Punjabi programme for a younger year group, although
even if T. had been eligible, it's not certain that he would have opted for this, given the
problems that he now had with the script due to his lack of sustained Punjabi literacy
instruction. It has been suggested in some sectors of Government that in the global village, Britain's linguistic diversity provides important commercial opportunities, but
so far anyway, there is little evidence of any coordinated thinking on this.

The emphasis has been on standard English as a common currency, and indeed it
has long been argued that the very plurality intimated in the cases of T. and Meryem
makes this the only practicable option – with children from so many backgrounds,
speaking so many languages, how could a national education system possibly cater
for everyone? Instead, the argument runs, state education should provide a centre
of gravity, a steady and unifying set of core orientation points. The trouble with this
is, of course, that it assumes that the groups and ethnicities in satellite around it are
fixed forever in completely separate orbits. In reality, ethnic essentialism of this kind
grossly misrepresents contemporary urban dynamics, as innumerable cultural commentators have explained, and as the case of T. attests. As Portes notes, when
critical mass is reached, diaspora connections and transnational activity become the
norm: new interpretive communities develop, generating new syntheses, seeking as
much to engage with difference as to suppress it (cf. Hall 1988; Mercer cited
above). In a global city environment of this kind, where there are high levels of
meta-cultural awareness, it's hard to imagine any curriculum – indeed any school
experience – managing to pass itself off as impartial, neutral, equal for all. The
upshot is likely to be that unless state education comes out of denial and starts to
engage with people on the moral, cultural and political grounds now emerging at
the intersection of globalization and diaspora processes, it will find them tuning out
in increasing numbers, pursuing their interests through alternative channels.

Notes

1   We are indebted to the editors for constructive critical feedback on an earlier version, to
    Amanda Bellsham-Revell for discussion of empirical cases, and to the students and teach-
    ers at 'Blackhill School' where fieldwork reported in the chapter was conducted. A
    longer and more detailed version of the paper is available from ben.rampton@kcl.ac.uk

2 This can be seen in its view of language: 'The English language is a central unifying factor in "being British", and is the key to participation on equal terms as a full member of this society. There is however a great diversity of other languages spoken among British families in British homes' (DES 1985: ch 7.1.1).

3 'We believe that discussion of the provisions of the EC Directive have to a very great extent over-shadowed and indeed distorted the debate about mother-tongue provision. It must be recognized that the Directive was explicitly intended to ensure that the children of *Migrant* Workers from EEC countries received an education which would enable them to return to their countries of origin. It is surely illogical therefore to seek to extend such provisions to ethnic minority children, born and brought up in this country, the great majority of whom are unlikely to "return home" and who neither perceive themselves, nor wish to be perceived as in any sense "transitory" citizens of this country' (DES 1985: ch 7.3.9. Original emphasis).

4 Similarly, the figures for the number of pupils for whom English is an Additional Language in maintained primary and secondary schools show 5.3 per cent for the North West and Merseyside and 3.7 per cent for the South East, but 29.4 per cent for Greater London (DfEE 1999).

5 'Typically, businesses in the informal economy tend to be low-wage and labour-intensive, often with a seasonal or irregular element to their work. Examples include: domestic service, household building, taxis and mini-cabs, market trading, tourism, hotels and catering, agriculture and fishing, fashion and clothing manufacture' (Grabiner 2000: 4).

6 Asylum applications in UK from 1985 to 1988 averaged about 4,000 a year, whereas in 1998 there were 46,000 applications (Watson and McGregor 1998). In 1998, the British Home Office estimated that it had an outstanding backlog of 93,000 asylum seeker cases (Fiddick 1999: 10).

7 Punjabi, for example, is described in the UK as a 'community language' rather than as a 'Modern Foreign Language', despite the fact that it has more than 60 million speakers worldwide, with 15 million in India and up to half a million in Britain (Dalby 1998).

8 Evidence from the last national census (1991) clearly indicates that 'The occupational structure for Black-Caribbean men is skewed towards the manual categories: two-thirds of the men are in such occupations in comparison with only half of the White male working population. Similarly, the proportion in professional occupations is the least of any of the ethnic groups (2.6 per cent compared with 7.1 per cent for White men)' (Peach 1996: 34).

9 During 1996–97, 'Blackhill' had more than 1400 pupils, among whom, according to its own data, 20 per cent were white and 78 per cent were of 'Asian origin'. A school survey claimed 'only 19 per cent of students stated that English was the principal language used at home': 27 of the class had South Asian connections, often with East African ones as well; 16 pupils claimed to have used Punjabi with their families before they first attended school; 9 claimed Gujarati; 1 Kurdish; 1 Mauritian French Creole; 1 Swahili; 1 Urdu. See also Harris 1999.

10 The dhol drum is a key instrument used in the production of bhangra, a traditional music of the Punjab, India.

11 This is based on a teaching vignette prepared by Anne Morgan and Amanda Bellsham-Revell to be published by the National Association for Language Development in the Curriculum (NALDIC).

12 In the UK at present, 'EAL' – English as an Additional Language' – is preferred as a term to ESL.

3 Globalization and the commodification of bilingualism in Canada

Monica Heller

Current transformations in the ideology and practice of bilingualism in Canada reveal a shift from an ideology of authentic nationhood to an ideology of commodification. These transformations are scarcely peculiar to Canada; we see them in all parts of the world where language has been tied to nation and state, and most obviously in those areas which have known linguistic minority movements since the 1960s (such as Catalonia, Wales, Brittany or Corsica). The shift is a complicated one, involving difficult contradictions between nationalist ideologies which have been at the heart of francophone (and other linguistic minority) political mobilization movements, and the diversity and involvement in international networks which have resulted from their relative success. It also involves contradictions between language as a mark of authenticity and belonging or identity, and language as an acquirable technical skill and marketable commodity. These contradictions have direct consequences for language teaching and learning, insofar as they affect what counts as competence, who gets to define what counts as competence, who is interested in acquiring that competence, and what is considered the best way to acquire it.

In this chapter I will first trace some of the economic and political shifts underlying this transformation as they have unfolded over the last forty years, since the Quiet Revolution and the emergence of Québécois nationalism, and through an ongoing shift from an economy based on the primary and secondary sectors (in which bilingualism was not valued and francophones were economically marginalized and exploited, thereby contributing to their successful social, cultural and linguistic reproduction) to one based on the tertiary service and information sectors (in which bilingualism is increasingly valued and commodified, but in ways which also provide new modes of social selection). The chapter examines social change in francophone Canada as a means to structure a narrative which involves multiple perspectives, but also because in many ways it has been social change from that community which has triggered a wider set of shifts in ideologies and practices of bilingualism across Canadian society, and, finally, because that case resonates with those of so many other linguistic minorities.

The bulk of the chapter will focus therefore on some ways in which the struggle between valuing French as the hallmark of an authentic community and as a commodity for exchange in an internationalized job market in the service and information sectors is manifested in certain key sectors, drawing on data from fieldwork in Quebec, Ontario and the Maritime provinces (New Brunswick, Nova Scotia and Prince Edward Island) which I have collected alone or with colleagues over the last twenty years or so.[1] These sectors are sites of struggle; struggle among various kinds of actors over access to French, English and other languages; struggle over the legitimacy of their access; and struggle over definitions of what is to count as bilingualism. Here, as we shall see, traditional insistence on 'monolingualist' ideologies of language has not changed; by this I mean that while bilingualism is valued, it is only valued as long as it takes the shape of 'double monolingualism'. One is expected to speak each 'language' as though it were a homogeneous monolingual variety (in social psychological terms, this is usually referred to as 'additive bilingualism'; cf. Landry 1982). Mixed varieties, which of course are common in bilingual settings, are frowned upon. This was certainly the case in the heyday of ethnic nationalism, in keeping with the dominant ideologies of language emerging with the European nation-state, and still is the case now that language is understood in more economic and less political terms. The ability to achieve the 'double monolingualism' ideal is not equally distributed among the population, although the ideology itself is quite hegemonic.

Along with this fairly continuous and dominant discourse of what 'good' bilingualism consists of, there circulate ideas about what constitute good English and good French. However, these processes also involve an interesting contradiction between the authentificating and legitimizing value of the local or regional vernaculars and their historical stigmatization as symbolic representations of the social conditions of marginalization, poverty and oppression from which francophone Canada has collectively been trying to escape. The obverse side of that coin is a valuing of 'international' French for integration into globalized networks and for the management of local ethnocultural diversity, accompanied by a fear of such a variety as being too distant from local realities, and as delegitimizing claims for national distinctiveness which still play a role in local struggles over the resources of the new economy.

These themes will traverse the substantive discussions of sites of discursive production in the next few sections. I will turn first to a brief overview of the social, economic and political shifts of the past forty years, before focusing on current processes of transformation in work, association and educational sites.

Francophone mobilization and changing ideologies of bilingualism

Canadian ideas about what constitutes bilingualism, and about whether or not it is a good thing, have always been tied to the material bases of reproduction of ideologies of language and identity. These have been inscribed in relations of power between conquering English-speakers and conquered French-speakers. While the conquest in question happened a long time ago (1755 for Acadia, 1759 for the rest of New France), it laid the groundwork for an ethnic division of labour which has informed Canadian society ever since. This division of labour was based on the reproduction of ethnic boundaries, and on the involvement of French Canadians in the exploitation of primary resources that is the basis of Canadian wealth, and in a variety of subsistence activities as well. These relations produced an elite that was bilingual because it had to deal with monolingual anglophones who controlled both economic and political power, and later a working-class whose bilingualism was directly connected to their conditions of marginalization. Elite bilingualism comprised standard and monolingual forms and practices largely acquired through literacy; working-class bilingualism was composed of much more mixed forms and practices largely acquired orally.

While social relations changed in the period following World War II, through a transformation of francophone nationalism connected to the rise and advancement of a new francophone middle class, ideologies of bilingualism did not. The new elite adopted the standard 'double monolingual' variety of bilingualism, and reinforced it through homogenizing ideologies of nation and state, as well as through the development of monolingual regional markets.

Now it is no longer the nation-state that unambiguously provides the legitimacy of discourse on language and bilingualism. Globalization, neoliberalism and the new economy all have their effects. The state is withdrawing from the scene; not only does this mean that the discourse of nationalism is less compelling than it used to be, but it is also the case that the state is providing less funding for associations and activities connected to linguistic nationalism. At the same time, both French and English are growing in importance in the service and information sectors of the globalized economy, attached as they are not only to the regional markets of Canada, but to the worldwide markets in which each language has currency. Here there is certainly a reproduction of longstanding ideologies of bilingualism among the new globetrotting elite, ideologies reinforced by discourses of 'quality' and 'standards' in the private sector. At the same time, many bilingual jobs in the new economy are at the lower end of the scale, and require bilingualism because they involve customer service – with customers who frequently do not master the standard themselves.

Elsewhere (Heller and Budach 1999; Heller in preparation) I have described these shifts as discursive changes, so as to capture a periodization which, while connected to changing material conditions, is far from strict, and to lay bare the ways in which ideologies of language and bilingualism are re-entextualized (Silverstein and Urban 1996) rather than replaced. These discourses can be thought of as *traditional*, *modernizing* and *globalizing*.

Traditionalist discourse was based on the importance of resisting English domination by remaining homogeneous (hence a great concern about linguistic purism, specifically with respect to traces of contact with English) and faithful to values which were (and still are) understood as traditional, in the sense of linking contemporary actors and practices with a legitimizing past (cf. Hobsbawm and Ranger 1983; Crowley 1996).

The *modernizing* discourse which emerged most strongly after 1960 focuses on the collective political mobilization of francophones in order to use the apparatus of the state to open doors for the economic advancement of francophones through participation in mainstream structures of political and economic power. In this discourse, francophones are still understood as a nation in the classic sense, with a modern overlay of state nationalism where possible (that is, Quebec) and an institutional form of that nationalism elsewhere. As a nation, francophones are understood to have collective rights, and to require control over an autonomous and homogeneous space.

[handwritten margin note: learn inglish as commodity]

Both traditionalist and modernizing discourses treat bilingualism as problematic, and associate linguistic holism with national completeness. However, whereas the traditionalist discourse still largely looks to France to define norms, while identifying local authentificating forms, the modernizing discourse actively seeks to construct native norms which help demarcate the boundaries of the nation-state, and which in addition help construct the new, modern face of francophone Canada (or more specifically, Quebec, Acadie, and so on). Indeed, a good deal of work by linguists in recent years has focused on the construction of indigenous norms for French, notably in Quebec (e.g. Cajolet-Laganière and Martel 1995) and Acadia (e.g. Péronnet and Kasparian 1998), norms which are meant to inform teaching programmes and practices.

Interestingly, this move on the part of francophones, and in particular of Quebec, generated a reaction on the part of Canada which in turn shifted the ground on bilingualism. Clearly, Quebec's position was a threat to the legitimacy of the Canadian state, as well as to the powerful position of English-speakers. While one does find attempts to reassert the dominance of English, the dominant discourse attempts to affirm the legitimacy of Canada through the construction of an ideology of bilingualism (Heller 1999b). This ideology responds to Quebec by first asserting Canada as a nation-state (cf. Breton 1984), and then characterizing that nation-state as simultaneously unified and diverse, first in terms of language, and later in terms of culture (a bilingual, multicultural country).

At the same time, the emergence of the modernizing discourse in Quebec went hand in hand with the development of a strong regional economic market which francophones were able to control. This also was not lost on anglophones, who realized that their privileged access to economic resources now had some competition. Many responded by going after the linguistic resources which they would now need in order to maintain their position, that is, they started to learn French or at least to make sure their children did. It is not surprising that French Immersion[2] as an educational response to the new state of affairs, emerged precisely at this time, and precisely in areas where anglophone power was most threatened, that is, Montreal and Ottawa (where indeed that programme remains most popular, despite having spread through much of urban Canada). Bilingualism, once the mark of the compromises of the francophone elite, and of the domination of the francophone urban industrial working and service class, became a mark of middle-class status and privilege for anglophones.

This process also marks the beginning of the decoupling of language and identity, at least through competition between middle-class francophones and anglophones over the resources of French, and eventually of French–English bilingualism. For successful middle-class francophones also discovered that ironically economic success necessitated dealing with English, not just because of its importance in the national market, but also because of its international value. Finally, the very success of the francophone modernizing ethnonational movement has created its own contradictions: (1) on the national and international scale, English and other languages are necessary; and (2) new, non-ethnic participants are drawn into francophone structures and networks (the anglophones described above, as well as immigrants and members of the First Nations population).

The modernizing discourse is the one with which we are most familiar; it is the one which has dominated Canadian public debate for the past forty years. However, in the past ten years the economic basis of that discourse has begun to shift, and with this shift we see emerging a new discourse, which we think of as *globalizing*. This discourse also emerges out of the consequences of the preceding, dominant discourse, and while constituting a distinct challenge, has yet to displace it entirely. The globalizing discourse picks up the importance of maintaining an outward focus, of participating actively in mainstream national and international networks and activities, and of doing so on the basis of a francophone collective identity with a political and economic power base. As we shall see in greater detail below, however, this discourse focuses more directly on the economy than on political rights and structures as a basis for the value of French, and attempts to confront the contradictions inherent in the success of the modernizing discourse, largely through diminishing discussion of identity through a focus on identity-independent language skills, or through replacing it with the concept of citizenship.

In what follows, I will examine three sites of discursive production in which the modernizing discourse is challenged by the globalizing one. While state and media discourses are certainly important sites (and which also therefore form the focus of much current work on discourse and globalization), I want to focus here on three areas which are more typical of the day-to-day functioning of discursive production: associations, education and work.

Discourses of modernization and globalization in association, educational and work milieux

In the history of francophone struggle over how to deal with anglophone power, associations, education and work provide important windows onto discursive shifts.[3]

Associations of all kinds have played a role as a kind of parallel set of political and social institutions outside the mainstream structures controlled by anglophones. In the absence of direct control over the state, in particular, francophones have often set up alternative and more locally based associations (although these associations have usually been brought together in regional or national networks, some of them centrally controlled). These associations were usually first initiated by the Catholic Church in the 'traditionalist' period; with modernization they became dependent on state support; and now with globalization and 'economization' they are having to redefine themselves and their basis of support once again.

Education also has historically been understood as essential to the survival of francophone Canada, as a primary institution of socialization. Linked initially to Church and family, education came under the control of the state, and took on greater importance as families and communities became increasingly heterogeneous and dispersed. Now the neoliberal discourse of education links it directly to preparation for the workforce. As a result, it is a key site of intersection between modernizing and globalizing discourses.

Work, of course, is a key dimension of the access to resources which lie at the heart of relations of power. For the most part in Canadian history, work meant either subsistence work within the francophone community, or it meant dealing with anglophones and English directly or indirectly, since they controlled the economy. Even the traditionalist discourse, with its elements of what Dumont (1993) characterizes as an agricultural 'utopianism', ambivalently issued periodic, and generally vain, calls for francophones to develop entrepreneurial skills which would allow them access to the anglophone-controlled economy. The modernizing discourse took on control of a portion of the private sector as a central goal, and is connected to what has come to be known in popular parlance as 'Québec Inc.' (the collection of enterprises of various sizes controlled by Quebec francophones and producing a francophone market and business network; cf. Fraser 1987). The globalizing discourse shares this focus on the workplace as key to the development of the francophone community, but must struggle now with the ways in which, having entered this world, this world is changing the meaning of what it means to be and to speak French.

Associations

In our research, we interviewed members of a large number of francophone associations of various kinds across Ontario and the Maritime provinces, ranging from provincial political lobbying associations to local folklore dance troupes, environmental associations and anti-racism activists. A few have existed since the early part of the twentieth century, but most were founded in the 1970s and 1980s in the wake of the expansion of the welfare state, and the commitment to bilingualism which was part of that expansion in Canada at the time. Now all face similar challenges in the form of neoliberal retrenchment and rationalization; the funds that were available, and on which these associations depended, are drying up, and centralizing efforts exacerbate competition for scarce resources. In addition, the client population is becoming more and more diverse from every point of view. In these associations, it is possible to see the struggle between the modernizing discourse from which the associations came forth, and the emerging globalizing discourse to which they themselves are contributing. I would like to illustrate this process through the example of one community association in a small town in Ontario.

This association grew out of a major struggle the town's activist francophones conducted over education: they wanted a high school in which French would be the language of education, and the school board refused to establish such a school until it finally lost the battle in 1980 (for a variety of reasons, many Ontario communities went through similar struggles in the 1970s, and they continue across Canada to the present day; see Heller 1994 for a more detailed discussion). That experience was a source of political consciousness-raising, at least for some members of the community, and the structures put in place during the struggle became the basis for a community association which was intended to build on the results by providing a place for francophones to continue to defend and extend their rights, and to build community in ways beyond the capacity of the schools to achieve. It was in many ways a classic modernizing association, with a view of the community as homogeneous, tied to a particular history and territory, and requiring state intervention and support in order to ameliorate its life conditions.

The centre had many ups and downs over its history, its most notable problem being how to change the ideological orientation of those potential members who saw things differently: who were happy sending their children to English-language schools, say, or who thought the activists were – well – too active. But the late 1990s saw the emergence of a more difficult challenge in the form of reduced state funding, since the centre relied almost exclusively on government support.

From 1997 to 2000, we followed the centre's activities quite closely, interviewing members of staff and of the elected *Conseil d'administration* (anyone who declares themselves a francophone in this town and surrounding area can vote at the General Assembly), observing and taping many of the monthly *Conseil* meetings, attending some activities it organized (such as a contribution to the town Winter Fair), and reading its documentation. The matter of how to react to the changed funding situation was a frequent topic; interestingly, it became embedded in a much broader set of concerns about how to actually run the association and about its mandate.

In the time we spent there, it was possible to see a number of processes developing simultaneously. First, the *Conseil* set about rationalizing its own organizational practices, drawing up job descriptions and contracts for its personnel. This is significant because it means that working for the centre becomes wage labour, not a mission, and staff become replaceable (which heroes are not, or at least less so). There was a confrontation between the *Conseil* and the centre director over this; in the end, the director was fired and replaced by someone who was hired according to bureaucratized practices (job advertisements, short-listing, interviews by a selection committee).

Second, the *Conseil* set about defining its mission. While earlier texts talked more about the importance of maintaining French language and culture in the region, a 2000 draft of the mission statement refers to the association as '. . . *un organisme catalyseur au service de la communauté francophone*' (a catalysing organization at the service of the francophone community). There are no assumptions about what the 'francophone community' might need in the way of services; the community is recast as a client group for whom services should be provided, as opposed to the body of which the centre is the voice. The association reorients itself: instead of speaking to the government on behalf of the community, it speaks to the community to find out what it wants. This is an important step in moving away from the rights focus of the modernizing discourse, and towards the economy focus of the globalizing discourse. Being francophone is, at least in part, about goods and services.

Third, the centre sponsored a separate organization with responsibility for initiating community development projects. This is significant because the centre had always in a broad sense been involved in 'community development'; clearly, here was an attempt to organize this activity in a different way, with separate funding and separate functioning. More importantly, that organization has increasingly taken over the initiation of activities which had been the centre's purview in the past, and has recast those activities with an economic slant. In a 2000 issue of the local newspaper, this new organization presented itself as having the mandate of the '*développement de biens et de services novateurs et la création d'entreprises et d'emplois qui montrent la valeur ajoutée des francophones et des bilingues de la (région) où l'on reflète leur impact considérable sur la vitalité de la région*' (development of innovative goods and services and creation of companies and of jobs which show the added value of the francophones and the bilinguals of the (region) where it is reflected their considerable impact on the vitality of the region). With this statement, the region's associations move squarely away from the modernizing discourse to focus on the economy, and on the economic value of the francophone community and of their language (note the inclusion of '*bilingues*'). The goal here is to sell the community and its linguistic capital to potential employers, in order to attract jobs to an economically depressed area, and jobs to which local French-speakers should have privileged access (but from which bilingual anglophones or people of mixed background would not be excluded, which was a problem with the modernizing discourse). These are, of course, the tourism and communications jobs of the new economy.

In this and in other cases, local associations have moved from a modernist view of themselves as the voice of a homogeneous community, a space for the maintenance of traditional language and culture, and towards a view of themselves as service providers, with a focus on jobs, training and settlement. The older view of the francophone population as community persists, in different forms, and for different reasons. In many ways, the institutional infrastructure currently in place necessitates its maintenance, or many jobs will be lost and resources will go elsewhere. In addition, though, the concept provides a kind of quality control regarding commodifiable linguistic resources, and also acts as source for an authentic identity which is commodifiable in and of itself (in tourism, for example, or in the arts and culture). This last form of commodification potentially performs the final separation of language and identity (one does not actually have to speak French to construct 'French' cultural goods), and is worth exploring in greater detail than I have room to do here. I will focus instead on the issue of the value of the linguistic resources of French and of French–English bilingualism in the arenas where debates on those questions are most evident: education and work.

Education

Education has been a major focus of both traditionalist and modernizing activism. Working in part through the state and in part through the courts, francophone activists have succeeded in setting up French-language elementary and high schools throughout Canada (although there are still areas where the issue remains current and unresolved), as well as some post-secondary institutions and some pre-schools and daycare centres. French-language schools are understood as key sites for the reproduction of the francophone community in minority areas. Indeed, they are perceived in much the same way in Quebec, where language legislation (the Charter of the French Language, 1977) aims at ensuring that immigrants integrate into the francophone community through their children's attendance at French-language schools; the future of the francophone community in Quebec is understood as being partly dependent on francophone education's ability to socialize new members into the community, and notably to socialize them into a knowledge of and preference for French as a language of public communication.

However, both in Quebec and in minority areas, the very success of the modernizing movement in establishing French-language education as a means to gain access to the newly valuable resource of the French language, has created conditions which challenge the modernizing understanding of what it means to be and to speak French. In Quebec, middle-class anglophone parents not only send their children to French Immersion classes, they also send their children increasingly to French-language schools. Immigrants attend those same schools, learn and use French, but do not necessarily take it the step further that many would like: they speak what they like amongst themselves, and that is sometimes French, sometimes English, sometimes yet other languages, and frequently a mixture of all of them. In addition, there is much dispute about what 'integration' means.

This is perhaps best illustrated in shifting categorial terminology. For a long time, labels were fairly unambiguously ethnic: people spoke of 'French Canadians', and even the term 'Québécois' could be understood in an ethnonational sense. In the 1970s, the term 'francophone' began to gain favour, as a potentially ethnically neutral term referring only to competence in French as a new, and inclusionary, criterion of membership. But quickly a new term emerged, one which is generally avoided in writing, and which when it appears occurs in scare quotes, even orally: '*francophones de souche*' (often translated as 'old stock francophones'). This term appears to maintain the delicate distinction between ethnic and non-ethnic francophones, reintroducing a modernist perspective into a process which again separates language and identity. So, it is possible to go to a French school, to speak French, and still not be sure to what extent one counts as a francophone. From the perspective of those doing the defining, the problem is how to maintain a notion of nationhood without practising the very kind of discrimination against which the modernist, nationalist movement fought. Schools are a key site where these conflicts unfold on the ground.

In minority settings, much the same issues manifest themselves, heightened perhaps by the greater presence and power of English and English-speakers. I spent many years doing fieldwork in French-language schools in southern Ontario (cf. Heller 1994, 1999a), and data from that work show the challenges that diversity presents to the modernist idea of *la francophonie canadienne*. These challenges can be understood as taking the form first of rights of participation; but quickly they turn also to questions having to do with language.

The participation issue turns on the question of who has the right to attend a French-language school, and thereby contributes to a definition of who counts as Franco-Ontarian. Choice of language of education works differently in minority areas than in Quebec. The Canadian Charter of Rights and Freedoms (1982) guarantees rights to French-language education outside Quebec to a certain well-defined population, so there are people whom these schools *must* accept. Beyond that, schools are free to accept other people as well if they so choose. Most schools so choose because otherwise they would not be able to maintain the level of enrolment the province imposes on all schools (minority or majority) for access to resources. They also so choose for the same reasons as in Quebec: a concern to not practise ethnic discrimination and a concern to reproduce the community.

However, the result is a conflict regarding participation in the structures of power, and therefore over who gets to define the schools' values and practices. In an interview in the early 1990s, a Haitian parent recalled for me what it was like for him when he engaged in struggles with the local French-language schools and other associations. Speaking for others like him, he explains that 'Franco-Ontarians' were afraid of including 'other francophones', because they thought it would diminish the legitimacy of their claims against anglophones, with the result that others felt 'rejected'. They decided to fight for inclusion, which they did both symbolically in public debates, and materially by organizing a slate to run, successfully, for office as school trustees.

Ils ont eu peur qu'on les fasse eux passer pour un autre groupe minoritaire (. . .) alors que nous-autres francophones on venait d'ailleurs, on s'est senti rejetés (. . .) le terme 'franco-ontarien' ne s'appliquait qu'aux autres Franco-Ontariens de souche 'pure laine', et alors il y a eu toute une bataille autour de ceci, et nous n'avons pas été acceptés à bras ouverts. (. . .) (mais) nous avons fait le choix de vivre en français en Ontario, nous avons fait le choix d'envoyer nos enfants dans les écoles françaises (. . .) nous avons préféré nous battre pour nous faire accepter par la communauté franco-ontarienne (. . .) c'est pourquoi nous nous sommes organisés et pis nous avons élu nos (xx) pis on s'est fait, nous avons été élus (. . .)

They were afraid that we would make them seem like another minority group (. . .) so us francophones we came from elsewhere, we felt rejected (. . .). The term 'Franco-Ontarian' only applied to the other Franco-Ontarians of origin 'pure wool', and so there was a whole battle about that, and we weren't accepted with open arms. (. . .) (but) we made the choice to live in French in Ontario, we made the choice to send our children to the French schools (. . .) we preferred to fight to be accepted by the Franco-Ontarian community (. . .) that's why we organized ourselves and then we elected our (xx) then we got ourselves, we were elected (. . . .)

This parent points to the problem of sharing power, with all that that implies. Importantly, later in the interview he points specifically to the question of language, arguing that newcomers like himself are actually more faithful to the modernist goal of creating monolingual institutional spaces than the so-called 'Franco-Ontariens' themselves. It is not only then that there is need for tolerance and openness, it is that the specific participants in question actually contribute to increasing the legitimacy of the claim that the school is a French-language institution. What has to be given up in order to achieve that is a uniform culture and identity.

Over the course of a three-year period in the early 1990s, in which I conducted intensive fieldwork in one high school, I was able to witness more of the unfolding of the kinds of processes the parent above describes. Students who felt marginalized followed their parents' initiatives in insisting on equitable participation. They also argued that schools should be preparing students not for a narrow inward-looking task of cultural preservation, but for access to the opportunities that the world provides, and that the diversity of the student body should be seen as representing a resource existing already within the school for enhancing that preparation, rather than as a threat to Franco-Ontarian cultural cohesion.

This view, which converges with the socioeconomic goals of middle-class francophones and anglophones in the school, is balanced in an interesting way in many versions of the school's public image. The most condensed symbol perhaps is the statue and plaque the school unveiled in 1994 on the occasion of its twenty-fifth anniversary. The school was named in 1969 after a traditional symbol of French

Canada, a French 'explorer' sent by France to lay claim to territory through claiming and settling land. The school commissioned a statue of this man, carved out of
wood, a material which itself is symbolic of French Canadians' association with the
Canadian forest in the fur trade and the lumber business, and in colonization. The
school placed the statue in the foyer, surrounded by student-made wall hangings
representing different countries of origin of the student body, and before it a plaque
explaining the symbolic significance of the statue in terms of the school's motto:
'*L'unité dans la diversité* (Unity in diversity)'. The attempt then, is to reconcile tradition, modernity and the diversity of the consequences of modernity through
constructing some kind of common symbol which is meant to balance the historical legitimacy of the school and its putative population, and the reality of the lack
of historical ties to that image on the part of the present student body.

   In the end, the most effective common tie turned out to be language. Everyone
involved in the school agreed that French is valuable as a language of international
communication, and that with both French and English, students would be well-
positioned to profit from the globalized economy (as one student said : '. . . *tu
connais l'anglais, tu connais le français, tu es bien parti dans la vie'* – you know English,
you know French, you are well launched in life).

   For many parents and students, these forms of linguistic capital were quite distinct from any sense of identity, quite divorced from the modernist discourse. For
them, language was principally a commodity. Here is how one set of parents put it:

Mother: I think it's such an asset to have another language, I mean I probably
          didn't . . . realize that until I moved to Toronto, I probably think that even
          more now . . . that when I see people speak three or four languages . . .
Father: Yeah maybe what should be now that your French is there good for
          because . . . we are a two language country, so that was good, for me it is
          worthwhile to . . . have that, and I think that from that now we say, here
          how about Spanish . . . because of the North-South free trade (*a reference
          to the North American Free Trade Agreement, signed in 1990, facilitating links
          among Canada, Mexico and the USA*) . . . how about Chinese or something
          like that because there's going to be big markets, you know, it would be
          nice to have this go on . . . to a third or fourth language . . .
Mother: I just think of it as being another thing that a person has, I mean, you
          could . . . take another subject, so why not know another language, I just
          think it is an asset.

This concern about the importance of French (and English) for the workplace,
and, more generally, as 'an asset', ends up converging with the historical preoccupation of francophone activists with the question of norms. This time, though, the
concern is less with French as the symbol of a unified nation, and more with French
as a means of international communication. This is understood to require a certain

degree of standardization (or else how will people in or from different parts of the world communicate?). It is also understood to require a certain 'quality', since the purpose of international communication is to do well on international marketplaces where competition from English is stiff. In many ways, while the ideological under-pinnings shift, the result is the same: a preference for a standardized language distinct from English. Nonetheless, two other things also change, with potentially important consequences: the location of those who decide what counts as good French is moved to an ethnoculturally diverse, educated middle class, and away from a nation-ally identified middle class; and language is treated more as a commodity and less as a marker of identity. The expectations regarding its use in contexts such as school thereby shift along with those changes; using French is less a matter of adherence to a collective political agenda and more a matter of individual wise investment.

Work

It is the (concrete or imagined) 'realities' of the workplace that increasingly drive the ways Franco-Ontarian (and other) schools approach language, and the ways par-ents and students make choices regarding language of education and language education. This education–work link is not only part of discourse in everyday life, it is very explicitly a core dimension of Ontario government educational policy (which not only treats schooling as preparation for the workplace but also treats education as encompassing workplace training), although there is deep ambiva-lence about whether or not bi/multilingual skills are important enough work skills to merit attention. In addition, as we have seen, traditional francophone associations and other institutions have been focusing more and more on the value of French in the new economy as a means to retain the value of their linguistic capital and to fur-ther the economic advancement of community members.

Some of our recent research has been examining French-language adult literacy centres and workplaces typical of the new economy as a way of discovering to what extent the image that is projected in public discourse matches experience on the ground (cf. Labrie *et al.* 2000; Roy 2000; Budach *et al.* 2000). Francophone lead-ers vaunt their communities as 'added value' for potential employers and investors; they urge francophones to start up small or medium sized companies, that is, to become entrepreneurs; and young people expect their bilingualism to translate into privileged access to jobs in the service and information sectors. The question is first, whether or not these language skills in any way actually make a difference to people's lives, and second, if so, what kinds of language skills are involved.

The answer so far seems to point again in the direction of the value of standard-ized 'monolingual' forms of language skills, at opposite ends of the economic hierarchy. For Québécois in particular, these language skills are an important dimension of job promotion, so much so that many francophone Québécois private sector managers arrange temporary transfers to an English-speaking milieu in order to perfect their English. Their French remains important for privileged access to control over the regional francophone market centred in Quebec, and is key to their rise in the Quebec branches of national and international companies. Once they speak English, of course, they are also well-placed for international duty. We know little, however, empirically about their trajectories. I suspect, in addition, that some forms of vernacular French retain their value among this group as a means of maintaining privileged control over their (historically) new status, that is, as a way to fend off competition from bi/multilingual anglophones and allophones who may compete for their jobs (with similar effects of closure, for example, as the use of Swiss German among Swiss bankers). There are similar competitions at the higher levels of the federal public service, although it appears there that the historically dominant anglophones have succeeded in using bilingualism as a means to retain their privileged position, fending off francophone competition.

Most jobs requiring bilingualism across Canada actually seem to be concentrated at the lower levels of the job hierarchy (Hart *et al.* 1990 may have been among the first to notice this trend). It is at the interface between enterprise and clientele that multilingual skills are most required, that is, at the front line of the provision of services and information. It is the telephone representatives in call centres; the wait staff and desk clerks at the hotels; the croupiers in the casinos; the sales clerks in stores who are bi/multilingual, and not the managers. It may even be the case that companies organize themselves to make sure that the bilingual staff they have remain where they are most useful, at the bottom of the scale, thereby actually creating obstacles to their advancement (Labrie, personal communication).

In addition, Roy (2000) has shown that there are contradictory pressures regarding the nature of the language skills valued for those kinds of jobs. On the one hand, service providers are meant to be able to make connections with clients, and this ought to mean being able to speak like them, or at least to understand them, even if they are vernacular speakers. At the same time, pressures to render uniform service, and of uniform 'quality', tend to push companies to implement language standards which are quite normative. It is the service providers themselves who are left to sort out how to manage those contradictions.

Bilingual skills seem, then, to be an advantage mainly for getting low-level entry jobs. In the communities in which we have been doing fieldwork, however, it is important to understand that these jobs are considered better than the real alternative, which is no jobs at all, or having to leave the community to find them. They are also understood as a potential life-line for the community; the problem is that it is usually precisely the kind of economic marginalization which may be being reproduced here that has also historically been the basis for social, linguistic and cultural reproduction. At the same time, the association of French with the workplace means that the language begins to acquire value more as a straightforward commodity, and less as a means for developing the kind of social cohesion which goes along with the distribution of other, quite different kinds of resources.

Finally, communities often tend to assume that the *fact* of being bilingual will be an advantage, when new economy companies actually pay a fair amount of attention to the *nature* of that bilingualism. The kinds of economically disadvantaged communities which have an interest in these kinds of jobs also possess bilingual linguistic competence of a fairly mixed, and vernacular, nature. This ends up being a problem both for job candidates, who can be refused hiring or bilingual bonuses (as risibly low as these usually are), and for companies, who have a hard time finding people with the kinds of educated, standardized language skills they look for and who are willing to take the poorly-paid and often insecure positions on offer. It is not clear where this will lead. At the moment, we are seeing companies adopt a variety of strategies. In the company which has been the focus of Roy's work, for example, we have seen attempts at finding a new labour pool (from Quebec, or among immigrants), as well as attempts to provide in-house language training. The group that seems best placed is students and others seeking part-time flexible work (including some retirees and some women with young children).

The workplace in the end has been at the heart of the language struggle in Canada. New developments seem to indicate that French–English bilingualism is shifting ground, gaining importance in the new economy, but perhaps in some rather unexpected ways. Its value remains tied to the existence of French monolingual markets, whether in Canada or elsewhere. The question is, where does that leave the monolinguals?

Implications for the teaching and learning of French in Canada

For a long time, the learning of French by anglophones and English by francophones was limited to an elite who often learned it first in school, the francophones to talk to the English, the English to appear educated. Whatever 'language of the other' learning took place informally on the streets among the working class (for example, between the Irish and the French) is recorded only incidentally in literature and journalism, and not well described or known.

The modernizing movement of the 1960s provided a power base for francophones, and thereby increased the value of French, both for francophones and for anglophones. Schools were the first to be called into reorganizing access to French–English bilingualism, but many other players besides educators were called upon to define the nature of the language skills to be valued and developed: translators, linguists, writers, journalists and politicians all have had something to say at one point or another. But the nature of the modernizing movement contained within it a paradox: the importance of legitimizing linguistic forms and practices symbolic of authenticity and identity, while valuing linguistic forms and practices that are inclusive of a diverse population and means of access to a diverse world.

The economic shifts that gave rise to modernization have unfolded in ways which only serve to underscore this paradox, and to move language increasingly away from a symbol of community to the form of a commodity. Nonetheless, community has not disappeared; instead, it reasserts itself in struggles over access to bilingualism, to valued forms of French and to the resources attached to them. The consequences manifest themselves in debates over when and if to introduce English teaching into French-language schools; over the relative importance of French versus other languages (Japanese or Spanish, for example) in language education in English-language schools; over the value of the vernacular versus standard French; over the very nature of standard French; and over how best to be bilingual; to name just a few of the debates current in Canadian society. They also manifest themselves in struggles over who gets to participate in these debates, and over whose interests should prevail in them.

However, the popularity of the view that language skills are technical (which does in many ways accompany commodification) fails to account for the reality of the social categories which are at play. We would not have such debates if it were not for the fact that linguistic resources are unequally distributed in Canadian society, and more importantly, if it were not for the fact that the possibility of defining their value and controlling their circulation is also unequally distributed. That unequal distribution is of course not random; rather, we see the effects not only of the old ethnolinguistic categories which have accompanied and organized us for hundreds of years, but also of new configurations of race, gender and class.

Language teaching and learning are about struggles over resources, not the least of which is knowledge about linguistic forms and practices themselves. In the age of globalization, there are shifts over how these processes unfold, which make them perhaps more visible, more amenable to description and analysis. The current age if anything makes language more obviously tied into processes of construction of social difference and inequality, not less, as globalization utopianists would have it. 'Skilling' language masks this process. Language teaching and learning are no less political now that we speak the language of economy than they were before.

Notes

1 The data come from a number of research projects funded by the Government of Québec, Multiculturalism Canada, the Ontario Ministry of Education, the Ontario Ministry of Education Transfer Grant to the Ontario Institute for Studies in Education, the Ontario Ministry of Training (Ontario-Quebec Exchange programme), the German-American Academic Council Foundation, and the Social Sciences and Humanities Research Council of Canada. Many people have been, and are still involved in this research in a number of ways, directly and indirectly; for the purposes of this chapter I would like in particular to acknowledge the role of Normand Labrie, Jürgen Erfurt, Annette Boudreau, Lise Dubois, Claudine Moïse, Patricia Lamarre, Deirdre Meintel, Sylvie Roy and Gabriele Budach.

2 French Immersion is a cover term for a variety of educational arrangements which have in common the use of French as a language of instruction for subjects other than French in schools for students whose first language is not French.

3 The Catholic Church has also played a crucial role historically. I leave it aside here partly because of its waning influence in the modernist period, but I recognize nonetheless that it is a revealing institution to examine. Some data on the Church were collected as part of the *Prise de parole* project; they are currently being analysed by Jürgen Erfurt.

Part II
Zones of contact

4 Globalization and the teaching of 'communication skills'

Deborah Cameron

> I think it's essential for us to be able – in this global community and as the global community becomes even smaller through the internet and through all kinds of electronics – that we *are* able to communicate. . . . It is essential that there be a uniform way of talking, for the economy, for national communications, for exchange of politics and even on the level of individual couples being able to communicate. . . . And there are rules for that.
>
> (Judith Kuriansky, psychologist and therapist, speaking on the BBC World Service, August 1999)

The epigraph to this chapter reproduces some remarks made by a well-known American expert on communication in response to my own arguments about the effects of globalization on language and language-use.[1] At the time of our encounter I was finishing a book about the contemporary obsession with 'communication skills' and 'communication problems' (Cameron 2000). One of my conclusions was that globalization had given new legitimacy, and a new twist, to the long-lived idea that linguistic diversity is a problem, while linguistic uniformity is a desirable ideal. My interlocutor did not dispute the factual part of this argument, but she did take issue with my negative attitude to the developments I had identified. What I regarded as a regrettable curtailment of linguistic diversity, she celebrated as progress towards increased global harmony and mutual understanding.

The argument which the two of us conducted in the last months of the twentieth century is not, in its general outlines, new. On the contrary, what Umberto Eco (1995) labels 'the search for the perfect language' – typically conceived in universal or global terms, and representing a mythical unity among the peoples of the world – has inspired arguments for at least two millennia. In the nineteenth century, the quest for linguistic unity was pursued through the creation of international auxiliary languages like Esperanto and Volapük. In the twentieth century argument came to centre on the desirability or otherwise of using English as a global lingua franca. That debate continues, and is addressed by a number of contributors to the present volume (see especially Chapter 1 by Kubota and Chapter 6 by Wallace). But it is not what was at issue in the disagreement between Dr Kuriansky and myself.

When she asserted the need for 'a uniform way of talking' in the global community, she did not mean that the people of the world should abandon their native tongues and agree to communicate in one language, be it English, Mandarin or Esperanto. Nor was she making a plea for standard English to replace every other dialect. When she said 'there are rules', she was not talking about rules of grammatical correctness, but rather about norms for relating to other people through talk. She went on to give some concrete examples of these norms. Speaking directly is better than speaking indirectly. Speaking positively is better than criticizing. Negotiating is better than arguing. Sharing your feelings is better than being silent and withdrawn.

Dr Kuriansky maintained that norms of this sort are applicable across languages, dialects, cultures and contexts. Where a community departs from them, the result will be problematic. Thus she claimed (citing her professional experience of working with Japanese organizations) that the existence of multiple levels of formality in Japanese is not just a problem for foreigners trying to communicate with Japanese, but an obstacle to good communication among Japanese themselves. When another participant in the discussion, a former Buddhist monk from Tibet, explained that he spent a certain period of each day in total silence, 'listening to what is within', Dr Kuriansky responded that meditation can be an aid to good communication; it helps to clarify thoughts and feelings so they can later be shared more fully and honestly with others. (The Tibetan shared with me later that he felt she had missed the point.)

What, it might be asked, does this have to do with the theme of globalization and language teaching? The short answer, on which I will elaborate below, is that in the rise of experts like Dr Kuriansky (most of them not trained in linguistics or language teaching, but in psychology, therapy or counselling), in their public utterances and in their activities as consultants to various organizations, I believe we are witnessing the consolidation of a new and powerful discourse on language and communication, which has significant implications both for language teaching and for discussions of its politics.

'Communication' and the international politics of language

In recent years, critical discussions of the international politics of language and language teaching have often been framed in terms of the concept of 'linguistic imperialism' (cf. Phillipson 1992; Pennycook 1994; Canagarajah 1999a). I have no intention of arguing that this concept is no longer relevant or useful, for clearly the phenomena it encompasses are still very much with us. However, I do want to suggest that there are other, newer phenomena which are less well accounted for in the conceptual framework of linguistic imperialism. For instance, the views on language and communication expressed by Dr Kuriansky are undoubtedly ethnocentric – they display intolerance of cultural difference and presuppose the superiority of the expert's own cultural/linguistic norms. But this ethnocentrism does not take the form of linguistic imperialism as that term is ordinarily understood, i.e. promoting one language over others. Instead it involves promoting particular interactional norms, genres and speech-styles *across* languages, on the grounds that they are maximally 'effective' for purposes of 'communication'. Ryuko Kubota (this volume) provides another example in her account of some recent changes in the practices of Japanese schools. Genres such as 'debate', and 'logical' styles of prose writing, have been imported from Western educational traditions with the intention of remedying alleged deficiencies in Japanese habits of thought and expression. However, there is no question of displacing Japanese itself as the medium for speech and writing. Rather students are expected to master new and supposedly 'better' ways of expressing themselves in Japanese.

What is imposed in cases like the one Kubota mentions is not someone else's language, but someone else's definition of what is acceptable or desirable in your own. I would argue that it is important to distinguish between this and more traditional forms of linguistic imperialism, not only because the effects are different, but also and perhaps more importantly because the underlying attitude to language and culture is different. In particular, it is (on the surface, at least) more inclined to view diversity in positive terms, as a natural and valuable aspect of human experience. This idea of diversity as enriching, however, tends not to be pushed to the point where it might threaten the very notion of a (universal or fundamentally shared) 'human experience' (see also Kramsch and Thorne, Chapter 5 this volume). Instead, the potential threat is neutralized in a rhetoric of 'unity in diversity'. This has become a favoured trope of the new capitalism, well illustrated by advertisements for transnational clothing retailers like Benetton and Gap, which pointedly feature models with a range of skin colours, all dressed in the same jeans and sweaters. Here the differences we conventionally think of as 'deep' (e.g. racial or ethnic identity) are portrayed as superficial; the young people in the poster are part of a global community defined not by ancestry but by preferred styles of clothing.

Discourse on the subject of 'global communication' contains analogous tendencies and similar contradictions. Rather than propose a wholesale levelling of difference through the adoption of a single global language, it has elaborated a version of 'unity in diversity', according to which the existence of different languages is not in itself a problem; problems arise only to the extent that these languages embody different or incommensurable worldviews. It is those 'deeper' differences that need to be levelled if global communication is to be effective. Hence the recommendation that, for instance, Japanese students should learn to write Japanese in accordance with Western norms of 'logic', or that Japanese businesspeople should adopt more 'direct' or 'informal' ways of interacting among themselves. On the surface, this approach preserves linguistic diversity, but at a deeper level the effect is to make every language into a vehicle for the affirmation of similar values and beliefs, and for the enactment by speakers of similar social identities and roles. Language becomes a global product available in different local flavours.

I have been focusing on the ways in which the new rhetoric of global communication *differs* from older discourses of linguistic imperialism, but there are also continuities. The dissemination of 'global' communicative norms and genres, like the dissemination of international languages, involves a one-way flow of expert knowledge from dominant to subaltern cultures. (I use the terms 'dominant' and 'subaltern' here in preference to the more familiar 'centre' and 'periphery' because globalization arguably calls into question the applicability of the latter terms as they are usually defined. Any detailed discussion of that issue, however, is beyond the scope of this chapter.) As will no doubt be evident from my listing of the communicative norms adduced by Judith Kuriansky, the ideal of 'good' or 'effective' communication bears a non-coincidental resemblance to the preferred speech-habits of educated middle-class and predominantly white people brought up in the USA. (Beyond that, the ideal reflects the principles governing a specific communicational activity, therapy, which is not confined to the USA but is particularly culturally salient there.) I know of no case in which the communicative norms of a non-Western, or indeed non-Anglophone society have been exported by expert consultants. Finns do not run workshops for British businesses on the virtues of talking less; Japanese are not invited to instruct Americans in speaking indirectly. The discourse of 'global' communication is not a case of postmodern 'hybridity' or 'fusion'.

The relevance of the foregoing discussion to language *teaching* can be seen if we ask how the dissemination of 'global' norms for 'effective' communication is actually accomplished. The process of dissemination does not depend exclusively on the activities of experts like Judith Kuriansky who produce texts for both professional and lay audiences, speak publicly via the media and provide consultancy services to organizations. At ground level, dissemination is accomplished through instruction and training in particular linguistic practices. Forms of instruction and training which aim to develop 'communication skills', typically defined in terms of the discourse outlined above, are increasingly common in all kinds of contemporary institutions, ranging from elementary schools to multinational corporations.

Here it might be objected that these forms of instruction are quite different from what is usually meant or implied by 'language teaching', and certainly from the kind of language teaching with which this book is mainly concerned, namely the teaching of foreign or second languages. Communication skills training is not necessarily directed at second language learners specifically: many or most recipients are either native monolingual or highly proficient bilingual speakers of the language in which (and through which) they are learning to 'communicate'. On the other hand, there are forms of instruction, many of them in the category of language teaching for specific purposes or for business, which incorporate concerns like 'negotiation', 'meeting skills', 'presentation skills', etc., into programmes aimed at particular groups of L2 learners such as managers in multinational companies. In future it seems probable that a communication skills element will be incorporated into L2 teaching for less elite occupational groups, for instance those who work or aspire to work in the internationalized service sector (as Monica Heller remarks (this volume), many entry-level service jobs in tourism, travel, leisure and hospitality demand foreign language competence). In sum, just as I have already argued that globalization poses a challenge to prevailing ideas about 'linguistic imperialism', perhaps it also demands that we revisit our assumptions about the nature and scope of 'language teaching'.

But to bring out the full force of this argument it is necessary to place the notion of 'communication skills' in a broader context than I have done so far. An illuminating analysis of 'communication skills' and the associated instructional practices must take account of how 'skills' are in general defined and what place they occupy in contemporary discourse on teaching and learning. It is also important to look closely at what 'communication' means in that discourse, and how it has come to be categorized as a 'skill'. Below, I will suggest that current understandings of 'skills', of 'communication' and of the relationship between them are themselves products of globalization: they are related on one hand to changes in the organization of work driven by intensified economic competition, and on the other to changing conceptions of knowledge in the wake of the information revolution.

Communication, 'skills' and the 'new work order'

'Communication' is among the keywords of the global age, just as it was a keyword, though with a different set of meanings, in the age of the industrial revolution (Williams 1983: 72–3). In contemporary usage we hear and read frequent references to '[information and] communication technologies (ICTs)' and '[mass] communications media', both of which, of course, are implicated in the processes of globalization. Global markets depend on the rapid information flows made possible by ICTs, while media corporations (like Disney and News International) are powerful players in those markets, whose products also contribute to globalization at the cultural level. When the word 'communication' collocates with 'skills', however, the reference is rarely if ever to computers, the internet or satellite TV. Rather it is usually to the oldest, least technologized and least mediated of all communication channels: spoken interaction, or talk.

In support of this claim we might note that in surveys undertaken to assess which skills are needed to maximize employability, employers almost invariably distinguish 'communication skills' from 'literacy' and 'ICT skills'. Furthermore, they consistently rate the 'communication skills' displayed by recruits to the workforce as *more important* than their literacy skills or their facility with ICTs — and also, in many cases, as less satisfactory. A survey reported in *People Management* in November 1997, for example, found that 'Oral communication was cited [by employers] as the most important soft skill but was perceived to be sorely lacking in recruits coming straight from further or higher education. While 91 per cent of respondents believed that this was an essential skill, only 32 per cent said it was present among this group'.

The obvious question here is *why* oral communication should be the object of so much concern. Why are key actors in the new economy – including politicians and policymakers as well as employers and other representatives of the commercial world – so preoccupied with something that used to be thought of as a mundane activity requiring little in the way of special 'skill', namely interacting with others via the medium of spoken language? The answer lies in what Gee *et al.* (1996) have called 'the new work order'. Although there is debate about the exact nature and extent of change, it is widely agreed that during the 1980s and 1990s there were important shifts in the conceptualization and the experience of work, reflecting the emergence of a deregulated, hyper-competitive, post-industrial, globalized economy. The resulting 'new work order' makes new demands on workers; Gee *et al.* are among a number of commentators (see also Fairclough 1992, and contributors to Cope and Kalantzis 2000) who draw attention to the specifically *linguistic* aspects of those demands.

It is true, of course, that linguistic abilities were an important factor in labour market stratification long before the current, global phase of capitalism. Individuals have long been, and still are, denied access to certain kinds of work because of their inability to read and write, or to use a standard language rather than a non-standard dialect, or to speak the dominant language of a multilingual society. But whereas the industrial economy required large numbers of manual workers, who were colloquially referred to as 'hands' and whose language skills were seen as largely irrelevant, the new capitalism is different. For one thing it is dominated by forms of work in which language-using is an integral part of almost every worker's function. In his influential text *The Work of Nations*, former USA Labor Secretary Robert Reich (1992) suggested that the traditional 'manual/non-manual' distinction was in the process of being superseded by a new division of labour, in which an elite class of 'symbolic analysts' – creative professionals skilled in the manipulation of words, numbers, images and digital bits – would dominate a much larger and less privileged group of workers providing routine services, either 'in person' or behind the scenes. While the work done by these service providers is not necessarily any more creative or demanding than traditional manual work, it does put more pressure on literacy skills (since service work often requires extensive data inputting and record keeping) and more generally, interpersonal communication skills (being pleasant and attentive to customers and clients in face-to-face talk or on the telephone). The implication, at least in those economically advanced societies where manufacturing industries are in decline while the service and creative industries are expanding rapidly, is that individuals will need a relatively high level of linguistic skill if they are to participate in waged labour at all.

Because of these developments there has been a marked 'skilling up' of talk at work. In the rhetoric and practice of many institutions, talking has been promoted from a taken-for-granted social accomplishment of all normal humans to a complex task requiring special effort to master. At the same time, mastery of this task is expected of workers across the occupational and social spectrum. Consider, for instance, part of the 'person specification' for a job in the UK's National Health Service (taken from *The Medical Monitor*, 1994). The ideal recruit is defined as someone who can, *inter alia*:

- demonstrate sound interpersonal relationships and an awareness of the individual clients' psychological and emotional needs;
- understand the need for effective verbal and non-verbal communication;
- support clients and relatives in the care environment by demonstrating empathy and understanding.

One might suppose that this advertisement is aimed at members of one of the 'caring professions' – perhaps the hospital is seeking a medical social worker or a clinical psychologist. In fact, the job on offer is that of a hospital orderly: in other words, a cleaner. There is, of course, nothing new or surprising in the assumption that hospital cleaners will talk to patients. But specifications like the one just quoted change what was previously understood as an informal, 'natural' and, in this context, incidental activity into a formalized professional responsibility. And this formalization of workers' responsibility to 'communicate' not only changes the status of the activity denoted by 'communication', it also implies that there are standards for the performance of that activity. Communication becomes not just something workers are required to do, but something they are expected to be, or become, *good at*. What counts as 'good' is defined by the institution: in the hospital case, for instance, the specification suggests that a cleaner must have particular conversational abilities (e.g. 'demonstrating empathy and understanding') and be able to give a quasi-theoretical account of why these abilities are important ('understand the need for effective verbal and nonverbal communication'). Defining what kinds of talk employees must be able to produce in a given workplace context (e.g. 'demonstrating empathy') makes it possible to consider designing instructional programmes in which those ways of talking are explicitly taught.

The practice of instructing people in speaking and listening is also gaining ground in educational institutions, not least because of politicians' and policymakers' concern that education should prepare students to meet the needs of the new economy. As I have noted already, employers who are asked to specify their needs consistently stress that what matters to them is not the specialist subject knowledge new recruits bring with them from education, but transferable or 'key' skills – among which oral communication skills are ranked as particularly important. Discussing the educational consequences of the 'enterprise culture' promoted by Margaret Thatcher's administration in Britain during the 1980s, Norman Fairclough notes 'a general shift towards seeing knowledge operationally, in terms of competence . . . and towards seeing education as training in skills' (1995: 239). In retrospect, Thatcherite 'enterprise culture' can be seen as part of the early stages of globalization; as that process has advanced, the emphasis placed on skills has become even more marked. There has been a move towards incorporating skills more explicitly into the educational curriculum, especially in post-compulsory education (in the UK this means education after the age of 16). For example, students following advanced level academic courses which qualify them for university entrance will in future be required to produce a portfolio demonstrating competence in communication (both oral and written), application of number and the use of ICTs. National Vocational Qualifications (NVQs), for which instruction is partly workplace-based and partly college-based, also include communication as one 'area of competence' in which students are assessed.

Yet it would be wrong to suggest that the present preoccupation with communication skills is solely a reflex of recent and ongoing changes in the economic sphere, or that instruction in oral communication is a purely vocational enterprise aimed at increasing the employability of entrants to the labour market. On the contrary, it may be argued that in its attitudes to communication, the new capitalism has followed rather than led, borrowing many of its ideas and techniques from what could loosely be called 'self-improvement culture'. That culture is also the locus for a good deal of informal (non-institutional) instruction in oral communication skills, undertaken by individuals voluntarily and for personal rather than professional reasons. Contemporary attitudes to 'communication' – and contemporary approaches to teaching it – cannot be fully understood without reference to the culture of self-improvement.

Communication and the culture of self-improvement

What I am calling 'self-improvement culture' comprises a range of practices and text-types focusing on the individual and her or his relationships with others, and particularly on the problems of modern personal life. Among the most accessible expressions of this culture are self-help and popular psychology books, and broadcast talk shows of the 'confessional' type where people talk about their experiences, problems and feelings, sometimes receiving advice from an expert (a therapist, counsellor or psychologist). Large numbers of people are at least occasional consumers of this kind of material, and it is so ubiquitous in contemporary popular culture that it is difficult for anyone to remain entirely unfamiliar with it. More active forms of self-improvement include taking a course in something like assertiveness training or positive thinking, transactional analysis or neurolinguistic programming, being 'in therapy', or participating in a groups with a quasi-therapeutic purpose, such as one of the twelve-step programmes of the 'recovery' movement (e.g. Alcoholics Anonymous). Commentators on the culture of self-improvement usually date its emergence as a salient phenomenon to the late 1960s and 1970s, and while some self-improvement activities have apparently declined since then (e.g. being in therapy for reasons of personal growth rather than clinical need), others (e.g. reading popular psychology books) have flourished and grown.

All the forms of self-improvement mentioned above place considerable emphasis on 'communication' (not surprisingly, since after all their roots are in therapy – the so-called 'talking cure'). Being able to 'communicate' – that is, talk openly and honestly about one's experiences and feelings, while listening non-judgementally to the talk of other people about *their* experiences and feelings – is held to be the key to solving problems and improving relationships with significant others. Many self-improvement activities not only emphasize this point in general terms, they also teach or model particular ways of 'communicating'. Assertiveness training for example teaches how to communicate 'honestly and directly' (e.g. by performing speech acts like refusals on record without mitigation); transactional analysis teaches trainees how to spot 'crossed' messages; twelve-step programmes model a particular narrative structure for presenting one's life experience (the story that begins 'I'm X and I'm an alcoholic').

Self-improvement practices concerned with 'communication' have had a direct and significant influence on the thinking and practice of the new capitalism. 'Therapeutic' approaches, particularly assertiveness training and transactional analysis, are widely used in workplace training. This is a good example of what Norman Fairclough calls 'the technologization of discourse' (Fairclough 1992), whereby communication techniques elaborated for a particular purpose are taken out of their original context and used for a quite different purpose. In the culture of self-improvement, people learn techniques for creating rapport for use in intimate personal relationships. In the business context these same techniques may be taught, but they will be used to *simulate* intimacy with customers to encourage them to buy, and then to return. Advocates of teaching oral communication skills in schools often refer approvingly to the idea that the same skills can be applied in many domains – they are not merely vocational skills, but 'life skills'. In the words of one advocate, 'all children benefit from learning skills that will make them better friends, better life-partners, better employees and better human beings' (Phillips 1998: 7).

The idea that communication skills training is capable of producing 'better human beings' can be linked with an argument put forward by the social theorist Anthony Giddens in his book *Modernity and Self-Identity* (1991). Giddens suggests that in 'late modern' societies – those which are furthest from 'traditional' or pre-modern ways of life – the individual self has become 'a reflexive project' – something the individual has to 'work on' rather than being able to take for granted. In traditional societies, people expect their own lives to follow a similar course to those of their parents; but in late modern societies the pace and extent of social change means that the experience of older generations does not provide a model for their children. Instead of being able to fit their experiences into a pre-existing social narrative, late modern individuals have to construct their own story. Hence the popularity of therapy and quasi-therapeutic activities which offer guidance on how to do this. Giddens also points out that in a highly mobile and individualistic culture where people no longer spend their whole lives in the same close-knit communities, the formation of intimate relationships presents particular challenges. In a world of strangers, people do not know who you are until you tell them. This, Giddens suggests, is another reason why late modern cultures place such emphasis on 'communication skills', and most especially, on the skills of self-expression and mutual self-disclosure.

Current concerns about 'communication' (in the sense of 'spoken interaction') are underpinned by a complex set of factors. New ideas about the nature of work and the demands it places on workers, recent trends towards skill-based or competence-led curricula in education, and therapeutic notions of the self as a reflexive project requiring work to perfect, all contribute to the increasing sense that speaking and listening, long taken for granted as things everyone could do 'naturally' without special help, are in need of more explicit and systematic attention. At this point, then, we must turn to the question of what form that attention actually takes – what is taught under the heading of communication skills, how it is taught, and what problems are raised by the enterprise.

Teaching talk in L1 – a curious enterprise?

Earlier in this chapter I pointed out that communication skills training is often aimed at L1 users rather than L2 learners. The examples I studied, some of which I will refer to here, were all designed on the assumption that trainees would be adults with native or native-like fluency in English. But this points to a striking peculiarity of oral communication skills training: it casts a group of people who would normally be considered fully competent linguistically and communicatively (adult native speakers) as needing expert assistance with an activity they have been performing since early childhood (interacting verbally with others). This is a case of what Giddens (1991) describes as the incursion of 'expert systems' into areas where previously people's ability to do things was acquired informally through observation and direct experience. Among Giddens's own examples is 'parenting', an activity (raising children) which now supports a huge expert literature and a cadre of specialist professionals, whereas not long ago knowledge about it was largely experiential and transmitted informally from older to younger generations (especially from mothers to daughters). The growth of expert systems in any domain tends to promote the attitude that knowledge acquired without expert support is somehow insufficient to meet contemporary standards (parenting is, again, a good example of this tendency). In the sphere of 'communication', the increasing salience of expert knowledge leads to native speakers being treated, for some purposes at least, almost as though they were second language learners.

There are, of course, much older traditions of instruction in spoken first language-use for specific purposes: classical rhetoric, for example, which prepared citizens of ancient Greece and Rome to participate in political and legal discourse; or more recently, the training given to lawyers in courtroom advocacy, ministers of religion in preaching, politicians in public oratory and therapists in non-directive counselling techniques. These forms of spoken discourse were and still are viewed as appropriate objects for formal instruction because they are part of the arcane knowledge of a particular profession: their conventions are unlikely to have been picked up in the course of everyday experience. But the kind of instruction in communication skills which I am concerned with here focuses on much more ordinary kinds of spoken interaction, and often on what might be considered quite basic and elementary aspects of communicative competence.

Consider, for instance, the fairly widespread practice (especially in workplace training) of teaching 'listening skills'. In the workplaces whose training I looked at (shops, supermarkets and call centres), listening was an object of considerable concern.[2] Many of the managers and trainers I talked to, as well as the authors of widely used training materials, believed that many people had great difficulty with listening because they had never been instructed in the relevant skills. In the words of one organization which required all employees to undergo training in what it called 'expanded listening', 'as important as listening is, it's the one communication skill we're never really taught'. Several organizations' training materials that I looked at stated that 'most people listen at a 25% level of efficiency' – though it was not made clear either how this statistic was arrived at or what it actually means. One organization had adopted a 'four-stage model' of listening – 'hearing, understanding, interpreting, responding' – and trainees were required to work through these stages in response to a prompt, by verbalizing each in turn. Communication trainers used various other classroom activities to promote better listening comprehension. For example, at one call centre whose training programme informants described to me, trainees worked in pairs, taking it in turn to read out a set of increasingly complicated instructions which their partner then had to repeat back accurately from memory.

As well as the ability to decode and retain information accurately, training in listening also covers the ability to demonstrate to an interlocutor that you are listening to them and understanding what they say. This is a particular concern in the context of telephone service, since the absence of visual cues makes it more important to demonstrate listening verbally; but I encountered the same concern in workplaces like supermarkets where contact between staff and customers is face-to-face. Training addresses the issue by explicitly teaching strategies like using minimal responses, asking clarification questions, paraphrasing and making checks to confirm you have understood the customer correctly. Here for instance is a listening skills checklist taken from a training manual used with call centre employees.

- Demonstrate that you are actively listening by your responses and your interest — make listening noises, e.g. *yes, I see, fine, I'm making notes*.
- Use your questioning skills to control the conversation at the same time enabling clients to communicate their messages logically.
- Ask specific questions.
- Use statements to clarify and give information.
- Paraphrase or repeat back your understanding of the client's requirements.
- Summarize to control the conversation and clarify the final position.
- Limit your own talking — you cannot talk and listen at the same time.

Some points on this list are expanded on elsewhere in the manual. The instruction 'use your questioning skills to control the conversation' refers back to an earlier unit describing different types of questions in English and their functions — yes/no questions, WH questions, disjunct either/or questions, tag questions, hypothetical questions. The idea is that different question forms will produce different kinds of answers from the customer. When the trainer has gone through the checklist, trainees are typically given a practice task, such as role-playing a phone call or an encounter with the customer, in which they try to use the recommended strategies.

The kind of instruction just described is based on the assumption that trainees are not already competent listeners, and moreover that this is the case because they have never previously been *taught* how to listen. From a linguist's perspective this is a strange assumption. It overlooks the possibility that most people are never taught to listen in their first language because they do not need to be: listening is a 'skill' extensively practised by hearing humans from infancy, and normal levels of exposure to spoken language input are sufficient to develop competence in it. No doubt some people on some occasions listen poorly, but this is more likely to reflect boredom or lack of motivation than some deep-seated deficiency in their ability to take in and interpret utterances produced by others. It is very unlikely that L1 users' problems with listening comprehension resemble, either in degree or in kind, the problems experienced by L2 learners whose knowledge of the target language is limited.

Nevertheless, the approaches used by trainers to develop communication skills might well remind us of approaches commonly used with second language learners. The activities described above include, for instance, structured listening comprehension tasks where the input becomes progressively more complex, and the provision of lists of forms that can be used for the same communicative function — asking a question, say — followed by a role-play exercise in which trainees practise using the various alternatives appropriately. The strategies taught under the heading of 'active listening' (such as paraphrasing, asking clarification questions and making confirmation checks) are examples of what the SLA literature calls 'negotiation for meaning': language teachers as well as communication trainers devise tasks which encourage the use of these strategies. Examining communication training materials, I was often struck by the resemblance they bore to a certain kind of foreign language teaching text. Some language textbooks contain units of work on topics like 'travelling' and 'going to the doctor': the unit starts with a fictional dialogue set in a railway station or a doctor's surgery, it introduces new vocabulary relevant to the topic, and then focuses on useful grammatical structures – in the travel case, for instance, time and place expressions useful for discussing your itinerary. Workplace communication training manuals, not dissimilarly, often contain units on topics like 'dealing with complaints' which include exemplary made-up dialogues and sections explaining which words, grammatical constructions and politeness formulae are appropriate in this particular communicative situation.

I am not suggesting that there are no differences between communication training manuals and language textbooks. But the resemblances which arguably do exist between them underline the point that communication training addressed to L1 users tends to assume a remarkably low level of communicative competence, the ability to make linguistic choices based on judgements of contextual appropriateness. There is also an assumption that the relevant choices need to be drawn explicitly to the speaker's attention, which implies that conscious knowledge *about* different language forms is necessary to ensure that the speaker in practice makes the 'appropriate' choice. Again, this is a curious assumption. How many adult speakers really need to be reminded that on the phone it is important to demonstrate attention using minimal responses – let alone have the relevant responses ('yes', 'OK', 'I see', etc.) modelled for them to practise? Who needs to be told that statements are used for giving information whereas questions are more appropriate for eliciting it? I was not surprised to find, in interviews with communication trainees, that many were critical of some parts of their training on the grounds that these just 'stated the obvious' and were to that extent a waste of time.

But wasting trainees' time on low-level skills is not the only or the most serious problem raised by communication skills training. At this point we must return to the more broadly *ideological* implications of what is taught under the heading of 'good' or 'effective' communication.

Effective communication – effective for who and for what?

Any kind of language instruction depends on selecting and codifying (systematically writing down in the form of rules) the particular linguistic norms that will be transmitted to learners; deciding what kind of grammar or pronunciation will be adopted as a model, or what style and level of formality will be presented as the norm. Language-teaching, then, especially when carried out on a relatively large scale, both requires and contributes to the process of language standardization, which may be defined in the terms of Milroy and Milroy (1998: 47) as 'the suppression of optional variability'.

The teaching of 'communication skills', just like grammar teaching or elocution teaching, clearly has normative and standardizing effects. In at least some workplaces, one explicit goal of communication training is to reduce or even eliminate variation in people's ways of interacting. Just as many organizations insist that their employees wear a uniform or observe a strict dress code, so an increasing number insist that employees subordinate their own linguistic personae to a centrally-designed corporate linguistic persona. Speech, like appearance, is treated as an aspect of 'branding', and in order to ensure that customers get a consistent experience of the brand, employees are required to deliver standard verbal routines in an approved style; at the extreme, they may have to follow a script specifying the correct form of words exhaustively.

The normative/standardizing impulse can also take less obviously coercive forms, however. Recall, for instance, the person specification I quoted earlier, stating that applicants for the job of a hospital cleaner should be able to 'demonstrate empathy and understanding'. This statement, like many other statements of the same kind (for instance the criteria used to assess communication skills in examinations like Britain's NVQs) represents a value judgement, on the basis of which a norm is constructed: it defines 'demonstrating empathy' as an aspect of good communication. There are many other communicative abilities to which the specification could have referred, but does not (e.g. 'be able to tell a joke' or 'be capable of defending yourself in an argument'). By implication, these abilities are not valued in the same way as 'demonstrating empathy'. As more and more organizations (businesses, hospitals, schools and colleges, public examination boards, etc.) institute programmes of instruction and assessment for spoken communication, and as this in turn obliges them to codify its norms, it is likely that an increasing consensus will emerge about what constitutes 'effective communication'.

This consensus will not be socially, culturally or ideologically neutral. Just as in the case of grammar or pronunciation, a standard for 'effective communication' is always in practice based on habits and values which are not cultural universals, but are specific to a particular cultural milieu. And just as in the case of grammar and pronunciation, the effect of institutionalizing some people's preferred practices as norms will be to define large numbers of other people as inadequate or 'substandard' communicators.

The potential for ethnocentrism here is particularly obvious. Much expert discourse about interpersonal communication is produced by psychologists, therapists and counsellors; though this kind of expertise is by now widely diffused, its roots are in Western modernity with its rational, goal-oriented and individualistic outlook. Many of the communicative strategies which are most enthusiastically advocated by experts in this tradition, such as speaking directly (the key recommendation of assertiveness training) and engaging in open self-disclosure, are problematic in cultures whose notions of personhood and modes of social organization diverge markedly from the Western/Anglo mode. Ethnographers and sociolinguists have documented the very considerable variation that exists in cultural attitudes to, say, reticence versus verbosity, what levels of directness or of verbal aggression are considered normal or tolerable, how and in what circumstances emotion may be expressed or personal information disclosed, how parents should relate to children, and so on.[3] But many experts continue to give the impression that they regard their own norms as universal desiderata – the standard for 'effective communication' rather than one possible, culturally and contextually specific version of it.

As multinational corporations and Western consultants extend their sphere of influence, there is every reason to think that particular, and basically American (US), norms of interaction are being exported to other parts of the world, even when no attempt is made to export the English language itself. In Hungary, for example, since the end of the communist era there has been an influx of Western business organizations, and controversy has been caused by the insistence of some of these multinationals that customers be addressed (in Hungarian) using the informal, egalitarian style which is the norm in most Western companies, though this flouts local expectations and well-established rules of Hungarian usage.[4] In Western Europe, small examples of American service-speak overlaying native conventions are routinely observable. British servers now say 'How may I help you?' when in the past they said 'Can I help you?'; French market traders end transactions by wishing you *bonne journée*. (On the other hand, an initiative whereby Scottish supermarket customers were greeted at the entrance by a staff-member who handed them a basket and exhorted them to 'enjoy your shopping experience' had to be abandoned because of the ridicule it occasioned.)

It may well be objected that the above examples, involving formulaic routines in service contexts, are trivial; I do not dispute it. What is not trivial, however, is the ideology of communication, of which these globalized politeness formulas are only the most superficial expressions: 'it is essential that there be a uniform way of talking . . . and there are rules for that'. If, as this chapter has suggested, 'communication' is emerging as the supreme value of language teaching, for first language users as well as second language learners, then it is crucial for language teaching professionals to engage with questions about what kinds of communication are valuable. Such questions are just as significant, politically speaking, as questions about which actual language(s) should serve as means of communication in a globalized world.

Notes

1 Dr Kuriansky is a clinical psychologist and therapist, who is also known to a large audience in the USA as 'Dr Judy', broadcaster and author of several popular advice texts.

2 Throughout this chapter I follow a general policy of not naming, or giving details about, the organizations whose training materials and practices I examined. No organization whose permission I sought agreed to the use of its real name in published work, on the grounds that this might compromise commercial interests. In addition,

some materials were obtained and examined without the knowledge of anyone who had the authority to grant or withhold permission. In these cases I have placed my obligation to protect my informants above my obligation to reveal my sources for the benefit of other scholars.

3 A good selection of classic ethnographic work on these topics may be found in Bauman and Sherzer (1974) (includes contributions on silence and directness); Brown and Levinson (1987) (politeness across cultures); Lutz and Abu-Lughod (1980) (the expression of emotion across cultures); Schieffelin and Ochs (1986) (carer-child interaction across cultures).

4 Thanks to Erika Sólyom for information on this topic.

5 Foreign language learning as global communicative practice

Claire Kramsch and Steven L. Thorne

The ease of access to foreign speakers and cultures provided by internet communication tools has been hailed as potentially transforming the learning of foreign languages from a decontextualized exercise into an engagement with authentic real-world contexts of language use (e.g. Blyth 1998; Warschauer 1999; Warschauer and Kern 2000). Some concerns have been voiced, however, that the type of communication students engage in over global networks might not fulfil the communicative goals traditionally associated with the learning of a foreign language. Whereas communicative language teaching was predicated on the authentic exchange of information and the development of mutual cross-cultural understanding (Breen and Candlin 1980; Savignon 1983), computer-mediated interaction seems to favour phatic contact and favourable presentation of self (Kramsch *et al.* 2000; Thorne 1999). Indeed, as Kern (2000: 255) points out: '[On the internet] students are certainly engaged in communication. But has the communication led to any new understanding?'

In this chapter, we reflect on the implications of global communication technologies for teaching and using foreign languages. After a short review of the role of communication in language teaching and of the possibilities of global communication networks, we examine the use of synchronous and asynchronous communication between American learners of French in the USA and French learners of English in France. We interrogate the presumption that computer-mediated communication (hereafter CmC) naturally helps learners understand local conditions of language use and builds a global common ground for cross-cultural understanding.

Communicative language teaching: transmission of information versus ritual of engagement

The concept of 'negotiation of meaning' has been at the heart of foreign language teaching since the 1970s. Communicative competence, first defined by Savignon (1972) and Breen and Candlin (1980) as the ability to 'share and negotiate meanings and conventions' (Breen and Candlin 1980: 92), became popular through Canale

and Swain's (1980) analysis of its grammatical, sociolinguistic, and strategic components, and Savignon's (1983: 307) later definition of negotiation as 'a process
whereby a participant in a speech event uses various sources of information – prior
experience, the context, another participant – to achieve understanding'. The concept of negotiation became operationalized in American second language acquisition
research and practice in terms defined by Pica (1995: 200), i.e. as 'those interactions in which learners and their interlocutors adjust their speech phonologically,
lexically, and morphosyntactically to resolve difficulties in mutual understanding
that impede the course of their communication'. By associating meaning with information, and understanding with the linguistic dimensions of speech, American
foreign language (FL) pedagogy grounded its notion of communicative competence in the Utilitarian discourse system prevalent in many sectors of American
public life (Scollon and Scollon 1995: 94).

Indeed, following a historical belief in the power of science and technology,
communication in the USA has been seen mostly as the transmission of information,
an activity that reduces distances between interlocutors in the same way as the pio-
neers conquered space by 'going West', or the Pacific Railroad connected people
across vast distances (Carey 1988). This view of communication hinges on the
belief that cultural Others can be known through an enlightened discourse of truth
(Foucault 1971: 19) that is based on a common rationality and communicative purpose (Habermas 1970; see Hymes's critique of Habermas in Hymes 1987: 225).

But there exists at the same time another view of communication, one based on
the need to identify with and belong to a community of discursive practice. This is
a view of communication as a ritual of engagement, referred to also as involvement
and solidarity (Tannen 1984), where trust takes precedence over objective truth.
Computer-mediated communication, that brings together individual speaking sensibilities in an a-historical cyberspace, can replace the traditional messy encounter
of historical speakers with their baggage of national allegiances and cultural practices. It can bring about the resolution of problems caused for example by national
or cultural stereotypes. Sociologist James Carey (1988: 35) describes this kind of
communication as follows: 'A ritual view of communication sees language as an
instrument of dramatic action, of thought as essentially situational and social, and
symbolism as fundamentally fiduciary.' It focuses on the sharing of experience,
ideas, values and sentiments. Here, the modern view of communication as the discourse of truth gives way to a post-modern view of communication as the discourse
of trust; it is more important that you are personally engaged than that you get to
the bottom of the 'truth'. In official FL pedagogy, the notion of communicative
competence has not, up to now, included communication as ritual except in its
more codified forms of social etiquette, although the symbolic or ritual uses of the
foreign language have been shown to be alive and well in learners' unofficial uses of
the language (Kramsch 1997; Rampton 1999a).

At the beginning of the twenty-first century, the teaching of foreign languages at educational institutions in the USA is being challenged by new global communication technologies. Cyberspace is perceived as a utopian middle landscape, where native speakers and non-native speakers can have access to one another as linguistic entities on a screen, unfettered by historical, geographical, national or institutional identities. The anonymity, the multiple audiences, the speed, and the ubiquity of the medium have been hailed as liberating (Lanham 1994; Turkle 1995; Jones 1995; Herring 1996) and as creating global opportunities for FL use. But to what extent does the medium itself change the parameters of communication and the nature of language use (Latour 1999)? And what kind of discourse is being promoted there: a discourse of truth or a discourse of trust?

Language learning and technology in a global context

Globalization, a highly contested term (Jameson and Miyoshi 1999; Giddens 2000; Harvey 2000), is often described using the analogy of a network (e.g. Castells 1996). A 'many to many' network enables, distributes, and arguably makes cosmopolitan all sorts of symbolic and material goods at the level of economic trade and its artefacts, and the exchange of cultural practices and images such as music, dance, film and language. Recently available communication technologies, particularly those associated with the internet but also cell phones, pagers, and increasingly personal digital assistants, are displacing conventional modalities such as the memo, note and letter writing. In addition to its ubiquitous material forms, the discourse around communication technology is globally visible and can be found in the Technology section of any national and most local papers, in reports on televised news programmes, and of course, on the thousands of websites that speak, indirectly, about the means of their own conveyance. In this sense, global communication networks, globalization, and the discourses of the two, are bound up together.

Global communication networks present a paradox. They encourage alienation by reducing face-to-face contact, yet this same technology, from an opposing point of view, provides a nexus of connectivity, social interaction and community building, albeit in novel formations. Undeniably, CmC has become a habituated and everyday dimension of social, academic and professional communicative activity and American students are reported to find it highly engaging (e.g. Beauvois 1998; Kern 1995; Lee 1998). As internet communication of both synchronous and asynchronous varieties is increasingly used to supplement or even replace face-to-face teaching methods in various formal educational settings in the USA, there is a need to look at these digital spaces as social places. Castells (1996: 356) terms this the 'culture of real virtuality' – a social-material space that enables individualism and community, but where social inequalities may also powerfully manifest themselves.

The pedagogical impetus (and assumption) behind FL educational uses of CmC is directly linked to the popularity of communicative language teaching that advocates language development through social interaction. Language use over net-works can provide various benefits, many of which are not readily available in foreign language classrooms (Cononelos and Oliva 1993; Warshauer 1996), e.g. regular interaction with spatially dispersed interlocutors, access to expert speakers of the language of study, increased peer–peer interaction, the development of on-line discourse communities (Warshauer 1998), and often an overall increase in the total production of language by students (Kern 1995). Putting students in direct written contact with one another has been argued to elevate thinking and writing in the classroom to a legitimate and co-constructed form of knowledge (Faigley 1992; Day and Batson 1995; Bruce *et al.* 1993). In this sense, network technologies have helped to initiate a significant pedagogical shift, moving many language arts educa-tors from cognitivist assumptions about knowledge and learning as a brain phenomenon, to contextual, collaborative and social-interactive approaches to lan-guage development and activity (Ferrara *et al.* 1991; Hawisher 1994; Noblitt 1995; Ortega 1997; Kern 1998, 2000; Thorne 2000b).

CmC use spans synchronous and asynchronous interaction. Synchronous CmC requires that interactants are simultaneously on-line and involves tools such as Internet Relay Chat, ICQ ('I seek you'), assorted web-based environments, and MOOs (Multi-user domain Object Oriented environments). Unlike synchronous CmC, where the interactional and linguistic dimensions of communication often show a medium effect (see Thorne 2000b), asynchronous communication tools such as email and threaded discussion continue to elicit the use of traditional epis-tolary conventions (openings, closings, and explicit references to prior texts). See Herring (1996) for a discussion of the 'basic electronic message schema'. New epis-tolary conventions have also accompanied the adoption of email, such as the inclusion of parts or the whole of a prior email message (or messages) in one's response, a coherence strategy which co-evolved with the medium to help users cope with the massive increase in textual communication that email afforded. Of relevance here is that expectations of language register tied to recognizable social conventions become blurred in both synchronous and asynchronous CmC. Asynchronous communication, for example, can show an extreme range of written and spoken registers, from formal letters, memos and essays, which ape their con-ventionally mediated or 'paper' counterparts, to virtual transcriptions of oral conversation emphasizing phatic communion. Most American students participat-ing in this study reported using CmC more than two hours a day, largely for social and/or phatic purposes.

We turn now to specific instances of the use of internet communication tools in foreign language education. Our examples are taken from an ongoing foreign lan-guage project using the internet to link together *lycée* students in France and college students in the USA, between 18 and 20 years of age. We begin by examining an early semester brainstorming activity, conducted in March 1997, in which three American students of French are using a synchronous form of CmC or 'chat' to consider possible issues and questions for their upcoming email interactions with students from the lycée Fernand-Léger in Ivry.

Synchronous CmC among Americans: seeking common ground

The stated goals of this intermediate-level French course were to increase intra-class interaction through the use of email and chat, to engage in a critical dialogue with French students from a suburb of Paris (email); and to culminate with web projects based on collaborative popular culture research carried out in tandem with the French students. The excerpt below is an example of the first effort by the American students, working in small groups, a few weeks after the start of their semester. The software used, a MOO server coupled with the MacMOOse client, automatically tags user messages with their names (Eric says, '. . .'; Matt says, '. . .'). Note that it does not allow for the use of accent marks. None of the orthography or grammar has been altered, though deletions have been made due to space limitations. For ease of reference, we have divided this exchange into three sections. The course instructor has provided a brief description of the Ivry students as primarily of North African descent or recently immigrated to France. The American students have also been told that a number of the Ivry students live in HLM, or subsidized public housing.

Section One: Brainstorming topics

1 Eric says, 'j'ai un idea . . . le diversity ethnic du Ivry, en comparison avec Berkeley . . . d'ou les immigres viens, en quelle quantite . . .' [I have an idea . . . a comparison of the ethnic diversity between Ivry and Berkeley . . . where do the immigrants come from, in what quantity . . .]

2 Ken says, 'voila une question . . . est-ce les bandelieus sont comme une exile, ou on ne peut pas partir?' [There's a question: are the suburbs like an exile, where one cannot leave?]

3 Eric says, 'c'est bon aussi. . . . est-ce que les persones dans les banlieus . . . est-que les parents aussi habitaient dans l'HLM . . .' [this is good also . . . is the people in the suburbs . . . do their parents also live in the HLM?]

4 Matt says, 'probablement' [probably]

5 Eric says, 'aussi . . . l'HLM . . . il existe depuis quand?' [also . . . the HLM . . . how long has it existed?]

6 Eric says, 'ils l'ont fait quand? Pour quelle raison?' [when was it made? For what reason?]

7 Matt says, 'c'est une bonne question' [this is a good question]

8 Ken says, 'mais ca n'est pas une question qui commence une discussion . . .' [but that is not a question which begins a discussion]

9   Matt says, 'non, mais c'est quelquechose que je veux savoir' [no, but it's something that I want to know]

10   Eric says, 'ce ne doit pas etre un discussion, un project du recherche . . .' [it doesn't have to be a discussion, but a research project]

11   Ken says, 'ce serait plus facile si le sujet est quelque chose qui commence une discussion . . .' [this would be easier if the subject is something which begins a discussion . . .]

In this initial brainstorming session, the American students disagree on the primary function of the planned email exchange with the French. Eric tentatively asserts that the goal is to carry out a research project (turn 10), while Ken and Matt stress the importance of topics that will catalyse discussion and engagement (turns 8, 9 and 10). These two goals correspond to the two divergent parameters of the assignment. On the one hand they have been given an institutionally mandated goal (to carry out research as class project), on the other hand they have their own personally motivated goals (to communicate with French students, and learn about their lives). Because they are able to use personal computers and email accounts to communicate with the French, outside of class, and without the instructor as an intermediary, they tend to blur the boundaries between institutional and personal, between public and private. This blurring of institutional and personal domains conceals from them the fact that 'conversation', 'academic discussion' and 'research project' are different genres, that are rooted in different local educational cultures and that put different constraints on the kind of knowledge the students are likely to gain from the upcoming exchange.

Section Two: 'je veux nous mettre au même niveau'

12   Ken says, 'alors, est-ce qu'il y a quelque chose que nous voulons savoir de les gens qui habit a Ivry?' [so, is there something that we want to know about the people who live in Ivry?]

13   Matt says, 'Je voudrais savoir leur opinions de la vie' [I would like to know their opinions about life]

14   Eric says, 'oui . . . de leurs chances dans l'avenir' [yes . . . their chances for the future]

15   Matt says, 'S'ils pensent qu'ils veut aller a l'universite' [If they think they want to go to university]

16   Eric says, 'mais tout ces sujets est . . . tellement . . . negatife' [but all these subjects is . . . so . . . negative]

17   Matt says, 'Oui, mais je veux savoir s'ils pensent comme nous' [Yes, but I want to know if they think like us]

18   Ken says, 'EST comme nous ou PENSE comme nous . . . ?' [IS like us or THINK like us . . . ?]

19 Matt says, 'si ils pensent comme nous pensons' [if they think like we think]
20 Eric says, 'vous ne pensez pas que si nous allions au Oakland, et demander au les etudiants le plus pauvre . . . "est'que vous pensez a l'University", il n'y a pas un problem avec ca?' [you don't think that if we were to go to Oakland, and ask the poorest students . . . 'do you think about University', there isn't a problem with that?]
21 Eric says, 'je veux nous mettre au meme niveau' [I want to put us at the same level]

While wanting to put themselves 'at the same level' as their French interlocutors, the three American students seem clearly aware of the social class differential as they construct the other as the counterimage of themselves. They picture the Ivry students to be: poor, unlikely to attend university, and (therefore?) with uncertain futures. Their own implied oppositional identity of affluence and opportunity accounts for their belief that they not only have the responsibility but also the power to level the playing field, even as the unevenness of that field is precisely the reality they say they want to explore. One could interpret this paradox in two ways, which we illustrate below in the form of a dialogue between the two authors of this paper.

STEVE: While it is clear that the Americans construct the French through negative homologies (e.g. 'poorest students in Oakland') and that social class permeates each contribution to this discussion, I should like to state that this analysis is not meant to condemn the participants in any way. Stated optimistically, they reflectively doubt the appropriateness of questions like intentions for university or the future and determine these to be insensitive and 'tellement . . . negatife' based on the information that they have about Ivry. I suggest that this illustrates an effort to understand matters from the (admittedly projected) vantage point of the Ivry students, hinting that this activity has *the potential* to displace norms of cultural and class reference for the Americans (the stated goal of the interaction).

CLAIRE: I don't think anyone would 'condemn' the American students. In the absence of further knowledge, they are clearly projecting their vision of Harlem or East Oakland onto the Parisian *banlieue* and their conception of America's inner city poor onto Ivry's *milieux ouvriers*. They are sensitive to difference, yes, but, rather than trying to understand this difference, they seek beyond difference to reach a common ground. So what do they mean when they claim they want to *understand* how the French think? What do they want to understand if all they do later is come to the conclusion that their lives are similar, after all, and that violence and racial conflict can be found everywhere?

STEVE: But perhaps this tendency for finding and affirming perceived similarity is a necessary step before they can go about exploring difference?

Section Three: The great equalizer – global youth culture

22 Ken says, 'je veux savoir comment on habite a Ivry, je sais comment un parisien vivre, mais je ne sais pas comment les etudiants d'Ivry vivre' [I want to know how one lives in Ivry, I know how Parisians live, but I don't know how students in Ivry live]

23 Eric says, 'comment ils vivent? Leur vie qouitedenment?' [how they live? Their everyday lives?]

24 Ken says, 'oui' [yes]

25 Eric says, 'qu'est ce que c'est les chose qui les inquetes?' [what are the things they worry about?]

26 Ken says, 'les parents, les drogues, la sexe? le SIDA, les politiques' [parents, drugs, sex? AIDS, politics]

27 Eric says, 'oui oui oui!!!!' [yes yes yes!!!!]

CLAIRE: So in order to find a safe common ground for discussion, they resort to familiar topics like family, drugs, sex, AIDS, and politics that they feel are universal in their conversational appeal. But in the absence of information about France, these are topics that are of primary interest to Berkeley college students, not necessarily to French *lycéens* from Ivry.

STEVE: In my view, the American suggestion to discuss the quotidian preoccupations of youth culture marks a desire to engage within a mutually shared horizon of social, cultural, and experiential knowledge. Through the deployment of youth culture themes, where participants can situate themselves along a personal/specific-to-objective/global continuum, the Americans are attempting to engineer a future interaction based on fairness, mutuality, and hope, where relationships might be built, understanding might occur, and insights might be gleaned.

CLAIRE: These 'mights' are full of good intentions and idealism, but how is that idealistic communicative agenda ever to be realized without a knowledge of basic facts and an understanding of the different social and cultural conventions under which each party is operating? This idealism, I am afraid, is not based on knowledge and information about the Other, but on some vague attempts at establishing trust based on a supposedly shared youth culture.

Asynchronous CmC between American and French students: clashing frames of expectation

The following excerpts are a follow-up on synchronous exchanges like the one discussed above. They were collected also in March 1997 between another group of Berkeley undergraduates in 2nd year French and French students, this time from the lycée Frédéric Mistral in Fresnes.[1] The initial contact was made by the French teacher in the USA with the English teacher in France (Contrepois 1999). Both the French and the American students had watched the feature film *La Haine*, made in 1995 by Mathieu Kassovitz, that depicts the experiences of three boys living in the housing projects of a Parisian *banlieue*. The film deals with racism, violence, gang culture, and the influence of American culture. The students' discussion of this film is the beginning of an ongoing exchange with the French students on a variety of topics during the semester. The American students wrote in French, their French partners responded in English. All postings are written by the students themselves, without any input from their teachers; however the American students posted their messages from their own individual terminals, whereas the French students gave their postings to their teacher who then sent them from her computer. The exchange started with this posting by the American students.

A qui de droit:
> Je vous ecrire de la part de la classe francais 13, instruire par Julie Sauvage, a UC Berkeley. Recemment, nous avons regarde le film 'Le Haine' en classe. Le contenue de ce film nous a choque car il y avait des images de France que nous ne voyons pas d'habitude ici aux Etats-Unis. Alors ce film etait un peu deroutant pour nous. J'espere que vous ou votre class peut nous aider avec notre confusion. Voici une liste de questions sur 'Le Haine' que nous avons preparé:
> 1. Est-ce qu'il y a des ressemblances entre la situation a la banlieue de Paris dans la film et la vraie situation?
> 2. Est-ce qu'il y a beaucoup de problems entre les jeunes francais et la police?
> 3. Est-ce qu'il y a des emeutes a la banlieue de Paris?
> 4. Est-ce que c'est difficile a obtenir un arme a feu en France?
> 5. Est-ce que c'est difficile a obtenir des drougues (comme marijuana) en France?
> 6. Pourquoi est-ce que vous pensez que les jeunes americains ignorent des problems sociaux en France?
> 7. Est-ce que vous pensez que la situation a la banlieue de Paris est en plus mauvais etat que les ghettos des Etats-Unis?
> Signed: Nat Chadwick.

[*To whom it may concern:*
> *I am writing you on behalf of French 13, taught by Julie Sauvage, at UC Berkeley. Recently we saw the film 'La Haine' in class. The content of the film shocked us since there were images of France that we don't normally see here in the U.S. So this film was a bit unsettling for us. I hope that you or your class can help us with our confusion. Here's a list of questions on 'La Haine' that we've prepared:*
> 1. *Are there similarities between the situation in the suburbs of Paris in the film and the real situation?*

> 2. *Are there many problems between young French people and the police?*
> 3. *Are there riots in the suburbs of Paris?*
> 4. *Is it hard to obtain firearms in France?*
> 5. *Is it hard to get drugs (like marijuana) in France?*
> 6. *Why do you think that young Americans are not aware of social problems in France?*
> 7. *Do you think the situation in the Paris suburbs is worse than in the ghettos of the U.S.?*
>
>   *Signed: Nat Chadwick*]

The group's itemized list of questions, with their specific requests for information and for personal judgements, shows evidence of a view of communication as the transmission of objective, valid, verifiable facts from authentic sources. At the same time, the American students' admission of personal weakness (*confusion*), their request for help and their sharing of personal sentiments, gives a ritual flavour to this exchange that is meant to display goodwill and to elicit trust. The students evidently consider the French students to be legitimate and qualified informants, even on such sensitive issues as 6 and 7. The written format of the medium and the asynchronous nature of the exchange impose a formality to this list of 'interview' questions that jars with the discourse of personal perplexity expressed in the opening paragraph. This stylistic dissonance is also due to the use of French 'false friends' such as *choqué* (E. shocked = surprised; Fr. *choqué* = scandalized) or *confusion* (E. confusion = perplexity; Fr. *confusion* = embarrassment). These and other rhetorical dissonances (e.g. the legal phrase *à qui de droit* sounds too formal in a friendly exchange), while possibly not impeding the transmission of information, might negatively affect the emotional tone of the communicative ritual. The linguistic ambiguity often found in unedited email exchanges further impairs credibility. For example, from the way the third sentence is constructed, it is not clear whether the reason given for the American students' 'shock' is that the film gives a picture of France which is different from the pictures they are used to seeing, or that this type of violence is not seen in the USA. Such dissonances and ambiguities are inherent in global exchanges on the Internet, when Internet users, sitting at their local computers, attempt to understand each other through variously valued requests for information and differently weighted expressions of trustworthiness. Moreover, these requests for information set up the French partners as ambiguous 'teachers'/ 'informants'/ 'interviewees'/ 'conversational partners'. For example, in France such a barrage of questions would be markedly impolite in an informal chat (note that the French don't ask a single question of the Americans). The ambiguity in tone is the result of the Americans' desire to be considerate and to avoid confrontation (Cameron 2000). However, the French cannot but take this list of questions as a class assignment, or as a kind of formal interview, despite the breaks in register noted above. They respond in kind with a formal report. In both cases, the chosen discourse style backfires, as we shall see below.

Five days after their initial posting, the American students receive the following message from three French students, who are anxious to transmit comparative, accurate and reliable information.

> Dear Nat,
> You shouldn't generalize, because there are three sorts of suburbs at least. For example, Sandrine lives in a very good suburb, in which all is quiet; Sophie lives in an area where violence is rising and Delphine lives in a suburb where violence is widespread: a bookseller was killed without any reason four months ago. However the situation in France is certainly better than the situation in America. As a matter of fact, delinquents have more difficulty getting arms than in the USA. Moreover, areas resembling the American ghettos don't exist in France. If you go to France, you will never see an area like Harlem, where violence is great. . . . So we can confirm that the suburbs you saw in 'La Haine' are not like this in reality.
> Signed: Sandrine, Delphine and Sophie.

The rational rhetorical progression of this posting, punctuated by clear logical connectors (*For example, However, But*) and the tripartite organization of the Parisian suburbs, illustrates a kind of logic that is typical of academic print literacy and that the French students are transferring to the electronic medium. Their electronic posting on the computer resembles an official letter that inspires trust through its institutional warrant. Here, the native speakers 'speak' with the authority of the French educational institution and with the legitimation of those who know the local conditions and can vouch for their validity. The French rhetoric of their English sentences is meant to convey all the more credibility as their English grammar is flawless. However, the French students don't have the expertise to give their American partners a larger sociopolitical picture of the situation of immigrants in France. Despite its academic rhetorical structure, their response remains anecdotal, personal, circumstantial, and thus vulnerable to misunderstandings. Moreover, the impersonal French expression 'il ne faut pas généraliser', translated by the French students into English as 'you shouldn't generalize', transforms what might have been intended only as an objective statement into a personal accusation through the use of the ambiguous second person pronoun.

And indeed, two weeks later, Nat and Eric protest vehemently:

> Chere Sandrine, Delphine, et Sophie,
> La premiere chose que vous ecrivez dans votre lettre etait: 'You shouldn't generalize', ou en francais, 'vous ne devriez pas generaliser' – ca, c'est incroyable. Innocemment, ma class de francais vous a pose des questions pour mieux comprendre la verite de la situation a la banlieue francaise. Tout que nous recevions de vous etaient des reactions nationalistes! Vous ne disiez rien sauf

des choses comme: 'The situation in France is certainly better than the situation in America', et 'If you go to France, you will never see an area like Harlem where violence is great.'

Avez-vous visite Harlem? Pouvez-vous dire franchement que vous connaissez bien les problemes sociaux des Etats-Unis? Avez-vous habite a Harlem ou Brooklyn, ou 'the Bronx', ou Oakland, ou Richmond, ou Compton, ou Long Beach, ou ici a Berkeley? Comment est-ce que c'est possible que vous connaissiez la situation des ghettos des Etats-Unis quand vous n'avez jamais habite ici? D'ou avez-vous obtenu votre information – Des films americains? Si je ne me trompe, vous etes coupable de faire des generalizations, pas nous. Et ca, c'est un peu hypocrite.

En plus, Christelle, une autre etudiante qui nous a ecrit, a dit que 'La Haine' etait d'aider les gens du monde a comprendre la realite de la banlieue de Paris. Alors, qui a raison?

Signed: Nat and Eric.

[*Dear Sandrine, Delphine, and Sophie,*
The first thing you wrote in your letter was :'you shouldn't generalize', or in French,
'Vous ne devriez pas généraliser' – that is incredible. Innocently, my French class asked
you some questions in order to better understand the truth of the situation in the French
suburbs. All that we got back from you were nationalistic reactions! You didn't say any-
thing except for things like: 'The situation in France is certainly better than the situation
in America', and, 'If you go to France, you will never see an area like Harlem where vio-
lence is great.'

Have you visited Harlem? Can you frankly say that you know the U.S.'s social problems
well? Have you lived in Harlem or Brooklyn, or 'the Bronx', or Oakland, or Richmond,
or Compton, or Long Beach, or here in Berkeley? How is it possible that you know the sit-
uation of U.S. ghettos when you've never lived here? Where have you gotten your
information – from American films? If I'm not mistaken, you are guilty of making gen-
eralizations, not us. And that is a little hypocritical.

What's more, Christelle, another student who wrote us, said that 'La Haine' was to
help the people of the world to understand the reality of the Paris suburbs. So who's right?
Signed: Nat and Eric]

Forgetting that they themselves had asked the French students to compare French banlieues and American ghettos (see list of questions above), Nat and Eric vent their anger. What they had posted as a list of information-seeking questions in French, now seems offensive to them when it comes back in the form of answers in English, their own native language. For, the French write in perfectly correct English, but without the social legitimation nor the trustworthiness of fellow native speakers of English. What happens is not a case of linguistic misunderstanding but a clash of cultural frames caused by the different resonances of the two languages for each group of speakers and their different understanding of appropriate genres. The French academic discourse expressed through the English language is perceived by the Americans not as having the ring of scientific truth, but as being unduly aggressive by displaying 'nationalist reactions'. The American ingratiating personal discourse expressed through the French language is not perceived by the French as enhancing the trustworthiness of their authors, but as lacking scientific rigour ('You shouldn't generalize'). While the French students write (in English) in the genre appropriate to their institutional status, the Americans write (in French) as autonomous individuals contacting other individuals. The Americans Nat and Eric attack the facts advanced by the French, not by placing them into their larger sociopolitical context, but by attacking the legitimacy of the authors themselves, their lack of personal experience ('how can you say anything about Harlem if you have not lived in Harlem?'). Despite the objective appearance of the first five interview questions above, it is subjective experience that seems to be, for the American students, a guarantee of trust, not larger explanatory discourse systems, like, for example, the prohibition to bear arms in France versus its legality in the USA.

Nat and Eric's ultimate attack draws on the negative resonances in American English of the word '*nationalist*' which they map onto the French word *nationaliste*. They seem to adhere to the myth of the internet as a person-to-person mode of communication, free from national and institutional constraints and ideologies, legitimized solely through human experience. Their sudden realization that the French students are not just individuals who happen to be talking French, but are actually enacting both an institutional identity as *lycéens*, and a French national identity which distinguishes them from the American students *qua* Americans, seems to fuel Nat and Eric's anger and disappointment.

A week later, Delphine responds. She attempts to return to a dispassionate exchange of ideas by redirecting the illocutionary force of Nat and Eric's rhetorical questions and making them into genuine requests for information.

> Dear Nat and Eric,
> I want to answer your letter which surprised me. To my mind, you didn't understand what we wrote. Now, to answer your questions, I have never been to America and all what I know is taken from books and films. The films we see, show us a bad image of the States. In American films, we always see violent actions and in the books we see photos such as I explained to you in my letter of . . . And to my mind, we are not 'hypocritical' like you wrote: we only wrote what we thought. I'm waiting for an answer from you to know what you think about my last letter.
> Signed: Delphine

In her response, Delphine does not seek to smooth out differences; instead she counters the Americans' accusations, verbalizes differences, and restates her position. But she does not go back to the list of questions asked by the American students in order to question the expectations raised by that list. Nor does she attempt to understand what put Nat and Eric so much on the defensive.

The last message in this series of exchanges, sent by the Americans, is as follows.

> Chere Emilie, Isabelle et Sabrina,
> Selon vous, y a-t-il d'autres films qui presentent la France mieux que 'La Haine'?. Pourquoi pensez-vous que la violence americaine a cause la violence en France? Nous pensons que vous avez tort parce que la violence et les conflicts raciaux sont partout. . . Nous ne savons pas quel films americains vous avez vu, mais nous pensons que les films avec beaucoup de violence ne montrent pas tous les exemples de la vie aux Etats-Unis. Quels films americains avez-vous vu qui selon vous sont des bons exemples de la violence americaine? Nous n'avons pas beaucoup d'information sur la situation en France. Alors, nous ne savons pas quel pays a la meilleure situation. Est-ce qu'il y a d'autres sujets auxquels vous interessez?
> Salut,
> Signed: Enrico, Beth, Cassie, Priscilla.

> [*Dear Emilie, Isabelle and Sabrina,*
> *Do you feel that there are other films that present France better than 'La Haine'? Why do you think that American violence is the cause of violence in France? We think that you are wrong because violence and racial conflicts are everywhere . . . We don't know which American films you have seen, but we believe that films with a lot of violence do not show all facets of life in the United States. Which American films have you seen that you feel are good examples of American violence? We don't have much information on the situation in France. Are there other topics you are interested about?*
> *Greetings,*
> *Signed: Enrico, Beth, Cassie, Priscilla*]

Here we see the four American students attempting to diffuse the conflict by resorting to such legalistic strategies as: (1) soliciting counter examples; (2) requesting objective evidence for claims made; (3) resorting to general philosophical truths; (4) claiming their own lack of expertise; (5) challenging the generalizability of the French claims; (6) offering to change the subject. They don't attempt to probe cultural differences by explaining the role played by Hollywood, the media or the entertainment industry in the image that America exports of itself. The tone is again on the defensive, as was that of the French students in their first reply. It is unclear how this exchange has in fact 'dissipated confusion' and led to a better mutual understanding, even if we consider the engagement itself as ultimately beneficial.

The American and French messages are characterized by different discourse styles that play themselves out on the national, institutional and personal levels.

Eric, who appears both in our synchronous and in our asynchronous data, had this to say retrospectively about the conflicting styles of the American and French students.

> *email is kind of like not a written thing.* . . . *when you read email, you get conversation but in a written form* so you can go back and look at them. That's neat. I've had that experience where conversational constructions appear in an email form from a native speaker of French, which is really neat. Because it doesn't fly by you and kind of 'look at that' – but in the [French] communications, *it felt like they were writing essays and sending them to us rather than having an email conversation with us.*
> – It seemed like you all would ask questions, right? Didn't you get responses?
> – sometimes we'd get long . . . but it's true we didn't get, *it seems true that they weren't doing the same thing we were.* It seemed like, you know, we had a task. And they, it seemed like, *I didn't know what they were doing.* [laughs] (our emphases).

He went on to attribute the difficulties they encountered with the Ivry students to differences in social class, although it is not clear why he associates 'socio-economic class' with the ability to interact and conduct a conversation.

> There was a clear socio-economic class difference between us and the French. We were doing different things so it was sort of an interaction, but it wasn't a discussion or conversation. When we [Americans] were talking to each other, it was debate and agreement and process. But with the French, we'd ask a question and receive a statement. . . .

Between global and local – genre

The exchanges above present a largely problematic scenario of the use of digital technologies for the learning of French in an American university context. Messages were sent back and forth, but is there evidence of 'communication' in the sense that this term is used in foreign language education?

The juxtaposition of the intracultural synchronous exchange and the intercultural asynchronous exchange has brought to light the expectations with which the American students entered the email encounters with the French. When faced with potentially divisive factors like social class, ethnicity and economic status, the Americans searched for common ground in an ostensibly global youth culture (all the while wishing they could find out how the local French thought and lived). They considered the electronic medium to be classless, colourless and economically neutral. But the medium only renders such differences less immediately visible, it does not make them disappear. In the intercultural exchanges above, what needed to be negotiated was not only the connotations of words (*banlieue*/suburb; *confusion*/confusion; *choqué*/shocked) but the stylistic conventions of the genre (formal/informal, edited/unedited, literate/orate), and more importantly the whole discourse system to which that genre belonged (Scollon and Scollon 1995). However, we see very little explicit negotiation going on, neither in the American nor in the French postings, despite the asynchronous nature of the exchange. These exchanges are characterized by an enormous amount of goodwill, personal investment and acknowledgement of limitations, but with very little understanding of the larger cultural framework within which each party is operating, and very little awareness that such an understanding is even necessary.

Communication seems defined here by varying degrees of information exchange and personal engagement across culturally different discourse genres. Most of the French interlocutors used factual, impersonal, dispassionate genres of writing. They were conscious of representing both their country and the French 'native speaker', even when they wrote in English, and therefore of possessing a cultural capital that gave them additional symbolic authority in this linguistic market. They made differentiated judgements about the situation in France. Now and then they corrected the American students' French, thus responding in a reliable manner to what the American students asked them explicitly to do. This pushed them into adopting the genre of the school report, even though their audience turned out to be the wrong audience for that genre. The French students believed their trustworthiness came from the objective truths of their statements and the transmission of those truths. But it is also possible that, faced by the prospect of being read by unknown recipients, who live in an unknown country and hold unknown views on them and what they represent, the French students only tried to use the 'hypercorrect' or 'hypercautious' style of delivery that characterizes exchanges across risky social and cultural boundaries (Bourdieu 1991).

By contrast, most of the American students, who initiated this exchange in order to 'improve their French and better understand the lives' of the French, viewed communication as a ritual of mutual trust building. They presented themselves as personally invested in the issues, and felt responsible for finding solutions; they adduced their own personal experience of violence, they voiced personal opinions, and they were frustrated when they sensed that their interlocutors spoke as members of institutional, educational, or national communities from which they as Americans were excluded. The oral style of their postings, full of questions and exclamation marks, suggests a high degree of affective involvement and emotional identification. It seems that the Americans, in their search for understanding the lives of the French, or for accessing 'la vérité de la situation', expected truth to emerge from direct contact with the French interlocutors on the basis of shared personal experience. The illusion of proximity offered by the medium seemed to call for engagement rather than requests for objective information or even the negotiation of foreign meanings and beliefs.

A matter of differing styles? Bakhtin makes the distinction between *style*, i.e. individual choice in discourse, and *genre*, i.e. the collective conventions of a discourse community, its 'accumulated experience' (Morson and Emerson 1990: 292). A community's stock of speech genres is the concrete repository of its common history, of the way it conceives of language, communication and interpersonal relations, and of the way it envisages its future (Kramsch 1998). For Bakhtin, a speech genre is 'the residue of past behavior' (Morson and Emerson 1990: 290), a 'relatively stable type of utterance' (Bakhtin 1986: 60) that implies 'a set of values, a way of thinking about kinds of experience and an intuition about the appropriateness of applying the genres in any given context' (Morson and Emerson 1990: 291). As Hanks (2000: 135) wrote recently: 'Genres can be defined as the historically specific conventions and ideals according to which authors compose discourse and audiences receive it'.

In that respect, the clash we witnessed in the data above is not between individuals choosing 'right' or 'wrong' styles of writing, more or less truth-based or trust-based, but between two local genres engaged in global confrontation. Because genre is bound up both with global communicative purpose (Swales 1990) and a local understanding of social relations, genre is the mediator between the global and the local. It is all the more pervasive as it is the invisible fabric of our speech. It should not be surprising, then, that at the end of our analysis we find genre to be the major source of misunderstanding in global communicative practice. Because we tend to take our genres for natural and universal (Fairclough 1992), we don't realize the local flavour they bring to the global medium.

Of course, genre wars also occur in face-to-face interactions. But there, the multiplicity of semiotic channels serves to diffuse the conflict and to disambiguate the nature of the genre. In the rarefied context of cyberspace, the problem is exacerbated. The partners in the exchange above were not aware that the seemingly transparent medium of the internet might itself be the source of their frustrations. Each group mapped the communicative genres they were familiar with onto their FL communicative practices in cyberspace (Thorne 1999, 2000b). But genres are part of the material, economic fabric of societies. There is a fear that those who own personal computers and email accounts may unwittingly impose their genres globally onto others and thus enforce deinstitutionalized forms of discourse, based on personal experience and trust, at the expense of other, more literacy-based discourses of truth. The danger is that those whose lives are less centred around the computer may not so much lose their language, as they risk losing the very genres that are the hallmark of their membership in their local social and cultural communities.

With regard to FL pedagogy, Kern (2000) has argued that, in foreign language uses of internet-mediated 'key-pal' partnerships, the instructor plays a key role in facilitating critical reflection and cultural awareness after the activity. As Kern says: 'The teacher's crucial task is to lead follow-up discussions, so that the chains of texts that students produce can be examined, interpreted, and possibly re-interpreted in the light of class discussion or subsequent responses from native speakers.' We agree that the teacher should use the rich material provided by these internet exchanges as 'teachable moments' in face-to-face classroom discussions. But in light of the genre wars described above, what is teachable is far more complex than usually thought. The teacher has traditionally been the representative of an acade-mic institution that gave him/her his authority, certified his knowledge, guaranteed his expertise, and sanctioned his pedagogic practice within the limits of a local educational system. The challenge is to prepare teachers to transfer the genres of their local educational systems into global learning environments, and to prepare students to deal with global communicative practices that require far more than local communicative competence.

Conclusion

Global technologies offer a mode of communication that provides at first sight convenient, authentic, direct, and speedy access to native speakers and their cul-tures. For American foreign language learners, increasingly computer literate and avid users of internet communication tools, the use of the internet to learn French encourages a notion of communication that is less the rational negotiation of intended meanings, or even the transmission of information, but a trust-building ritual, that offers the prospect of a global interaction based on fairness, mutuality, and hope in a common global future. However, as we have seen above, this is not the way the French students used the medium. Neither the French nor the American students were aware that the global medium only exacerbated the discrepancies in social and cultural genres of communication. Without a knowledge and under-standing of these genres, no 'understanding of each other's lives' and no reconfiguration of one's own is possible.

Between the global and the local lies genre, the social and historical base of our speech and thought. An understanding of this neglected dimension of foreign lan-guage teaching may lead to a reassessment of what we mean by 'communicative competence' in a global world and what the communicative contract will be, upon which trust is built.

Notes

1 The following excerpt is taken in part from Kern (2000: 252–54). We are most grate-ful to Rick Kern for giving us permission to reproduce it here.

6 Local literacies and global literacy

Catherine Wallace

The future of English as a global language seems assured. Although there are other world languages, only English is used transnationally with a majority of its users now those for whom it is a second language (Graddol 1999). In response to this expansion, and going against the grain of mainstream values and discourses, many teachers and scholars have wished to defend and valorize the local over the global. Vernacular speech or literacy is set against standard, institutionalized and mainstream language varieties. 'Little' languages are seen like little people as needing to be defended. At the same time, there is a strong implication that the local offers the best means for the expression of 'authentic' identity and political resistance on the part of subordinated groups. In this chapter I wish to challenge some of these assumptions. I want to argue that, as teachers of English, our best response to the global future of English is not resistance to the language which provides us with a living, nor even an apologetic defence, but a rethinking of what *kind* of English best serves the needs of its users for the twenty-first century.

Literacy and literacies

Just as local or indigenous languages are privileged over English in critiques of linguistic imperialism, so local and vernacular literacies are favoured in much of the current work in literacy, particularly the research carried out under the auspices of what has come to be known as the New Literacy Studies. This has investigated not mainstream, institutionalized literacy in languages of high national and international prestige such as English, but local, vernacular literacies. These vernacular literacies may be in languages other than English as documented, for instance, in Martin-Jones and Bhatt (1998). Or they may take place in English but for local, everyday purposes. In each case literacy is seen not as something possessed as a skill, but something done or performed as a contextualized practice (Barton 1994; Baynham 1995). Local literacies operate in private domains, such as family life, as opposed to public ones, such as the media and education (Wallace 1988). The interest in documenting the everyday literacy practices of children and adults is reflected in a number of recent titles, such as *City Literacies* (Gregory and Williams 2000) and *Local Literacies* (Barton and Hamilton 1998).

The preference for seeing literacy as context dependent and situationally contingent has led to the now widely preferred pluralization of literacy. Gee (1990: 153) claims: 'Literacy is always plural.' Rather than a single monolithic literacy we have multiple *literacies*: school sanctioned literacy becomes just 'one of a multiplicity of literacies which take place in people's lives, in different languages, in different domains and for a variety of purposes' (Gregory and Williams 2000: 11). The challenge to an overarching, universal literacy came originally from Brian Street in his influential book *Literacy in Theory and Practice* (Street 1984). This first proposed a difference between not literacies as such but two major conceptualizations of literacy: *autonomous* and *ideological* literacy – 'autonomous' suggesting that one is talking of a universal skill or aptitude, being able to read and write; to combat this technicist, skills-based view of literacy the 'ideological' view has it that literacy is a social construct, taking on complex cultural and ideological meanings and diverse forms in specific settings. Hence the widely preferred plural form.

Street's original characterization was a powerful one. It offered an important challenge to a hitherto exclusively Western understanding of literacy, as well as developing an awareness of cross-cultural differences in literacy practices, which Gregory and Williams (2000) draw on in their account of culturally distinctive literacy practices of language minority children and the implications for schooling in the mainstream. However, the continuing preference for conceptualizing literacy both as plural and as broadly autonomous or ideological in orientation, presents several problems. First, the emphasis on the multiple character of literacies may trivialize and relativize their significance; there is a danger that in emphasizing parity we may fail to acknowledge those power relations which are so strongly associated with certain literacies, as opposed to others, most evidently school literacy. Certainly 'power' is a central theme in New Literacy Studies discourse, but the implications are not clearly followed through. For instance, does school sanctioned literacy, often linked to English, offer perceived or real advantages? Is its power merely symbolic? Moreover, the emphasis on discreteness in statements such as: 'Practices each require different skills . . . learned in different ways' (Gregory and Williams 2000: 9) leads one to wonder how far this knowledge has the potential to cross boundaries, how far it might be put to productive use in a range of settings, including school. Indeed in many of the ethnographic studies, though Gregory and Williams's book is a notable exception, educational or school literacy gets scant mention.

Finally, the autonomous/ideological characterization has led to a tendency to see autonomous literacy as necessarily and exclusively represented in educational contexts. Street and Street (1995), for instance, appear to equate schooled literacy with autonomous literacy. It is taken for granted that schooled literacy in the sense of classroom literacy instruction is constructed and practised largely as neutral technology, with reading 'taught as a set of skills which can be broken into parts and taught and tested' (Barton 1994: 162). Certainly much of the discourse in recent documents such as the British National Literacy Strategy seems to favour a view of literacy as involving the unproblematic teaching of skills, with little contextualization of practice, and little acknowledgement in the case of bilingual learners that they may have distinctly different literacy experiences, and different language repertoires including understandings gained from knowledge of the vernacular or home language. However, schooling does not need to be interpreted in this manner. It is not that teaching and learning decontextualizes so much as, in Bernstein's (1996) terms, *re*contextualizes, reshaping everyday experiences and knowledge. Although school and home are necessarily different domains, it is not the case that school focuses necessarily on skills-based work and out of school contexts on more creative, more 'authentic' activities. There is a danger of taking a romantic, over-celebratory attitude to contingent, everyday and out-of-school literacies; after all, in many out-of-school cultural contexts literacy will be perceived as the learning of skills or routines of the 'listen, learn, and repeat' kind, documented as one literacy practice of the Roadville parents in Heath's (1983) study of the literacy practices of two communities in the United States. At the same time school literacy practices can be misrepresented as inevitably and inherently mechanistic. The job of educators is to acknowledge the differences, to build bridges between the domains of school and everyday life, but not necessarily by privileging the primary literacies of learners nor by taking a narrow view of school literacy as skills-based.

Notions of primary and secondary kinds of knowledge, experience and identity are suggested by Gee's (1990) characterization of primary and secondary Discourses, where he uses the term Discourse to mean 'ways of being in the world' – that is, more than just language, but ways of displaying membership of a particular social group. Schooling is a secondary Discourse, as opposed to the Primary Discourse of early social settings. As children move from home to school they move from familiar domestic worlds which are part of their primary socialization to take on other identities, ways of behaving and ways of using language. Literacy is part of this. As Gee (1990: 153) puts it: 'Literacy is mastery of, or fluent control over, a Secondary Discourse.'

Halliday (1996: 353) characterizes this shift less in terms of identity than of knowledge: he describes the difference between everyday life and school as one between what he calls primary and secondary knowledge: the latter is more heterogeneously constituted and specific to educational settings. Similarly, Bernstein (1996) talks of vertical and horizontal literacies. The latter are segmental and embedded in ongoing practices and directed to specific goals, and are often acquired through apprenticeship. It is these local and contingent literacies which have been investigated ethnographically in the studies described earlier. Vertical discourse and its associated literacy is scaffolded in schools and learned rather than acquired or 'picked up on the job'. It is not that school literacies are inferior attempts at 'the real thing' (cf. Street and Street 1995: 106) – they are *qualitatively* different. Schooled language, which is literate-like rather than necessarily delivered through the medium of print, is, as I argue more fully later in this chapter, a code for learning and for wider communication rather than for day-to-day use. Nor is it the case that primary knowledge, including, most importantly, knowledge of home languages and literacies, is to be discarded; rather it is rearticulated among a greater diversity of voices and experiences, which accompany the move into secondary socialization. It becomes, in the term that Halliday uses, 'heteroglossic'. It takes on some of the characteristics of written language; it is 'construed out of the dialectic between the spoken and the written' (Halliday 1996: 353). Cummins and Swain (1986) make a similar point in talking about the shift from embedded, primarily oral language towards disembedded, written or literate-like language that educational development in school represents. The question then arises as to how one supports the entry of learners who are skilled in vernacular literacies into the more elaborated, vertical discourse required for success in school or other educational settings. For language minority children, moreover, this shift or switch may involve not just a new language variety but a new language code, frequently English.

A further difficulty with the major focus in the New Literacy Studies on practice and practices in non-school settings is a relative neglect of process and processing. This is partly because of a wish not merely to diversify literacy in terms of domains but also in terms of media. An important point of difference between Gee and Halliday, for instance is that Gee does not wish to privilege print over other kinds of technologies. Therefore the linear processing unique to print is of less interest. Halliday, however, takes the view, which I follow here, that the specific features of print literacy offer particular educational advantages:

> The written world is a world of things. Its symbols are things, its texts are things and its grammar constructs a discourse of things, with which readers and writers construe experience. Or rather, with which they reconstrue experience, because all have been speakers and listeners first, so that the written world is their secondary socialization. This is critical for our understanding of the educational experience . . . the language of the school is written language.
>
> (Halliday 1996: 353)

It will be seen that Halliday continues to use the terms 'readers' and 'writers' in orthodox ways, to refer to the interpreters or producers of continuous print texts. There has been a diminished interest, in much of the social and anthropological literacy literature at least, in print literacy. *Reading* is not included in the glossary to an influential new collection of papers on literacy, *Multiliteracies* (Cope and Kalantzis 2000). And yet social subjects in a common-sense way continue to see themselves as readers and writers, and to value skill in these activities. Print is still the medium we mainly deal with, albeit in different forms – email and hypertext being the most obvious ones. And for many language minorities in Britain whose primary socialization will be in their home, community language, the written world of secondary socialization is in English.

Literate English and critical literacy

I want to push the case for literacy further by arguing not just for the unique role of print literacy, but for the value of sustained engagement with written text; to claim, moreover, unpalatable though it may be in a relativist age, that some texts are more linguistically and cognitively challenging than others, and that it is particularly important such texts should be made available in English to a wide range of students. For foreign and second language learners that means access, not so much to the oral everyday English favoured by many contemporary teaching approaches, but to English language literacy.

Nakata, writing from a postcolonial perspective, comments thus on the demand for English literacy on the part of Torres Strait Islanders:

> At present when Islanders call for English literacy we are told we need literacy in one of our traditional languages first. Why do we need to read and write in our first language which is after all still a robust oral tradition? Simply because it works in French Canada! This standpoint assumes that learning English at school cancels out children's previously acquired and ongoing acquisition of their first language competencies and communicative patterns.
>
> (Nakata 2000: 112)

Nakata's point here about the vitality of local languages echoes Halliday's about a distinctive 'written world of secondary socialization' which is not threatening to the mainly oral world of primary socialization. It also meshes with the argument made by Joseph Bisong (1995) who proclaims the ethnolinguistic vitality of Nigeria's indigenous languages, which are not threatened, he claims, by English, because of the differing functions which local and global languages fulfil.

I would wish to extend the scope of Nakata's point to include not just English literacy but *literate English,* meaning the kind of English (which may also be spoken) most like formal written English such as we encounter in broadsheet newspapers, quality novels and non-fiction texts. It is important to say what I am *not* talking about here: I am not talking about standard or of native speaker English. It is irrelevant for my argument here that, often only with some effort, one can identify a speaker as Russian or Danish or Ghanaian. Indeed the still ongoing debate on what *kind* of English to teach in terms of say British or American – or Nigerian or Singaporean – now seems a rather arid one, because the kind of English we admire for its elegance and eloquence is frequently not produced by those whose first language it is. It is a supranational global English which does not necessarily emanate in any direct way from the centre, as suggested in over-polarized accounts of centre versus periphery English; it will clearly demonstrate a whole range of functions but as a secondary Discourse is most powerful when used discursively rather than experientially. In the terms used by Habermas (1979) it is *constative speech* in that it carries with it obligations to provide grounds for what is said. Transnational English will need, not to be reduced or simplified, as some accounts of its role as a lingua franca seem to suggest, but on the contrary, to be elaborated to take account both of its likely expository function in formal settings, and of the reduction in shared world knowledge that is associated with transcultural exchanges.

Apart from its role in argument, 'literate English' is valuable in talk for learning in classrooms. Clegg (1992) drawing on the work of Gordon Wells, calls this *literate talk* – not just for content learning but for learning more about language itself, testing the limits, especially for L2 learners, of what they can do with their language. As Clegg (1992: 17) puts it, this involves students 'trying to get a foothold in new cognitive territory'. Literate talk – or literate English, defined to include oral and written language – is language which is not spontaneous but planned. It is more elaborated than informal speech, makes explicit its grounds and provides a useful bridge into expository written language. It is talk which is exploratory, where 'partners engage critically but constructively with each other's ideas' (cf. Mercer 1996), as opposed to the spontaneous and fluent speech which tends to be favoured in the foreign and second language classroom. Moreover it is not just in structure that the language is more complex, which may after all be a matter of empty elaboration, of mere verbiage, as Labov (1972) pointed out in his well-known defence of the logic of non-standard English. For this reason a term used by Granville *et al.* (1998) is helpful. They talk of the need for an 'enriched English', in the process of making a case for the role of good quality English teaching as subject (rather than medium) in post-apartheid South Africa. A pedagogy for an 'enriched' English will clearly need to attend to the complex manner in which structure, content and function inter-relate in the production of effective, literate English.

It should be emphasized that there is nothing inherent in English as a *language* which makes it more suitable than any other language for this role. As Granville *et al.* point out, it is rather that English has developed extensive resources as a result of its dominance across many domains of use. It is English, with its global reach, which is likely to take on public functions as opposed to the private and solidary functions of vernacular languages and literacies. Elaborated to fulfil this role, literate English, for both centre and periphery users, faces outwards rather than inwards. As Nakata (2000: 112) says with reference to the Torres Strait Islanders (but the point has wider implications): 'An English education will enable us to negotiate our position in relation to these outside influences'.

To summarize, I want to defend the position of global literate English as what Chew (1999) calls 'an international auxiliary language'. The kind of English serving this function will not necessarily be standard in form, there will inevitably be (usually minor) regional variations phonologically, lexically and syntactically; but functionally it will be elaborated to serve global needs, the most crucial one, as argued later in this chapter, being as a tool for resistance.

Global English will inevitably be differently inflected in different contexts. Language minority children in English medium schools will draw on different resources and have different immediate needs from adult EFL learners. But the commonalities will be more significant than the differences. Literate English is part of vertical rather than horizontal discourse. While local languages and literacies tend to serve horizontal, contingent and solidary functions, global English spans a wider range of contexts, and has universal applicability and resonance.

The value of the studies done by literacy ethnographers is not in doubt; teachers need an understanding of the full range of students' identities and languages. However, our business as language educators is ultimately with the wider picture, with forms of language which have currency beyond the particular and contingent, which will prepare our students for the unpredictable futures of the era of fast capitalism; which will offer tools to resist, not English itself but meanings which are frequently conveyed through English, often via powerful genres such as news and advertising and, as evidenced by its position as a major export industry for Britain, the English Language Teaching global textbook (see Gray, Chapter 9 this volume).

Pennycook (1994) acknowledges a 'writing back' role for English, whereby English is refashioned to serve the aesthetic and political purposes, particularly in postcolonial contexts, of new generations of users. These new users participate in the dismantling of the colonial legacy of English. This is also the spirit of Pierce's (1989) proposal, writing in the context of South Africa, by which the citizens of post-apartheid South Africa opt not for the replacement of English as a lingua franca by an indigenous language, but for a new kind of English – Pierce calls it 'people's English' – inflected with different kinds of meanings. The principle that one can draw variously on the resources of a single language, reshaping the discourses which have established its hegemony, is very much linked to critical discourse analysis and critical literacy, which I turn to next.

If *literacy* and *global* are terms fraught with difficulty then so is the term *critical* in general and *critical literacy* in particular. A major figure in critical literacy studies was Paulo Freire (1972), who saw the power of literacy as a way of reflecting back to learners their own lived experience, not in a direct and immediate way but systematized and amplified through dialogue, as part of the educational process. What critical educators who follow a broadly Freirean ideology share, is a belief in the empowering potential of literacy, a potential which is articulated in different ways: for Lankshear *et al.* (1997) critical literacy is powerful to the extent that it offers a vantage point from which to survey other literacies. It achieves this through acting as a secondary Discourse in Gee's terms and thereby providing a metalanguage, a language to talk about not just literacy itself, as a form of social and cultural practice, but about features of texts and aspects of the reading and writing process. Critical reading involves gaining some distance on our own production and reception of texts; we are not just involved ongoingly in these as we process or interpret texts but take the opportunity to reflect on the social circumstances of their production, on why they come to us in the form they do, and on the variable ways their meanings may be received in different cultural contexts. Thus, in gaining a degree of distance on what we typically take for granted we may become aware of what other discourses might replace the ones actually present; how else might this text have been written? At the same time, we are encouraged to ask what other ways there are of reading a text beyond our own currently preferred one, or that favoured by the writer.

The ability to engage in this level of critical analysis is not easily achieved. It will elude many native speakers of a language. However, the indisputable power of English as a global language necessitates a high level of critical literate English if it is to serve the 'writing back' or 'talking back' role of resistance. This is not provided by an instructional 'lingua franca' model of English which restricts communication to immediate, utilitarian contexts. Edward Said, visiting a Persian Gulf university in 1985, observed that students following the English programme proposed to end up working for airlines or banks in which English was the lingua franca. This view

> all but terminally consigned English to the level of a technical language stripped of expressive and aesthetic characteristics and denuded of any critical or self-conscious dimension. You learned English to use computers, respond to orders, transmit telexes, decipher manifests and so forth. That was all.
>
> (Said 1994: 369)

Global English teaching and the ELT profession

I have proposed that English language teaching, like globalization itself, does not need to be seen to bring only negative consequences. This is not to deny that English language teaching agencies, in particular some international publishers, have sometimes quite explicitly taken a market view of English language teaching as a commodity. There is some justification for the view expressed by Phillipson and Skuttnab Kangas (1999) that Eastern Europe has become the new postcolonial world (cf. Gray, Chapter 9 this volume). Asked to comment on recent English language teaching projects in Eastern and Central Europe Widdowson talks of there being 'rather too much of people coming in from outside "bringing in the good news" with scant knowledge of local traditions of scholarship and education' (Widdowson, quoted in Thomas 1999: 125). However, our resistance as language teachers need not be to the teaching of the language itself so much as to the grosser kinds of cultural and linguistic imperialism which continues to characterize some ELT discourse and practices. The reductive thrust of this, as argued above, fails to make available to learners an English which can serve the 'writing back' or 'talking back' function of critique. The answer, however, is not to throw in the towel but to do the job better, whether as language teachers or as teacher educators.

If we accept the need to deal with the realities of the globalization of English in the broad ways outlined above, what more specific implications arise in terms of the kinds of second language learners we teach in different contexts and the way we might draw on, adapt or reject prevailing methodologies and materials?

One effect of a general ideological preference for specificity and localization is the identification of subgroups of learners, the development of specific competencies of the kind noted by Said, and a consequent proliferation of specialist fields in English Language Teaching: ESP, EAP and, particularly in British ELT discourse, the long-standing division between EFL and ESL. While the EFL/ESL divide makes sense in school contexts, where children of immigrant or refugee families are receiving their schooling through the medium of English rather than learning it as a subject in the curriculum, in some adult learning contexts in Britain the value of the distinction is more dubious. It is based on outdated and essentialist assumptions that there are two clearly defined groups: one being short-stay students, mainly from European countries, and the second, refugees or asylum seekers who are judged to have different educational needs, even though these same students may in an earlier era have found themselves in the EFL 'European' group. In a recent study of one London Further Education college, Cooke (2000) found that the so-called ESL learners are currently likely to be asylum seekers or refugees from many parts of the world. They are assumed, in many instances quite wrongly, to have low educational levels and consequently judged to have literacy problems. Moreover, their supposed literacy needs are addressed with competence-based instruction and assessment, a clear example of Street's autonomous literacy pedagogy at work. The EFL 'European' group in the same college study with a standard global textbook, which is reductive in a different way, offering what we might call the three Ds view of consumerist EFL culture, *dinner parties, dieting* and *dating*, and reflecting the preoccupations of the textbook writers rather than their likely readers. Indeed, as Gray (this volume) also notes, one of the ironies of the so-called 'global' textbook is its typically narrow and parochial discourse. Consequently neither the group designated 'EFL' nor that designated 'ESL' is offered quality English language teaching provision, which, I am arguing here, is educationally demanding, rooted in literate language and designed to prepare students for longer term and relatively unpredictable needs as continuing learners and users of English.

In overseas contexts learners may be in EFL settings or in postcolonial periphery settings. Canagarajah (1999a) documents the bizarre situation in which learners in Sri Lanka are, in the guise of following communicative approaches, frequently working with old texts long abandoned in centre contexts, and which even in their heyday were gross caricatures of the ways of life they claimed to represent. Canagarajah (1999a: 87) notes: 'What we cannot tell is whether the authors and publishers of [American Kernel Lessons] and similar courses understand how little relation their subliminal messages bear to the life of students and teachers in periphery contexts'. One could add that these messages bear little or no relation to the lives of anyone anywhere. In the next section I take a closer look at how far contemporary favoured methodologies are able to offer access to global literate English of the kind argued for here.

In ESL school contexts literacy and literate talk have received more attention than in typical adult ESL and EFL contexts. Clegg (1996: 3) makes a plea for other than merely narrowly defined linguistic goals in the education of ESL children. 'The main point of their learning English as an additional language is so that they can use it for their cognitive, academic and curricular development'. However, in many English language teaching contexts favoured methodologies take a more restricted view of communicative ability. These methods or approaches cluster under the broad umbrella of communicative language teaching (CLT). CLT has been under attack for some time on the grounds that – as interpreted in actual ELT materials if not applied linguistics texts – the goal tends to be talk for its own sake; simply talking is enough, and it is immaterial *what* you talk about. Pennycook (1994: 311) refers to the phenomenon as the 'empty babble of the communicative language class'.

In spite of the recent challenge by Pennycook, and others such as Cope and Kalantzis (1993) who also question the dominant progressivist ideology, versions of communicative language teaching are still not seriously challenged, in particular the premise that the goal of language teaching is to enable communication with native speakers in natural, everyday environments. This resonates with the emphasis in the New Literacy Studies described earlier: everyday, lived experience is perceived as more legitimate or authentic than what Gee (1990) has called 'contrived educational settings'. As I note in Wallace (2001: 213) educational settings are *necessarily* contrived; it is the job of teachers to contrive situations for learning. The teacher's skill is demonstrated though the manner in which the classroom can offer learning opportunities not readily available in everyday life situations. Admittedly this goal becomes obscured in some progressivist language teaching methodologies. A major one is Task Based Learning, for some time now the most popular methodological offshoot of CLT (cf. Block, Chapter 7 this volume). Like CLT, it is also experientially grounded in the everyday worlds of learners and concerned with the achievement of immediate outcomes, such as solving a problem or carrying out instructions. It is, claims Kramsch (1995: 48) 'characterized by its local treatment of local problems through local solutions'.

We need, in short, to question the contribution of Communicative Language Teaching and Task Based Learning to the development of what I have called literate English, in so far as both prepare learners to deal with small-scale, day-to-day encounters between friends or intimates in familiar settings such as at parties, school or the workplace, or to engage in everyday transactions. We might expect to have moved right away from the following objective for EFL programmes offered by

Van Ek, with reference to the Threshold Syllabus of the 1970s, which nonetheless continues to inform much current methodology and materials: 'the learners will be able to survive (linguistically speaking) in temporary contacts with foreign language speakers in everyday situations whether as visitors to the foreign country or with visitors to their own' (Van Ek 1976: 24–5).

What might alternatives to CLT or TBLT look like? What are feasible ways of promoting a global critical literacy through the medium of English? What options are available to those who do not wish to merely translate the shallow preoccupations of British and American popular culture on to the world stage? Several scholars, most notably Pennycook 1994 and Canagarajah 1999a, have proposed critical pedagogy as a necessary underpinning to any English Language Teaching project which wishes to address the global reach of English. However, there are different interpretations of critical pedagogy. Some emphasize humanistic, learner centredness (e.g. Kanpol 1994). Others acknowledge the dangers of a romantic over-celebratory approach to the validation of learners' experiences: 'we must resist the somewhat misleading tendency in critical pedagogical circles to romanticize student opposition and minority discourses as being always liberatory and progressive' (Canagarajah 1999a: 97). Nonetheless Canagarajah is learner centred to the extent that he supports the need for teachers to 'unravel the hidden cultures of their classrooms and students' (Canagarajah 1999a: 193), and believes 'that pedagogies of resistance need to be rooted in the everyday life of our students' (1999a: 194). I take a different view: that we should acknowledge and respect but not appropriate or incorporate the underlife, as Canagarajah calls it, of our students; that it is not our role to nurture those sites; that the concerns of teachers should be less with personal or local empowerment than with a longer-term challenge to social inequity in a wider sense (Wallace 1999).

Practically, such a critical pedagogy involves addressing issues which may resonate locally but which have global implications; in terms more specifically of *language* teaching, it means developing literate English as a priority. This is not an imposition from the centre; it requires not the acquiescence of subordinated groups but their participation, if English is to be constantly recreated to serve emancipatory rather than oppressive goals. An attenuated, reduced English cannot serve this purpose. Literate English is also creatively more flexible than the restricted, horizontally embedded English of CLT. In other words the critical and creative use of English which Canagarajah rightly calls for is the end point rather than the starting point of critical pedagogy.

A key factor in the students' progress to critique and creativity by way of literate English is their ability and willingness to resist. Canagarajah (1999a: 182) notes the necessary role for reflective resistance, in view of his observation of the 'largely non-reflective' ways in which students 'display their strategies of linguistic appropriation'. This relates to a distinction first made by Giroux (1983) between *opposition* and *resistance*. Opposition can be seen as an instinctive, unreflected upon response to domination; resistance as a considered, reflected upon, rational stance, where earlier instinctive responses have been subjected to analysis.

The goal then is to lead students from opposition to resistance, from knee-jerk hostile response to reflective, considered judgement. For Canagarajah the route is pluralized English which he sees as 'standard grammars and established discourses being infused with diverse alternate grammars and conventions from periphery languages' (1999: 175). My proposal favours not pluralism but universality. I would argue, reconfiguring the role of hybridity and pluralization, that vernacular codes, which will be in local varieties and languages, possibly not written, not elaborated to serve wider needs, will be multiple and shifting, while English as a global literate language will expressly serve the purpose of embracing a range of settings; it requires greater stability as a 'syncretic' language, to take a term used by Searle (1983), that binds diverse periphery and centre communities together. Once this is established, as noted above, it can be put to critical and creative use, challenging and dismantling the hegemony of English in its conventional forms and uses.

To turn instinct into reflectiveness, opposition into resistance, means forging English as a critical analytical tool which is elaborated to serve those purposes. In terms of currently favoured teaching methodologies, it means a radical rethinking of both Communicative Language Teaching and Task Based Learning, at least as both of these tend to be translated into current teaching material. It means teaching a kind of language which is not for immediate use, not to be taken out into the streets and the clubs, but which can serve longer-term needs.

The proposal I want to consider here, necessarily briefly, centres around print literacy and literate talk and comes broadly under the auspices of Critical Language Awareness (e.g. Fairclough 1992). The purpose of Critical Language Awareness is to make language itself the object of critical scrutiny – both language as social practice and language as social process, evidenced in the reading and writing of texts. In the course of learning about these social practices and processes learners are made aware of how language might be differently shaped to meet needs beyond those which are closest and most familiar to them. Practically speaking in the classroom this involves the provision of a wide range of text genres, frameworks for analysis and opportunities for talk around text (Wallace 1992).

The teacher may start with analysis of texts brought into the classroom by herself or the students; however, ultimately the aim is to encourage students to respond to texts within wider contexts of use. This means being aware of the placing and meaning of texts in a range of settings beyond the classroom. The text is necessarily recontextualized within the classroom and takes on cultural meaning by being brought into a pedagogic setting by students or teachers. Canagarajah (1999a) describes the way commercial English language texts can be appropriated by students to their own ends. But *any* text, designed as pedagogic or coming from an everyday source can be made use of in a range of ways within the classroom. Indeed the point of critical language study is to read texts in different ways, to subject everyday texts to other than everyday readings. An example of the kind of response I have in mind occurs in this 'think aloud' reading of an article about Singapore by a Japanese student of mine on a Critical Reading course, as she reacts to the way in which oriental people are exoticized in popular news and magazine articles: 'I don't like this article so much because I think in this kind of text generally speaking I think the British people, and other European people, seem like they are looking at Far Eastern people in some different way – as if looking at some complete strangers, like people who's mad or who act beyond their comprehension.'

We are familiar with the idea of 'text as linguistic object', in English Language Teaching, where texts are gutted for linguistic structure. Indeed much reading instruction has traditionally taken this form. We can equally see texts as *cultural* objects or artefacts in the sense that they embody the values and belief systems of the societies and communities from which they arise, as my student observed in the case of the text about Singapore. Moreover, it is clearly advantageous to examine not just texts in standard English but in a range of forms, genres and discourses. In particular it is revealing to look at texts across linguistic and cultural boundaries, for instance at the way genres are interpreted in different cultural settings. This macro awareness of texts can then be refined by more micro analysis of specific linguistic and discoursal selections of the kind promoted in Critical Discourse Analysis (CDA) approaches (cf. Wallace 1992).

Critical literacy and literate talk are mutually reinforcing in the sense that talk around texts offers opportunities to check out our own preferred readings against those of others. Such talk also creates the occasion for multiple interpretations of texts, each of which can be argued through, defended, modified or abandoned in discussion with others. This is when literate talk is both put to work but also is enhanced in the *course* of critique. It is talk which is literate in the sense that, as I noted earlier, like formal modes of writing it makes its case explicit and the grounds for claims are open to scrutiny by others. In this sense it is constative in Habermas's (1979) terms. It involves not talk as social action, doing things with words, which has prevailed in the foreign language classroom, but 'the acquisition and development of more complex conceptual structures and cognitive processes' (Wells and Chang-Wells 1992: 55).

In the CLA classroom students are encouraged to deploy literate talk in critiquing a range of texts. One way of doing this is to offer opportunities for students to first rehearse in small group discussion their contributions to subsequent public debate, where views are shared and reconsidered in a wider forum, thus allowing space for more extended, planned discourse than is usually available to students in communicative language classrooms, where short-burst informal talk is privileged. It will be argued that foreign language learners have these abilities well developed from their first language. This is often true. However, such learners then welcome the opportunity, denied them in most language classrooms, to exercise their discursive abilities at the same time as developing literate English.

Conclusion

My defence is not of English but of a particular kind of literate English. This more widely contextualized form of English, often in written form but also used in formal spoken contexts, coexists with vernacular literacies, with each occupying distinct domains. For its users, literate English offers a form of secondary socialization into the world of global English. We need to ensure that this world is not exclusively represented by the Murdoch press or CNN or the commodified worldview of the ELT textbook; but that learners of English as a foreign and second language can participate in its critique and recreation. Modes of resistance to English are available through English, but a critically nuanced literate English. We resist global tyranny with global means. For today's world we might reverse Van Ek's counsel of twenty-five years ago to say that the need today is to help our learners to deal with 'ongoing contacts with a world community of intellectuals, most of whom will not be native speakers of English, in the public arena beyond the national boundaries either of their own country or any other, English speaking one'.

Part III
Methods and materials

7 'McCommunication'

A problem in the frame for SLA

David Block

Task-based Language Teaching (TBLT) is at present the most discussed methodology in language teaching and learning contexts. The term 'task' is on the lips of just about anyone attending a language teaching conference in any part of the world. It appears in language teaching coursebooks and increasingly is becoming part of the discourse of language teachers around the world. Most importantly, it is sustained by the most coherent and well-developed research strand in the field of second language acquisition (SLA) today, that revolving around the Interaction Hypothesis (see Long 1996 and Gass 1997, for in-depth presentations). The Interaction Hypothesis is based on the notion that language learners learn by using language in context whilst concentrating on the completion of communicative tasks. Communicative tasks are understood to be real-world-like speech events during which interlocutors exchange information. Central to this understanding of communication as information transaction is the construct known as *negotiation for meaning*. This chapter is about the shortcomings of this construct as a way of 'framing' communication which is part of a general global tendency towards the rationalization and technologization of discourse.

Globalization and framing

Globalization has become a familiar and much used term over the past two decades. In the introduction to this volume, there is a discussion of the many ways in which it has been defined and the relevance of these definitions to language teaching and learning. In this chapter, the important point is that globalization, as Held *et al.* (1999) point out, makes possible the extensive, intensive, rapid and high-impact spread of culture (understood here to comprise, among other things, the concepts, information, images, objects and practices of a particular society). In so doing, it also allows for the diffusion of particular ways of 'framing' various phenomena. Here I am using the term 'frame' following the work of Donald Schön (e.g. Schön 1979; Schön and Rein 1994), who believed that the first step towards understanding individuals' discourse about any number of phenomena in the real world is to try to reconstruct the basic metaphors around which that discourse is organized.

One aspect of framing which is particularly relevant in this chapter is the way frames are often transferred from one domain of experience to another. Thus, in the same way that frames originate in metaphorical process of seeing A as B within a particular domain of experience, entire domains themselves often come to be seen in terms of other domains. This process is often at the collective sub-conscious level, a form of conceptual seepage whereby groups either suddenly or gradually come to see a domain of experience in a different way. An example is interpersonal relationships which in late modern industrialized societies have, in a very subtle and gradual way, moved from being framed as traditionally deter-mined (e.g. as an alliance between kin groups) to being framed as constructed by the constituent parties (marriage as something which has to be worked at, as described by Quinn 1987, and exemplified by Gray 1992). Giddens (1991) charts this development, which is part of a larger move from biological and social deter-minism, that so dominated the framing of society in the social sciences, to more agent-centred approaches which attribute to individuals the capacity to transform and change their surrounding environment and their life conditions. This increas-ingly heightened sense of agency in effect transmutes into newly developed conceptualizations of a variety of events and phenomena. The process is effortless and not attributable to any one agent; rather it arises from the coming together of a constellation of events and phenomena, in this case the consolidation of tech-nologically and industrially advanced societies and their later movement into the post-industrial age.

Events, experiences and phenomena in our day-to-day lives are always subject to framing and reframing processes. These processes work both at the subconscious and conscious levels, at both the individual and collective level, and the exact source of new frames is often difficult or impossible to pin down. More impor-tantly, the increasing time–space compression associated with globalization, means that frames which might have remained local now circulate very rapidly around the world. This applies to the subconscious changes in the *zeitgeist* of a particular domain (e.g. the framing relationships cited above) as well as conscious policy pro-posals emanating from concrete sources (e.g. the conscious attempt by the USA government to impose the so called 'Washington Consensus' on countries around the world).

Reframing communication

An example of reframing, as described above, is the spread of what Fairclough (1992, 1995) calls the 'technologization of discourse', a process whereby a partic-ular sphere of discourse practices is colonized by methodologies and practices which previously had been foreign to it. Fairclough is particularly interested in the ongoing struggle between the tendency of some people to embrace enterprise and marketing frames for an ever-increasing number of discourse practices which were previously organized around different frames (e.g. education in Britain, which has moved from an 'education as public service' frame to an 'education as market' frame) and the resistance of others to these forces as they attempt to retain local control over those elements of their lifeworld which have not been colonized by the enterprise/marketing frame. A specific example of the technologization of discourse provided by Fairclough (1995: 100–1) (and elaborated on by Cameron 2000, Chapter 4 this volume), is what he calls the 'conversationalization of institutional discourse', that is, the recent tendency for service providers, selling face-to-face, by telephone and on-line, to adopt what is conventionally considered to be the discourse of interpersonal relationships in an effort to establish stronger affective links with their customers. However, this conversationalization of institutional discourse is inherently technologic as the service providers attempt to control every aspect of its implementation as a selling strategy. The end result is what Cameron (2000: 86–87) calls 'styling', that is, 'a kind of grooming of surface appearances . . . where there is little engagement with the underlying purposes and principles of verbal interaction, but rather an intense concern to manage what might be called its aesthetics'. The kinds of aesthetic which Cameron discusses have to do with elements such as voice quality (speaking with a 'smiley' voice), as well as rather naive pragmatic notions like 'speaking in adult persona' (e.g. dealing with problems with colleagues on the job in neither condescending nor evasive style, but in assertive adult-to-adult style). However, 'styling' might also be used to refer to recipes for how best to carry out successful information transactions, where recommendations for proper turn taking, lexical choice, and conversation repair come into play (see further discussion below).

Cameron and Fairclough's discussion of the colonization of interpersonal interaction by Taylorized, technologized and stylized communication, articulates well with George Ritzer's dystopic portrayal of the pre- and post-millennium globalized existence of many citizens of this planet. Ritzer (1996, 1998, 1999) believes that the lives of people around the world are becoming progressively more Americanized, over-rationalized and ultimately dehumanized, using the term 'McDonaldization' to name 'the process by which the principles of the fast-food restaurant are coming to dominate more and more sectors of American society as well as of the rest of the world' (Ritzer 1996: 1). Ritzer sees fast-food restaurants and other rationalized social phenomena, such as shopping malls and theme parks, as examples of Weberian mini-bureaucracies. These mini-bureaucracies are characterized by five key tenets: efficiency, calculability, predictability, control and standardization. Efficiency means that tasks, as goal directed processes, are carried out from beginning to end with minimal expenditure of human, technical and financial resources. Calculability means that success can be measured or counted and that what is valued is the number of units despatched and the price which it costs to dispatch them, as quality comes to be seen in terms of quantity. Predictability means that there is an assurance that a task will be done in a uniform manner and that the result will be similar if not the same, no matter who is responsible for carrying it out. Control over these three tenets is via careful design and monitoring mechanisms and this control ultimately leads to the final tenet of McDonaldization, standardization, as the mini-bureaucracy functions in the same way for all people in all places, all the time.

As Cameron and Fairclough point out, in recent times there has been a tendency to frame interpersonal and workplace-based communication as a set of technical skills that can be defined, made more efficient, quantified, predicted and ultimately controlled. Cameron and Fairclough might prefer to call this process the 'technologization of discourse', or more specifically, the 'conversationalization of institutional discourse'. Ritzer, however, would call it 'McCommunication', emphasizing not only that process relies on a frame which over-rationalizes communication, but also that this frame is commodified and spread around the world. This commodification and spread of McCommunication is manifested in the worldwide sales of books (e.g. Gray 1992) which engage in what Cameron (1996: 36) calls 'verbal hygiene', that is, 'a diverse set of normative metalinguistic practices based on a conviction that some ways of using language are functionally, aesthetically or morally preferable to others'. This raises the rather depressing possibility that not only will consumption soon be globalized to such an extent that eating, shopping, and holidaying come to be very similar across different geographical locations, but that our ways of communicating in institutional contexts and our personal lives, will also come to be similar as we all follow the same recommendations on how we should and shouldn't talk.

SLA research does not take place in a vacuum and it too has been influenced by the tendency to technologize or 'McDonaldize' communication. However, in SLA research, the details of the frame are very different from those found in the contexts that Fairclough and Cameron discuss. Indeed, while these authors focus on the colonization of institutional discourses by interpersonal conversational discourses, in SLA we find a consensus view that it is *referential* communication, an institutionalized discourse of information exchange, which is a priority for individuals in their day-to-day interactions with others. Yule describes referential communication as follows:

> It is the kind of talk needed for communication when we are not at home among those who know us and recognize what we are likely to mean and how we typically express ourselves. As such, it is the obvious kind of talk required of most of those who are using an L2 to accomplish some transactional goal, whether in education, business, technical communication, or any of the extremely wide range of contexts where a language . . . has become a common lingua franca.
>
> (Yule 1997: 14–15)

Once communication is considered to be primarily referential, this particular frame then colonizes the entirety of communicative contexts which are worthy of investigation. If we examine the interaction-based SLA research published in major applied linguistics journals and books over the past two decades, we see that the kind of tasks employed and presumably offered as models conducive to successful language acquisition, are for the most part referential in nature.[1] The kind of communication which comes out of such a bias is a rationalized information exchange, what I am calling 'McCommunication'.

McCommunication and negotiation for meaning

McCommunication may be understood as the framing of communication as a rational activity devoted to the transfer of information between and among individuals in an efficient, calculable, predictable and controllable manner via the use of language, understood strictly in linguistic terms (syntax, morphology, phonology and lexis). An emphasis on communication as efficient is evident in the preoccupation of many SLA researchers with communication as information transfer, i.e. negotiation for meaning (herefter NfM). Two typical definitions of this term are:

> Negotiation for meaning is the process in which, in an effort to communicate, learners and competent speakers provide and interpret signals of their own and their interlocutor's perceived comprehension, thus provoking adjustments to linguistic form, conversational structure, message content, or all three, until an acceptable level of understanding is achieved.
>
> (Long 1996: 418)

> Negotiation between learners and interlocutors takes place during the course of their interaction when either one signals with questions or comments that the other's preceding message has not been successfully conveyed. The other then responds often repeating or modifying the message. The modified version might take the form of a word or phrase extracted or segmented from the original utterance, a paraphrase, or a synonym substitution thereof.
>
> (Pica *et al.* 1996: 61)

As several authors have recently pointed out (e.g. Yule 1997; G. Cook, 2000; Thorne 2000a), and as we observed above, in the NfM model of interaction, communication is framed as referential in nature, that is as primarily about the exchange and transfer of information. Such a model is not new and dates back to the work of Shannon and Weaver (1949) who developed what became know as mathematical information theory. According to this theory, communication is a matter of an individual transmitting a message via a particular channel to a receiver who then unpacks and interprets it. This model of communication was later to be critiqued by Reddy (1979) who said that it operated according to the conduit metaphor, which entails the following four beliefs about language:

1   Language is a conduit used by human beings to transfer thoughts, feelings and ideas from one person (the sender) to another (the recipient).
2   In the process of speaking and writing, human beings package their thoughts, feelings and ideas *in* the words.
3   Words maintain the meanings intended by the sender.
4   The receiver unpacks or extracts the intended meanings from the words.

In the above-cited definitions by Long and Pica *et al.* interlocutors are seen to 'provide and interpret signals' (in Reddy's terms, 'package and unpack'). More importantly, language is seen to have self-contained meaning which can be accessed without reference to the social context or the intervention of socio-psychological factors. As Tarone (1997: 139) puts it, 'the learner continues to be imagined as a logical mind which generates linguistic input, totally impervious to influence from interactional context and the presence or absence of an interlocutor'.

Another aspect of NfM which is directly tied to efficiency is the notion of 'successful communication' in the completion of tasks. Tasks are seen as goal and outcome oriented, the result of hard work (see G. Cook 2000), and there is a belief that, at least to some extent, judgement of success is possible, particularly where tasks are convergent (i.e. requiring agreement on one set answer). However, in order for the NfM to be successful, the individuals involved have to be attentive, efficient and willing communicators who are aligned in their goal to sort out communication problems as they arise. As Gass (1997: 108) puts it, '. . . negotiation comes when there is some recognized asymmetry between message transmission and reception and when both participants are willing to attempt a resolution of the difficulty.'

The second tenet of McDonaldization, calculability, is evident in NfM in the way that many authors frame communication first as a phenomenon which can be broken down into individual units which can then be counted. In a recent article, Foster *et al.* (2000)[2] discuss many of these calculable units, classifying them as relating to semantics (e.g. propositions, c-units and idea units), informational units (e.g. tone unit clause, idea unit and utterance) and syntactic units (e.g. sentences, idea units and t-units). Not content with what they themselves see as a proliferation in terminology, they carefully define and exemplify a unit of their own, the analysis of speech unit (AS-UNIT) 'which is psycholinguistically valid and reliable in its application to speech samples . . . [and is] an international standard which would enable comparisons to be made across data sets, and ideally, across different languages' (Foster *et al.* 2000: 356). Presumably such a unit would be countable in that more AS-UNITS might substitute for c-units in the following explanation of how oral performance can be measured:

. . . accuracy is measured by dividing the number of correct clauses by the total number of clauses . . . Complexity is measured by dividing the total number of clauses by the total number of c-units . . . Fluency is measured by the number of total seconds of silence per subject per five-minute task.

(Skehan 1998: 108)

Another construct often used to qualify performance is 'lexical range' which, according to Ortega (1999: 124), may be 'calculated following the simplest formula of number of different words (i.e. types) divided by the total number of words (i.e. tokens)'. Elsewhere, Ellis (1997: 224–6) writes of participation in terms of the number and length of turns taken by students engaging in group speaking activities. What we can see in these examples is a tendency in much SLA research towards measuring the quality of language in quantitative terms. Performance is judged in a favourable light where the most turns are taken and where these turns show high lexical density, there is a high success rate (correct clauses divided by total clauses) and silence is at a minimum.

The third tenet of McDonaldization, predictability, is evident in some authors' references to the so-called 'devices' which will be used by interlocutors when they are negotiating for meaning (see Long 1996, for a thorough summary). These devices include recasts, repetitions, confirmations, reformulations, paraphrasing, comprehension checks, confirmation checks, clarification requests and lexical substitutions. The key idea here is that we can predict that these devices will be used if we can get people to negotiate for meaning, while doing carefully designed tasks. Referring to findings from a range of researchers, Skehan (1998: 134) argues that they 'suggest that it is possible to produce greater negotiation of meaning, so that, assuming this to be a desirable quality in task-based interaction, one can engineer a greater degree of active involvement, in order that clarification requests, confirmation checks, and so on are used more, with the possibility that they lead to better quality input and more malleable interlanguage systems'.

Control, the fourth tenet of McDonaldization, is the overriding concern of SLA researchers interested in TBLT as a pedagogical recommendation. The literature on TBLT is full of references to the right task design to engineer the most negotiation for meaning. From Long, Skehan and others, the reader understands that in general the most profitable negotiation will take place when the task type is relatively unfamiliar to participants (but not so unfamiliar that it leads to cognitive overload); the task is two-way (involving the exchange of information held exclusively by task participants) as opposed to one-way (involving transmission of information from one participant to another); the task is convergent (oriented towards agreement) as opposed to divergent (oriented towards differences of opinion); and the participants' interventions are planned as opposed to improvised.

NfM, seen as efficient, calculable, predictable and controllable, leads quite naturally to the fifth characteristic of McDonaldized phenomena, standardization. SLA researchers interested in TBLT appear to be heading towards a model for language teaching which will be applicable across contexts worldwide, what in essence (and despite protestations by authors such as Willis 1996, and Skehan 1998, that their pedagogical recommendations do not constitute a method) will be a new global method for language teaching.

A new frame for communication in SLA?

At this point, the reader might well ask two questions: (1) What is wrong with the McDonaldized view of communication encapsulated in NfM? and (2) What do I propose as a substitute for McCommunication? First, I should point out that I do not envisage the wholesale replacement of this utilitarian model of communication with another, presumably less utilitarian, as I believe that at the level of information transfer, it works quite well, and to some extent, this is what communication is about. I agree with Thorne (2000a) who suggests that challenges to SLA orthodoxy need not be taken as attempts to dismiss the work of many researchers over the past thirty years; rather, they should be seen as complementary, as a means to 'help explicate the processes of SLA, and subsequently, to develop more accurate heuristics which model these processes and conditions' (Thorne 2000a: 221).

The problem I have with McCommunication is that it is a *partial* view of communication and one that is not powerful enough to capture much of what language acquisition is about. As regards efficiency, I do not doubt that in face-to-face interactions, interlocutors engage in NfM; however, I also believe that these same interlocutors are engaged in acts of identity affirmation, face saving, and outright survival. And, while I might agree with Gass that NfM takes place when there is some recognition of communication problems by interlocutors willing to resolve these problems, I nevertheless wonder how often such conditions apply. Surely recognition of difficulty is often partial or even non-existent; and as for Gricean co-operative principles, authors such as Norton (2000) and Rampton (1995) discuss interesting research which suggests that these are far from default conditions in many interactional settings. Norton (2000: 8) makes the point that '. . . many applied linguists . . . take for granted the conditions for the establishment of communication: that those who speak regard those who listen as worthy to listen, and that those who listen regard those who speak as worthy to speak.' Yet, this cannot be taken for granted, as I shall suggest below.

As regards calculability in communication, I have no doubt that it is necessary to elaborate clear constructs which can then be operationalized in subsequent research. The problem I have is that this leads to the measurement of communication and a view of quality in terms of quantity. Thus, in NfM, a learner's performance is judged in a favourable light where the most turns are taken and where these turns show high lexical density, there is a high success rate (correct clauses divided by total clauses) and silence is at a minimum. Adopting such a position towards a concept like fluency, to cite one example, means that those who speak fast are automatically considered more fluent than those who speak slowly, and that silence is in itself a sign of dysfluency, a questionable notion if we are to believe what authors as diverse as Basso (1972), Saville-Troike (1989), Tannen (1993) and Blum-Kulka (1997) have argued, namely that it is simply not the case that silence is synonymous with non-communication.

Equally problematic are the predictive and controlling aspects of NfM, whereby, 'one can engineer a greater degree of active involvement, in order that clarification requests, confirmation checks, and so on are used more' (Skehan 1998: 134). Outside of very controlled formal contexts, typical of so much current SLA research, I do not believe that one can engineer exchanges in such a way that one set of variables will lead to events taking place in certain ways (e.g. constructing a task in such a way that it causes those engaged in it to implement the conversation devices listed above). I might add that I am not alone in this belief. Skehan (1998) himself is sceptical about this prospect and he cites studies by Aston (1986 1993) and Foster (1998), both of whom found that negotiation devices do not neatly emerge once the teacher has managed to engineer a task in the most propitious manner.

Rampton (1997) has argued that SLA needs to move away from strictly psycholinguistic models of language learning to ones which take into account a number of socio-psychological and sociological factors such as resistance and ethnolinguistic identity. He argues that two obstacles to such a change are to be found first, in the tenacity with which many researchers hang on to the notion of a Chomskyan ideal speaker-hearer inhabiting an ideal and homogeneous speech community and second, in their propensity to view the natural sciences as a model of inquiry. Indeed, it seems that the closest some researchers come to acknowledging that there is a place for social context in SLA, is to observe that just about all biological and cognitive processes take place in social context of some sort:

> SLA is certainly, in large part at least, a mental process: the acquisition of new linguistic knowledge. Language acquisition usually takes place in a social setting, to be sure, as do most internal processes – learning, thinking, remembering, sexual arousal, and digestion, for example – and that neither obviates the need for theories of those processes, nor shifts the goal of inquiry to the settings themselves.
>
> (Long 1998: 93)

As Rampton (1997) points out, the current problem with SLA is that it is too 'modern'. Drawing on the analogous case of social theory, Rampton argues that currently there is a need to embrace more recent views on the complexity of the realities explored and investigated by sociologists, which have variably been termed 'late-modern' (e.g. Giddens 1991) or 'postmodern' (e.g. Bauman 1992). Taking on more recent social theory in SLA would mean attempting to account for

phenomena such as 'fragmentation, contingency, marginality, transition, indeter-
minacy, ambivalence, and hybridity' (Rampton 1997: 330), adopting a different
'conceptual kit'. At the same time, it would mean leaving behind the 'overly hasty
pursuit of universals, referential above indexical meaning, disembedded cognition,
value-free inquiry, progress as a natural condition, and assimilation to the norms of
an idealized monolingual U.K. or U.S. national' (Rampton 1997: 330).

Such a change in orientation, in essence an attempt to rescue language use in
context from the most banal forms of McCommunication, is not in principle
rejected by many SLA researchers firmly situated inside the field of TBLT. Skehan,
for example, acknowledges the predominant focus in SLA on the technical aspects
of task design as opposed to research into task participants:

> There have been a small number of studies of participants within tasks. . . . The
> focus of such studies has not tended to be on variables such as personality or
> ethnic background, but rather on the capacity of the researchers to engineer
> more effective task completion.
>
> (Skehan 1998: 112)

Still, calls to 'sociolinguistify' SLA (e.g. Firth and Wagner 1997; Rampton 1997)
have met with dismissive replies (e.g. Long 1997 1998; Gass 1998) along with
challenges to provide evidence that such a change would be worthwhile:

> Instead of dismissing all past work as 'narrow' and 'flawed', and simply assert-
> ing that SLA researchers should therefore change their data base and analyses
> to take new elements into account, [critics] should offer at least some evidence
> that, e.g., a richer understanding of alternate social identities of people cur-
> rently treated as 'learners', or a broader view of social context, makes a
> difference, and a difference not just to the way this to that tiny stretch of dis-
> course is interpretable, but to our understanding of acquisition.
>
> (Long 1998: 92)

What is needed, it seems, is a broader and richer frame for communication, if it is
the goal of researchers to document interaction as a context for acquisition in a balanced and thorough manner. Such a frame would take into account both social and
psycholinguistic aspects of communication and would be able to account for all
interactions which are in any way either obviously or potentially language acquisition contexts.

This latter point is important because I disagree with authors such as Gass (1998)
for whom the division between language acquisition and language use contexts is
easy to establish; rather I think that most day-to-day interactions engaged in by individuals living in immigrant contexts can be potential acquisition opportunities,
even when these occur after five, ten, fifteen, or even twenty years of life in what

was originally a foreign culture. To demonstrate this point, below I reconstruct and analyse two exchanges which took place during the eighteen years which I lived as an immigrant in Barcelona.[3] In both cases, I was positioned as the less competent interlocutor in exchanges with bilinguals for whom Catalan was their first language and Spanish was their second language. And, in both cases, while there surely was some negotiation for meaning, as defined above, there was also negotiation for identity and face, two far more important aspects of my sense of competent self as a speaker of another language.

SLA in Barcelona: a question of identity and face saving

The first exchange took place in January 1979, shortly after I arrived in Barcelona. At this time, I was minimally proficient in Spanish and knew no Catalan, and if there was one communicative context which I found particularly face threatening and frustrating, it was telephone conversations: whereas I was increasingly confident in face-to-face encounters, I dreaded picking up the telephone when it rang. This exchange took place in just such a context. I was alone in a flat which I was sharing with a friend, who was Catalan herself and a bilingual Catalan and Spanish speaker. At the time of the phone call she was out with several friends, one of whom was named Dolors. The phone call was from Dolors's mother. In the reconstruction of the conversation which follows, I have written in bold the English translations of what was said, along with supplementary comments to help the reader understand what was going on.

David: ¿Sí?
           Hello. *(In Spanish, but the response would sound the same in Catalan)*
Mother: Què hi és la Dolors, si us plau?
           Is Dolors there, please? *(in Catalan)*
David: ¿Qué? . . .
           What? *(in Spanish)*
Mother: ¿Qué está María Dolores?
           Is Dolores there? *(N.B. In Spanish with Catalanized use of 'que' to begin the question; a change in the name, from Catalan 'Dolors', to Spanish 'Dolores'; and an uttering of the full name 'María Dolores', probably for emphasis.)*
David: ¿María Dolores?
           Maria Dolores?
Mother: Sí, María Dolores, ¿está?
           Yes, Maria Dolores. Is she there?
David: No, no está. Ha salido.
           No, she has gone out.
Mother: ¡Ah! ha salido. Pues, por favor, cuando vuelva . . . ¿le puedes decir que me llame? Soy su madre.

> **Ah, she's gone out. Uhm, could you please tell her to call me when she comes back. This is her mother.**

David: . . .

> **. . . (silence)**

Mother: Oye, ¿aún estás ahí?

> **Hello, are you still there?**

David: Más despacio – es que tengo problemas con la lengua.

> **More slowly – I have problems with my/the tongue/language**
>
> (N.B. 'lengua' could be either language or tongue.)

Mother: ¿Tienes problemas con la lengua? Pero qué . . . Mira, volveré a llamar más tarde.

> (impatiently) **You have problems with your tongue? But what . . . Look, I'll phone back later.**

David: ¿Cómo?

> **What?**

Mother: (Hangs up the telephone)

In this conversation I was involved in a process of NfM in that I was trying to exchange information with my interlocutor, Dolors's mother. There are several examples of the kind of devices outlined by Long (1996) and others which are believed to contribute to linguistic restructuring and language acquisition. For example there are confirmation checks (e.g. when I say '¿Maria Dolores?' after the mother has asked to speak to her); clarification requests (e.g. when I indicate that I do not understand, saying '¿Qué?', '¿Cómo?' or 'Más despacio . . . '); comprehension checks (e.g. when after a silence, the mother asks if I am still there) and a form of reformulation, when the mother switches to Spanish after beginning in Catalan. Nevertheless, despite the fact that Dolors's mother and I effectively negotiated for meaning as regards our use of negotiation devices, I would say that we failed to successfully complete our information exchange as the conversation came to an abrupt end with one interlocutor thoroughly frustrated and the other still in the dark about exactly what he had been told.

If we examine the actual language I used, there are no grammatical errors as regards syntax and morphology, although my pronunciation no doubt left much to be desired. My lexical choice with regard to 'lengua' was certainly a problem for my interlocutor: a more appropriate response would have been to simply say 'No entiendo' (I don't understand). The biggest problem, however, would appear to be one of listening comprehension in that I was having a great deal of difficulty following what my interlocutor was saying to me.

However, to reduce this exchange to negotiation devices, linguistic factors and skills is to miss out on what was uppermost in my mind at the time, and that was to be a plausible interlocutor for the caller and to save face. I was in essence negotiating my identity (van Lier 2000), as there was nothing more important to me at this time in my life than to be accepted as a valid Spanish speaker. However, this was not to be, as my interlocutor apparently did not take into account my obvious foreignness and treated my difficulties with impatience. Following Norton, we might say that Dolors's mother did not consider me to be 'worthy to speak', or in any case, worthy of engagement. And contra Gass, while there might have been 'some recognized asymmetry between message transmission and reception', Dolors's mother certainly did not seem 'willing to attempt a resolution of the difficulty'.

Another interesting aspect of this incident is what happened after the phone call took place. Several hours later, Dolors and the others returned from their outing. I forgot to tell Dolors that her mother had called and only remembered this when the phone rang. Dolors was called to the phone in the next room and when she returned, she was laughing. When asked why, she said that her mother had phoned and that the person who answered the phone (i.e. me) had been 'so stoned' that she couldn't engage him in conversation. Laughter broke out among all present and I laughed as well. However, inside I could only believe that I had failed in the exchange and made a fool of myself.

As a second language acquisition experience, this exchange taught me something about how to express a lack of comprehension. However, this moment of acquisition occurred not as a direct result of negotiation devices, but as a result of my public humiliation several hours later, which in turn provided an incentive to linguistically restructure my discourse in the future. In reference to Long's comment about SLA reproduced above, I would say that my experience was necessarily 'a mental process of some sort', which did lead to 'the acquisition of new linguistic knowledge'. However, contra Long, I would say that a lack of consideration of social setting and a rejection of a 'shift [in] the goal of inquiry to the settings themselves' would make it impossible to qualify this process and above all to make any sense of the conversation.

The second exchange took place some eight years later, by which time I was by most estimates fully proficient in Catalan and Spanish, with a marked preference for communicating in the former. Part of my job at a large language school was to carry out placement interviews with prospective students. I normally began such interviews by speaking in Catalan as I wished to establish rapport and engage the prospective student in an informal conversation about his/her background and needs before I proceeded to test his/her English. Beginning in Catalan instead of Spanish was not only a way of communicating to my interlocutor how I wished to position myself in the exchange, but also was an implicit recognition that most of our prospective students were Catalan dominant bilingual speakers. However, much to my dismay at the time, on many occasions I participated in conversations in which I was denied competent Catalan interlocutor status. The following exchange begins as I extend my hand to greet Jordi, a prospective student.

David: Bon dia, sóc David.
       (speaking in Catalan) Good morning. I'm David.
Jordi: Hola, soy Jordi, uh, Jorge.
       **Hello, I'm Jordi, uh Jorge (speaking in Spanish, changing
       'Jordi', Catalan for George, to 'Jorge', Spanish for George)**
David: Hola, Jordi. Molt de gust.
       (still speaking in Catalan) Hello, Jordi. Pleased to meet you.
Jordi: Ah, hablas Catalán. Muy bien. Estupendo. ¿Y cómo es eso?
       **(still speaking in Spanish) Ah, you speak Catalan. Very good.
       Great! And how is that?**
David: És que fa molt temps que visc aquí.
       (still speaking in Catalan) I've been living here for a long time.
Jordi: Sí, pero hay mucha gente que después de muchos anos aquí, no saben ni el
       castellano. Mira . . . por ejemplo, los extranjeros del Barça.
       **(still speaking in Spanish) Yes, but there are a lot of people
       who after many years here, don't even know Spanish. Look at
       the foreigners [who play with] Barça (Barcelona Football
       Club).**
David: Sí, supongo que sí. Bueno, . . .
       (switching to Spanish) Yes, I suppose so. Well, . . .

This excerpt contains a greeting + introduction, an information question followed
by a response and then further comments related to the same topic. The conversation continued with me asking Jordi for background information and there ensued
an abundance of information exchange along with numerous confirmations, confirmation checks and clarification requests. However, the most notable feature in
this conversation is how Jordi and I negotiate what language is to be used. Given my
sense of investment in Catalan, it seems that it was far more important for me to
carry on the conversation in this language than it was for Jordi. It is worth noting
that Jordi would have been accustomed to carrying out nearly all of his day-to-day
interactions in Catalan, the exception being those with monolingual Spanish speakers or foreigners, who could be assumed not to be competent in Catalan. As the
reader can appreciate in the excerpt, after the opening greeting and introductions,
Jordi acknowledges that I can speak Catalan. However, he does not consider this to
be sufficient reason for him to switch from Spanish to Catalan and he carries on in
the former. I continue in Catalan for one more turn but then desist, switching to
Spanish when I realize that Jordi is not going to switch to Catalan. And all of this
happened despite the fact that both of us would have expressed ourselves much
better in Catalan.

   The two examples I have discussed here make the point that in interactions
between native speakers and non-native speakers, there is much more than NfM
going on, and that the task at hand, overtly the exchange and transfer of

information, is conditioned by a number of social and socio-psychological phenomena. In particular, there is my perhaps exaggerated sense of identity as an acceptable interlocutor, first in Spanish and later in Catalan, which is interacting with the specific syntax, morphology, pronunciation and lexis which I draw on as I adapt to contingencies arising in the flow of conversion. As Norton (2000: 13) puts it, my 'language is constitutive of and constituted by [my] identity' and we can only carry out a partial analysis of it if we exclude a careful consideration of several of the particulars of the interactions in which I engaged. The NfM frame for communication is thus inadequate if our aim is to understand the complexity of my language development.

Conclusion

In this chapter I have argued that ways of framing and reframing a variety of phenomena can spread rapidly around the world via the kind of information flows and time-space compression discussed by sociologists such as Giddens (1990, 1991). In particular, I have focused on how in recent years there has been a tendency to frame communication in workplace and interpersonal contexts in a rationalized and technical manner. I have attempted a connection between Fairclough (1995) and Cameron's (2000) discussions of this 'technologization of discourse' with Ritzer's (1996, 1998, 1999) views on the over-rationalization or McDonaldization of an ever-increasing number of aspects of our day-to-day lives. Rebaptizing the 'technologization of discourse' as McCommunication, I have then argued that the tendency to frame communication in this way has spilled over into SLA research, where communication is seen as referential in nature and framed as efficient, calculable, predictable, controllable and standardized negotiation for meaning. The problem with this frame is not that it is incorrect or inaccurate, but that it is partial and fails to capture the complexities of communication as a site of SLA. Following authors such as Firth and Wagner (1997) and Rampton (1997), I suggest that there is a need to 'sociolinguistify' communication in SLA, taking into account any number of the features of interaction which have been identified by sociologists and sociolinguists. Recalling my own SLA experiences with Spanish and Catalan, I have attempted to make the point that phenomena such as ongoing identity projection and face saving were an important part of my SLA experience and indeed, that they were inextricably linked with NfM in the day-to-day communicative tasks which I carried out.

So what has any of this to do with globalization and language teaching, the theme of this book? As Ritzer points out, the McDonaldization of our lives is a global phenomenon as ways of doing, thinking and being (what we might call culture), most of which originate in the USA, flow outwards and eventually are taken up in some form or another around the world. This is not to say that traffic is completely one-way, from the USA outwards; however, it is to say that the USA is undoubtedly the key instigator and propagator of world culture (see Ritzer, op. cit., as well as Billig 1995 and Latouche 1996). The technologization of discourse/McCommunication is a way of framing communication which has its origins in the USA and is an out-growth of the enterprise culture which developed in the USA from the late 1970s onwards. At about the same time, in SLA research, the framing of communication as NfM originated in the USA,[4] and has since spread around the world via commu-nications systems specific to global academia but which generically are common to all information flows (international associations, international publications and information technology). An accidental parallel?

While I do not believe in conspiracy theories and certainly do not believe that researchers such as Long, Pica and Gass, subscribe to the tenets of the enterprise culture, I do believe that NfM is inherently enterprise-like in nature as it is consis-tent with a more general technical-rational frame which reduces human existence to the principles of efficiency, calculability, predictability, controllability and stan-dardization. Thus, while it makes SLA research easier to organize and more productive (where productive relates to the number of publications and to theory building), it ultimately dehumanizes a social/psychological phenomenon that deserves a broader frame. What is needed, then, is more talking back to the master frame of McCommunication, in the form of studies of SLA experiences which (1) are based on a broader framing of what the phenomenon involves and (2) take place in more diverse contexts than is presently the norm. Thus far, this call has been met by researchers such as Firth and Wagner (1997), Rampton (1997, 1999b) and some of the contributors to collections such as Hinkel (1999), Lantolf (2000) and this one. One can only hope that more is on the way.

Notes

1   For example, in the Autumn, 1998 issue of *Modern Language Journal* devoted to the role of input and interaction in SLA, the tasks used by the authors of contributions were based on the principle of the information gap necessitating information exchange, along the lines of jigsaw story telling and spot the differences.

2   Researchers such as Foster and Skehan do not see themselves as working within the Interaction Hypothesis and the NfM frame, as they focus more on fluency, accuracy and complexity than interaction. However, I feel justified in grouping them with Long, Gass and others here because they share the same general psycholinguistic perspective and a belief that tasks involving verbal interaction are an essential part of SLA (see Ellis 2000, for a more nuanced view, and Block, in preparation, for a more in-depth explanation of my position).

3   The two examples discussed here are not based on recordings and subsequent tran-scriptions; rather, they are based on my recollection of what happened and as such may be classified as personal narrative. In using personal narrative, I align myself with authors such as Schumann (1997) and Pavlenko and Lantolf (2000) who have shown how such accounts can illuminate important aspects of SLA. Schumann (1997) uses a wide variety of diary studies (e.g. Bailey 1983) as well as autobiographies of language learners (e.g. Hoffman 1989), all as evidence to support his neurobiological model of

SLA. Pavlenko and Lantolf (2000: 159) cite a growing tradition in psychology, sociology, sociolinguistics and anthropology to use personal narratives 'as legitimate and rich data sources for a variety of investigations' before going on to use language learner autobiographies (again Hoffman 1989, is cited) as evidence that 'ultimate attainment in second language learning relies on one's agency' (Ibid. 169).

4   The turn towards interaction as essential to SLA is generally attributed to Hatch (1978), although it was her student, Long, along with others, such as Gass and Pica, who were most instrumental in carrying the research agenda forward.

8 Globalization, methods, and practice in periphery classrooms

A. Suresh Canagarajah

For some time now, language teachers and applied linguists in third world communities have been concerned about the use of teaching methods and pedagogical paradigms developed in the West. Questions have been raised about the cultural relevance and appropriateness of these methods for local communities (Mukherjee 1986; Sampson 1984; Miller and Emel 1988). The need for developing teaching methods based on indigenous pedagogical traditions has also been articulated often by ethnographers in English Language Teaching (Watson-Gegeo 1988; Hornberger 1994). But this line of dichotomous thinking (East versus West; local versus foreign) is complicated by increasing cultural hybridity, human migration, and media expansion. We now acknowledge that cultures and languages of former colonizing nations have attained nativized status in many third world communities. In fact, to identify indigenous teaching methods is not easy. Local intellectual traditions have developed in contact with other cultures and communities. Institutionalized schooling since the Enlightenment has taken a fairly uniform direction everywhere. It is also not clear that third world students do not want to be acquainted with foreign language teaching methods and materials. After all, some of them will migrate to those European and North American communities to continue their educational and social life.

The geopolitical reality of globalization is sometimes exaggerated by discourses of postmodernism that scoff at dire scenarios of linguistic and educational imperialism. Challenging static ways of defining constructs like language, culture and identity, they envision idyllic forms of social relations. That identities are unstable is taken to mean that we can never be dominated by a single discourse to think and behave in preconstructed ways. That cultures are unstable means that powerful cultures cannot dominate minority community practices as they themselves would lose their identity and shade into the cultures they come into conflict with. That languages are unstable means that the linguistic system is always deconstructing itself, opening up to multiple meanings and ideologies, never having the stability to dominate other languages or communities. Taken to an extreme, such premises can prompt a cavalier attitude towards domination. They can nurture visions of a democratic global environment and mutual sharing. These trends give impetus to the already flourishing trade in the production and export of language teaching methods/materials in which the developed communities enjoy a near monopoly.

While negotiating diverse cultures and knowledge traditions is certainly important to become literate today, we shouldn't equate globalization with greater freedom. That identities are fluid doesn't mean that society and nations don't fix certain negative identities on minority students and discriminate against them accordingly. That cultures are mixed doesn't mean that certain values and practices aren't defined as the cultural capital required for success in mainstream institutions, including schools. That languages are hybrid doesn't mean that certain codes don't function as the linguistic capital (with a clear hierarchy of valued registers, dialects, and discourses) to obtain social and educational rewards. The global village is still stratified unequally according to differences in power and material resources (Luke 2000).

The methods trade parallels in many ways the traditional commercial relations in industrial products in the international market. Just as the technologically and economically developed nations of the West (or centre) hold an unfair monopoly over less developed (or periphery) communities in industrial products, similar relations characterize the marketing of language teaching methods. The dominance of centre applied linguistic circles is helped by their resources for conducting sophisticated research with hi-tech facilities and then popularizing the knowledge globally through their publishing networks and academic institutions (Canagarajah 1996). Therefore, it is not surprising that many teachers in periphery communities believe that the methods propagated by centre applied linguistic circles through their textbooks, research journals, teacher training programmes, and professional organizations are the most effective, efficient, and authoritative for their purposes. As in other areas of commerce, it has also been the case that new methods (or sometimes the same methods) have had to be marketed under different brand labels in order to create the need for these products. Business has been helped (sometimes unwittingly) by language teaching experts who hail the new methods in various media as the most advanced, revolutionary, or successful yet constructed. Greeting each new method that is shipped out of the centre with awe and bewilderment, periphery teachers and institutions spend their limited resources on purchasing the new teaching material. To learn to use these, periphery institutions have to spend more resources for getting the assistance of centre experts for re-training their teaching cadre. This becomes a vortex of professional dependence into which periphery communities get drawn ever deeper.

Furthermore, we now realize (thanks to philosophers like Feyarabend 1975) that methods are not value-free instruments validated by empirical research for purely practical teaching functions. Methods are cultural and ideological constructs with politico-economic consequences. Methods embody the social relations, forms of thinking and strategies of learning that are preferred by the circles that construct them. This orientation applies to language teaching methods too (Pennycook 1989).

Centre methods may make an assault on alternative styles of thinking, learning, and interacting preferred by other communities. They may limit critical thinking and impose homogeneous values and practices. This danger is accentuated by the assumptions motivating pedagogical relations in the past. Phillipson (1992: 238) characterizes the governing assumption of centre language teaching circles in the following way: 'Part of the professional identity and image of the Centre applied linguistics institutions is that their skills are universally relevant'. Similarly, Widdowson sums up the expectations of centre pedagogical activities hitherto in periphery contexts as holding 'that somehow it is the local conditions that have to be adjusted to the packaged set of concepts we bring with us rather than attempt to look into the real issues, practical as well as ideological, of implementation and innovation within those contexts' (quoted in Phillipson 1992: 260).

In the context of such heightened ideological sensitivity in language teaching circles today, some applied linguists in the centre have attempted to devise ways of transferring methods to other socio-educational contexts in a culturally harmless and politically neutral manner. I will explore the assumptions of two such models that propose a more effective transfer of methods in periphery communities. I will then proceed to consider the burgeoning professional realization that there is nothing called the 'best' method and that the notion of 'method' itself is not borne out by classroom research. I will consider how this 'postmethod' condition liberates us to think of pedagogical relations and practices in new ways, empowering periphery teachers and students to conduct language learning in a more creative and critical manner.

Critiquing models of methods transfer

In recent publications, Adrian Holliday (1994) and Martha Pennington (1995) have attempted to come up with models that explain the possibility of introducing new methods in culturally diverse contexts. While Holliday presents his model explicitly in the context of centre-periphery relations, Pennington's enterprise is more general in scope. She endeavours to explain the process by which teachers universally adapt to pedagogical change in any teaching context. Since she also claims that her model explains 'adoption of innovation' (1995: 705), and derives her model from research in a periphery ELT context (trying out a process-oriented approach among Chinese teachers and students in Hong Kong who previously employed a product-oriented writing pedagogy), her model will be treated seriously by periphery teachers as explaining what it takes for a new method to successfully get implanted in a different pedagogical environment. What makes the models of these scholars significant is that they profit from the debates on pedagogical politics to show a sensitivity to the challenges of cultural adaptation and ideological contestation. Therefore their models are remarkably interactive and dialectical – open to negotiating with periphery cultures for appropriate adaptation. The scholars are prepared to acknowledge that the method itself could go through changes when it gets adjusted to the periphery culture, even as it modifies the beliefs and practices of periphery teachers. Thus Pennington (1995: 725) insightfully allows for 'two-sided adjustment'.

Though the work of Pennington and Holliday represents a laudable attempt to correct/reform the problematic pedagogical mission of centre agencies in periphery classrooms, there are larger problems with the models they construct. Before critiquing the common principles and assumptions underlying both models, it is important to understand the unique features of each scholar's approach. Labelling his work as an effort to develop an 'appropriate methodology' (borrowing insights from industrial/engineering/agricultural circles to develop appropriate technologies for periphery communities), Holliday explores ways of evolving methods that are relevant to and effective in periphery contexts. But the solution he comes up with is questionable. He argues that it is possible to define the communicative language teaching (CLT) approach in a suitable manner to carry out his purpose. Though he initially acknowledges that the communicative approach is itself a centre-based method, he goes on to define and develop it as a culture-neutral (universal?) method. He integrates the different definitions CLT has been given by various applied linguists at different times to develop a broad/generalized understanding of the method. In some ways, this method is treated as an 'etic' model that can find 'emic' application in different cultural contexts. At other times, it appears to be presented as a 'meta-method' that needs no radical cultural adaptation as it can fit all situations. After defining CLT in such generic terms, Holliday is spared the need to explicate or demonstrate the complex process of adaptation underlying the employment of the method.

Holliday's choice of CLT is also motivated by his view that it is at the pinnacle of methodological development in language teaching. Arguing against the 'serial' view of methods – that all methods are of equal status and can be used variably befitting the concerns of the teacher – he posits the 'developmental' view. By the latter notion he indicates that each method adds a qualitative change to the state-of-the-art, and that it is impossible to go back to a chronologically earlier method without compromising one's newly achieved pedagogical and philosophical beliefs.

To turn now to the main features of Pennington's model, the primary interest for her is to explain the processes by which teachers internalize new methods. The model is largely a psychological one that attempts to explain universal processes of pedagogical adoption and adaptation. Her model is claimed to derive from empirical research. Pennington incorporates sufficient loops in her flow-chart to allow the model to take into account the complications teachers would face at each level as they proceed towards deeper awareness. She takes into account the fact that there could be significant teacher resistance to new methods and that the values/interests/predispositions of the teachers will mediate the reception of the new method. She admits also that the pedagogy will be internalized in accordance with the constraints teachers experience from the context (student motivation, cultural influence, availability of facilities).

Despite its flexibility, Pennington's model fails to accommodate more disturbing outcomes. Although the method may change, this model assumes that teachers will work with the same pedagogical paradigm. In other words, the changes teachers make will be on the pedagogical approach or method they start working with. They would tailor it to suit their specific purposes and needs by incorporating the necessary features from the context. But what about teachers who may wish to give up this method altogether to take on a totally different teaching approach? To capture such radical processes of opposition, Pennington needs to accommodate paths that move outside the uni-directional flow in her 'teacher change cycle'. Moreover, her model assumes progressive movement towards ever more mature and refined levels of competence. This is therefore a model that doesn't assume the possibility of conflict and dysfunction. In fact, whenever Pennington considers that teachers could get stuck at a particular level, she recommends that with additional support, teaching/research material, and encouragement teachers should be made to move towards more mature stages of internalization. Furthermore, there is no awareness that behind the façade of progressive development teachers could nurse hidden levels of suspicion, ambivalence, opposition, and disinterest (as has been discovered in other classroom centred ethnographic research, e.g. Kennedy 1987; Canagarajah 1999a: 104–24). There is no effort to encourage teachers to develop their own pedagogical paradigm for their own teaching contexts on the basis of their critical reflection on the methods used.

Though Pennington's model is more detailed and complex than Holliday's in considering the challenging process of pedagogical transfer, it shares with Holliday's model certain basic limitations. While both scholars acknowledge that there can be competing cultural values informing alternative language teaching methods, they don't see this as having implications for ideological and political domination. Their understanding of culture is shaped by the positivistic anthropological tradition, devoid of power-related concerns. Furthermore, both models are deductive approaches that start with a method before they understand the teaching context. The models display a top-to-bottom approach in imposing a pre-conceived method on local teaching contexts. Having decided on the superiority of a chosen method, they explore the complications in classroom practice. But there are other starting points available when one attempts to devise an appropriate teaching practice for a specific context: for example, one can begin inductively by taking a good look at the contextual features of the local classrooms/communities or begin with certain broad pedagogical principles that may require creative construction of new teaching strategies as befits the local context. In fact, although Holliday initially announces a preference for adopting an empirical approach by first observing the context and then developing pedagogies in response to ground realities (in what he labels the 'action research cycle'), he then posits a model that already starts with a method (i.e. CLT) that requires adaptation. This approach limits the process of cultural and pedagogical negotiation in classroom practice.

That both scholars choose process-oriented language teaching methods for implementation also requires questioning. (Holliday situates CLT within the general 'process movement' and the related Bernsteinian paradigm of 'integrationist' curriculum.) The scholars adopt this approach probably because the process paradigm currently enjoys much popularity in the centre professional circles. Note how Holliday (1994: 54) specifies the ideal condition for language learning as endorsed by his understanding of the research tradition: 'This learning group ideal sets the conditions for a process-oriented, task-based, inductive, collaborative, communicative English language teaching methodology'. He refers to this ideal as what is established in ELT research and professional circles as 'the optimum interactional parameters within which classroom language learning can take place' (54). It is not surprising therefore that Pennington too doesn't think too hard about why she and her team of researchers should attempt to impose a process-oriented pedagogy in a previously product-oriented learning context. But there is a growing tradition of scholarship by periphery applied linguists that challenges such assumptions. Minority scholars have pointed out that there is active resistance to process-oriented approaches in some of their communities (Delpit 1995; Muchiri *et al*. 1995). They point out that when minority student groups lack the very codes/rules required to enter the mainstream, to deny them these is to perpetuate their disadvantage. From the point of view of these student groups and communities, process methods are based on the linguistic needs of the dominant community (in L1 contexts) whose students have the required codes/skills and simply need to develop higher level skills of usage through active interaction and practice. Muchiri *et al*. (1995) further note that in the context of limited material facilities in many African communities, the product-oriented approaches work better. They don't have the time, resources and material to prepare tasks for an inductive learning approach. They would rather introduce the grammar rules in a teacher-led pedagogy and allow students to practise them instead. Others challenge the assumption that process-oriented methods always ensure effective language acquisition and/or that product-oriented methods may serve no useful pedagogical functions in certain communities (Casey 1968; Levin 1972; Smith 1970; Von Elek and Oskasson 1973). Such a tradition of scholarship shows the immense complexity of the social, cultural and historical contexts that can mediate the use of the method in the language classroom. We cannot therefore take for granted the effectiveness and relevance of process-oriented pedagogies in all contexts.

The pedagogy of postmethodism

While Holliday and Pennington operate within the dominant pedagogical assumptions, we now have with us a more radical paradigm to consider classroom practice.

A series of research and theoretical advances have challenged the whole concept of method, and have led to what I like to call the 'postmethod condition'. Many scholars realize that, purely from a pedagogical point of view, what teachers practise in language classrooms rarely resembles any specific method as it is prescribed in manuals or materials. What is supposed to be the same method can differ from teacher to teacher, and class to class, depending on the many logistical, cultural and institutional forces at play (Sheen 1994). It has been pointed out that classroom realities rarely correspond to any recognizable methods (at least as they are packaged by the research and publishing industry). Even when teachers start with a specific method in mind, they are influenced by classroom contingencies to introduce radical changes as they teach. Furthermore, applied linguists now recognize that we can never discover the 'best method' (Prabhu 1990; Kumaravadivelu 1994). They are ready to abandon the positivistic search for final solutions for the complex process of second language acquisition (SLA). As Sheen (1994: 127) argues, 'The frequent paradigm shifts in the field of second and foreign language teaching have not resulted in significant progress in language learning. The fault seems to lie in the overstatement of criticisms directed at existing paradigms and the failure to challenge the validity of the advantages imputed to replacements'. He goes on to analyse the tradition of Method Comparison Research to confirm that no method can be empirically proven 'the best' for all classrooms. Research only shows the different levels of effectiveness of different language teaching approaches in different learning contexts. All this has led to the emergent situation where teachers are compelled to give up thinking in terms of predefined/prepackaged methods and creatively devise pedagogical strategies from the bottom upwards to suit their specific classroom conditions (Kumaravadivelu 1994).

How does classroom practice proceed in a context where there are no formalized, formulaic methods to deal with? This is perhaps the right moment to empower the local knowledge of teachers, deriving from their years of accumulated experience, wisdom, and intuitions about what works best for their students. Though terms like experience, wisdom, and intuition are unscientific to base a pedagogy upon, in the post-Enlightenment period we are quite comfortable with them. After all, empirical research hasn't produced for us the best method that answers with finality the challenges of learning another language. On the other hand, people have been teaching languages quite successfully even in pre-modern communities from pre-scientific times. These are the teachers still working in the remote corners of the world in small village classrooms often meeting under trees in farms and fields away from the eyes of the professional pundits of the centre. These 'English teachers' are village elders, parents, and priests who may often possess only a smattering of English. Some of them don't have any advanced professional training (other than a post-high school training). I am not ashamed to say that it is such a charismatic rural teacher in Sri Lanka who initiated my own learning of the language which has sustained me to this point in earning a doctorate in English linguistics and serving in the faculty of an English department. Obviously, much more than applied linguistic knowledge or an awareness of the range of established methods were required by my village school teacher to do the magic of providing a solid foundation for my English education. My teacher instilled in me his own curiosity towards the language, the ability to intuit linguistic rules from observation of actual usage, a metalinguistic awareness of the system behind languages, and the ability to creatively negotiate meaning with speakers and texts. These are the secrets of successful language acquisition that were passed on to me by my village teacher. This solid training in learning strategies still sustains me as I continue to explore the discoursal and grammar rules of *both* my vernacular and English. It is through such language teaching practices that teachers in remote parts of the world are succeeding in developing linguistic proficiency among many students today – whatever the pundits in the centre may prescribe.

I must confess that besides the attitudes and strategies the teacher imparted to us, the formal instruction sometimes constituted something resembling a grammar translation method. We translated expository paragraphs from one language to the other, did grammar exercises, memorized new words and verb forms, and answered reading comprehension questions. But, for some reason, we appreciated this detached learning of the language. The teacher probably understood that generations of Tamil students brought with them a visual, reflective, analytical, and extroverted learning style. He would have known that our community has had a tradition of such learning approaches. While the well-known Dravidian scholar, Emeneau (1955: 145–6), outlines the fundamental influence of Hindu linguistic tradition on Western descriptive linguistics, he also notes: 'Intellectual thoroughness and an urge toward ratiocination, intellection, and learned classification for their own sakes should surely be recognized as characteristic of the Hindu higher culture. . . . They become grammarians, it would seem, for grammar's sake'. In fact, as late as the colonial period, the teaching of local languages to European administrators was primarily based on studying and memorizing learned grammatical treatises (Wickramasuriya 1981). The fact that we lacked fluency in oral communication wasn't an issue as we didn't have opportunities for intra-community conversation in English. English was used mostly for literate and formal functions in largely educational and institutional domains. There was thus a mysterious coherence behind the local knowledge and pedagogical practice of our teacher!

But it is unsatisfactory to leave language teaching to an uncritical and unsystematic 'folk lore' of teachers around the world. Even local knowledge can be developed in constructive ways. Other heuristic models or explanatory paradigms can be used to compare the local knowledge and systematize it for one's own teaching context. It is also important to learn from other pedagogical traditions – including Western models – to attain a critical and reflective understanding of one's own intuitive approaches. I want to interpret how the notion of 'strategies' may provide a means of tapping and developing local knowledge for teaching purposes. Though the learner strategy models of Oxford, Chamot and others are well known, there are others discovering useful strategies in diverse geographical and teaching contexts.

Before describing some of these models, it is important to understand how they are different from the hegemonizing methods we critiqued earlier. Methods are, for me, teaching approaches that come with an integrated set of theories and instructional techniques (Richards and Rodgers 1986). They are predefined and pre-packaged for use by those outside the specific classroom. Though teachers may adopt slight variations to suit their contexts, methods exert a pressure to mould teacher and student roles and activities in carefully orchestrated ways. Employing a more exploratory approach to language learning, strategy models attempt to understand the typical strategies learners use in everyday life to negotiate language acquisition. The underlying assumption of this approach is that making students aware of learning strategies will motivate them to discover their typical learning styles for greater optimization of the acquisition process. This awareness also enables them to be more self-directed and independent to achieve greater control of the learning process. Since learning strategies can differ from student to student, according to their personal and community-based styles of learning, there is scope to develop a context-sensitive and community-specific approach to language teaching pedagogy. Strategies are therefore different from methods in that they are not prescriptively/rigidly defined approaches that have to be used almost universally in any learning context. They do not constitute a method but function as a *heuristic* to develop an appropriate pedagogy from bottom up. As Kumaravadivelu is perceptive enough to clarify regarding his own somewhat more macro-strategic approach to language learning: 'Method neutral does not mean methodless; rather it means that the framework is not conditioned by a single set of theoretical principles or classroom procedures associated with any one particular teaching method' (1994: 32).

A typology of learner strategies would look like the following (to illustrate from the ones popularized by Chamot and O'Malley 1994; Oxford 1990; Wenden 1991):

1   Affective strategies for anxiety reduction, self-encouragement, and self-reward.
2   Social strategies such as asking questions, cooperating with native speakers, and becoming culturally aware.
3   Metacognitive strategies for evaluating one's progress, planning for language tasks, consciously searching for practice opportunities, paying attention, and monitoring errors.
4   Memory-related strategies, such as grouping, imagery, rhyming, moving physically, and reviewing in a structured way.
5   General cognitive strategies, such as reasoning, analysing, summarizing, and practising.

6   Compensatory strategies (to make up for limited knowledge), such as guessing meanings from context and using synonyms and gestures to convey meaning (Green and Oxford 1995: 294–5).

The choice of these *strategies* would vary according to the different learning *styles* students bring with them (e.g. visual, auditory and hands-on; reflective and impulsive; analytic and global; extroverted and introverted, etc.).

For this pedagogical approach to be effective, learners have to be made sensitive to the range of strategies available and the strategies that work for them. The fact that students are taught learning strategies so that they become aware of them and manipulate them to their advantage holds great potential for developing a meta-pedagogical awareness. Available research shows that successful L2 learners are aware of the strategies they use and why they use them (Abraham and Vann 1987). If learners already display a certain level of meta-pedagogical awareness, active steps can be taken by teachers to further develop this awareness among students by undertaking learner training. Oxford (1995: 264) describes this process in the following manner: 'The best learner training includes an explicit and clear focus on specific strategies, has frequent practice opportunities for strategies, is integrated with regular classwork, and shows students how to transfer strategies to new situations'. In fact, students continue to learn themselves, as they reflect on strategies that produce better results for them, and then consciously employ such strategies in future acquisition process.

We must note, however, that while the strategies are defined usefully at the most micro-level of analysis, without a larger set of pedagogical principles the strategies can lead to a use that lacks direction. Though eclecticism is desirable, there should be clear principles guiding the employment of strategies according to divergent contexts and student groups. Kumaravadivelu has articulated a set of macro-strategies that are well motivated by research considerations to function as the larger framework within which learner strategies should be employed. Kumaravadivelu (1994: 32) defines his macro-strategies as 'a broad guideline, based on which teachers can generate their own situation-specific, need-based micro-strategies or classroom techniques'. He lists the following:

- maximize learning opportunities;
- facilitate negotiated interaction;
- minimize perceptual mismatches;
- activate intuitive heuristics;
- foster language awareness;
- contextualize linguistic input;
- integrate language skills;
- promote learner autonomy;
- raise cultural consciousness;
- ensure social relevance.

To some extent, these strategies sound like the common-sense maxims many teachers live by. Letting the teachers foster these strategies according to the preferred styles of learning of their students is less intrusive than the implementation of traditional methods.

Others are working in their own pedagogical contexts to understand the strategies that work for their students. Ilona Leki (1995) has come up with a taxonomy of strategies based on an ethnographically based case study with ESL graduate students in an American university. She inquires into the ways in which these students negotiate the development of literacy in English in the midst of their commitments to other courses, family, work, and lifestyle. The strategies she identifies are as follows:

1 Clarifying strategies (e.g. talking to teachers or colleagues to understand the nature of the assignment better).
2 Focusing strategies (e.g. rereading the assignment several times, or rereading books, to narrow down the scope of the assignment).
3 Relying on past writing experience (e.g. evaluating the strategies used in the past and making connections to the present assignment).
4 Taking advantage of first language/culture.
5 Using current experience or feedback to adjust strategies.
6 Looking for models (e.g. consulting books, research articles, and book reviews for examples of format and language suitable for one's assignment).
7 Using current or past ESL writing training.
8 Accommodating teachers' demands (e.g. trying to satisfy the teacher by doing the project totally according to her interests and opinions).
9 Resisting teachers' demands (e.g. completing a project in accordance with the interests of the student).
10 Managing competing demands (sudivided into managing course loads, managing workload, managing the demands of life etc.) (e.g. making modifications in the project according to the other commitments one has).

Labelling these *coping strategies*, Leki offers an empirical account of the strategies she discovered without judging the effectiveness of these in language learning. These strategies help students to manage the conflicts and challenges they encounter in the educational domain. Understanding the strategies preferred by the students to accomplish their pedagogical tasks will help teachers to encourage students to adopt their own styles of learning rather than imposing methods from the outside.

But it is important to display to students the implications of using their chosen strategies. They have to realize the consequences for the representation of their identity, discourse, and voice. I find it useful to orientate to students in terms of a set of strategies I have discovered in the context of writing pedagogy. In keeping with the practices of critical pedagogy, I make some value judgements on the extent to which these strategies would help writers communicate critically and independently. A socially engaged, ideologically informed orientation to writing strategies will go a long way towards coherent and critical text construction. I offer the strategies discovered through an ethnography of writing practices by ESL and African American students (Canagarajah 1997, forthcoming), which are summarized in Table 8.1.

Table 8.1 Writing strategies used by ESL and African American students

Strategy	Voice	Ideology	Textual realization
accommodation	monological	uncritical	coherent
avoidance	monological	uncritical	incoherent
opposition	monological	critical potential	incoherent
transposition	dialogical	critical	coherent
appropriation	dialogical	critical	coherent

Faced with conflicting discourses from their native community and the academic community, what do minority students do to develop their own voice in English essays? Those who use the strategy of *accommodation* align themselves with the dominant discourses and take 'safe' argumentative positions. They consider this the best strategy to score good grades in that assignment and to be successful in their writing. But this leads to a voice that lacks complexity and positions that are stereotypical, which eventually leads to ineffective performance. Students who adopt the second strategy, avoidance, may avoid negotiating the discoursal conflicts in favour of simply getting their assignments accomplished in a perfunctory way. They may thus produce texts that are incoherent, embodying conflicting positions and voices. This uncertainty in footing will also lead to ineffective writing. Those using the strategy of *opposition* ignore the dominant discourses completely and express the values and positions from their own native communities in their mainstream writing. Although these students are ideologically well motivated, their strategy is rhetorically inappropriate. In writing to a specific audience one has to work with and through the established conventions to make a space for one's own interests. Failing to negotiate with the dominant conventions will lead to that community rejecting the text as having no relevance to them or inappropriate for their purposes. This too produces unsuccessful writing. The final two strategies are different ways of negotiating with the competing discourses for the student to represent his/her interests. The strategy of *transposition* leads to discovering a 'third space' – a space that reconciles the competing discourses and moves beyond them to form a synthetic voice for the writer. Such writers may draw from the competing discourses but may eventually also adopt a critical position towards either discourse, benefiting from the detachment they achieve from their multilingual subjectivity. (We can think of the writing of those like Wole Soyinka who creatively adopt a critical position beyond both the colonial and indigenous discourses, while also drawing from their conflicting literary traditions.) The strategy of *appropriation* manipulates the dominant conventions to represent one's own interests. One may think of Chinua Achebe's practice of using the Western literary conventions and novelistic form of the English tradition to critique colonialism and celebrate the indigenous culture.

Having devised this typology, I have an interesting array of options when I teach writing to ESL students. If the students adopt the first three strategies, I make them alert to what their writing will lead to. In order to critically engage with the competing discourses and construct more creative texts, I adopt a range of techniques based on the preferred styles of learning of the students. If the students are more analytical, visual, extroverted and reflective, then I use more product-oriented activities (constituting grammar exercises, reading model essays, and critiquing writing structure) to lead them to the strategies of transposition or appropriation. If the students prefer more holistic, hands on, introverted and involved styles of learning, I adopt a combination of peer critiques, serial revision, conferences, and collaborative exploration of content. Again, students may adopt the strategy of transposition or appropriation as it seems fit to their interests and ethos.

In a context where cultures and codes are in flux, the project in language teaching is not to make students move from a 'native' language to a target language, or host culture to receiving culture. Rather, the need is to shuttle between cultures and communities. This requires a certain amount of reflexivity as students are expected to develop a meta-linguistic and meta-cultural awareness of codes and conventions. We are not in fact dealing with binary languages or cultures anymore. We are simultaneously having to negotiate multiple languages and values. It is far better to teach students the skills of negotiating languages and cultures than to make them accommodate to one language/culture at a time. We also now know that becoming 'native' in another language or culture is out of the question. That the languages and cultures that we bring with us will mediate our understanding and appropriation of the new discourses is well accepted. We are now more concerned about giving the confidence for students to insert themselves in the other community's ways and words. The teaching methods we have, on the other hand, are based on the assumption of moving from one language to another, one at a time. They are also instrumental and objectivist, keeping the assumptions and processes opaque, making students and teachers focus on the target to be reached rather than on the path to be taken. Strategies are more transferable across languages, communities and cultures. They also develop useful meta-linguistic skills of negotiation.

It must be emphasized that it is not adequate to simply use the strategies students are comfortable with. Using, alternately, the strategies that are uncomfortable to them enables students to gain different skills/competencies in language. It is such an approach that will enable students to gain a meta-pedagogical awareness into the different potentialities of a range of strategies. Students need the practice of moving between strategies and perceiving one from the perspective of the other. This may help them understand the limitations of strategies they prefer and, contrastively, the advantages of strategies they are not comfortable with. While the models of Holliday and Pennington attempt to arrive at a stasis at the point the method satisfies the psychological comfort level of teachers/students, this approach would maintain a tension all the time. The aim is to negotiate and expand the comfort level. It is significant that Green and Oxford (1995: 289) find in their research that successful learners 'reported using a number of strategies more often than other students, and they reported using them in combination with other strategies used frequently or moderately so by students at all levels'.

Letting students participate in the negotiation of appropriate pedagogical strategies and styles empowers the students to take control of their learning experience. This lets them take responsibility for what they learn according to their linguistic and social needs. This process of negotiating pedagogies is more egalitarian than that envisioned by Holliday and Pennington who keep the students out of this search for cultural adaptation (except in the limited sense of providing feedback on the methods used by teachers). At a time when the authority of the teacher in the classroom has been questioned in many circles, the hold over methods offers perhaps the last vestige of power for the teacher. Opening up the domain of pedagogy to students, so that they can hold equal responsibility for negotiating the relevant strategies for their purposes, democratizes the language classroom. But this is not to say that the classroom has no place for the teacher. The authority of the teacher is instead 'earned' (Grossberg 1994: 19) by negotiating it with students according to the changing contexts, rather than uniformly and absolutely imposed in all circumstances.

The kind of teaching practice I propose may suggest that learning strategies need not totally displace methods. In response to the set of strategies proposed by Kumaravadivelu, Liu (1995) asks whether strategies are 'an alternative to' or 'in addition to' methods. Favouring the latter position, he argues that teachers have always been adopting this kind of approach – they pick and choose methods according to the contextual needs of the classroom. But I find that still using the framework of methods may limit the teachers as they are under pressure to think in terms of packaged techniques that come with the method. My proposal here is to shift our orientation radically to first think of the students and the contextual realities before adopting a suitable pedagogical practice. Also, one doesn't have to choose one's classroom techniques from the existing packaged methods. Teachers may choose techniques that have worked for them in their instructional experience and are stored in their local knowledge.

Is the learning strategies model another version of the currently popular process paradigm in the West? Not really. We see in the examples above that teachers may adopt product oriented techniques if they find that students' learning strategies are inclined that way. We now acknowledge that adult learners of English tend to favour product oriented activities, compared to children who profit greatly from a holistic, involved, introverted, hands-on style of learning. Other differences in learner identity (gender, culture, educational level, etc.) may lead to learning strategies that favour either product oriented or process oriented methods. So the learning strategies approach stands outside both camps, functioning as a heuristic to decide which approach would work in a specific context.

The citation of names and schools from the West in this article may lead some to believe that the postmethod paradigm is another centre-based imposition. But as is evident from the account of my village schoolmaster above, such strategies have been used by those in the periphery always. They simply haven't been documented in the professional literature. What is available in published form are pedagogical approaches from the communities that enjoy literate/publishing resources. Periphery teachers have shared their teaching strategies orally in their local contexts. So it is inevitable that we cite only the strategy models available in published form in the West such as those of Oxford and Leki. (Even Kumaravadivelu and Canagarajah cannot avoid but publish their models in the West, though their thinking has been considerably shaped by their educational backgrounds in India and Sri Lanka, respectively.) On the other hand, I have earlier stated that negotiating with different pedagogical cultures to critically reflect on one's classroom practice is important. It is the one-sided, top down imposition of pedagogical methods that is being questioned in this essay. Negotiating with the traditions of diverse communities and appropriating them for one's own purposes is in fact encouraged.

Implications for periphery students and teachers

How does the learning strategies approach deal with the thorny problem of centre-periphery inequalities in pedagogical transfer? In what ways does it combat the hegemonic agenda behind methods? The chief merit of this approach is that it is thoroughly context-dependent. Rather than prescribing the course of teaching practice as most methods do, this approach encourages teachers and students to become more reflective and critically conscious of the strategies they themselves find useful according to a variety of contextual determinants. This is an ongoing process of development for students as they try out and exploit strategies that work for them. Apart from the affective, cultural, material and ideological peculiarities of the students' context, there are other more pedagogically related shaping factors behind the choice of strategies: task demands, proficiency, aptitude, situation, attitude, motivation, previous success, anxiety, self-confidence, sanctions against strategy use, goals, and criteria for success (MacIntyre 1994). A model of strategy-use that takes into account such contextual features and defines itself in a context-dependent manner adopts a grounded and localized orientation to learning.

It is important to realize that the abandonment of the notion of methods is empowering for periphery teachers as well. They are freed from thinking that effective/efficient methods come from centres of research and expertise in the

West. In the absence of ready-made methods, they are thrust into the classrooms to discover their pedagogical approaches in negotiation with students. Rather than looking at the classrooms through spectacles offered by preconstructed pedagogical models, they open themselves more fully to the realities of their educational context. They are liberated from centre expertise to become more sensitive to their local classroom and socio-cultural context. This also makes periphery teachers truly creative in integrating experience, imagination, and knowledge to devise learning strategies with/for students. It is from this perspective that Holliday's ideal of the action research cycle – where teachers start inductively with the classroom situation to devise appropriate methods – gains its true meaning. This approach also helps periphery teachers develop their own tradition of professionalism and expertise. In fact, this calls for a fresh pedagogical and research agenda. Teachers now need to study many things: the strategies preferred by their students; the effectiveness of the strategies adopted; the social and educational consequences of the differing strategies employed. They must realize that expertise doesn't necessarily come from abroad, but needs to be developed in terms of local knowledge. Although they will profit from reading publications by centre researchers – reporting research on strategy use in other contexts – there is no compulsion to slavishly adopt the ways in which strategies are used by those communities.

Interestingly, this pedagogical approach also takes away the crutch many expatriate teachers use when they travel to teach in the periphery. Armed with the latest methods, centre teachers think they are qualified to teach in whatever socio-cultural context they find work. For many, it is the techniques/methods authoritatively learnt from centre institutions that gives them the licence to teach in a foreign classroom (supported, in addition, by their status as 'native' speakers). Methods can thus blind expatriate teachers to the socio-cultural context of the classrooms they are entering. But postmethod pedagogical practice would compel them to understand the uniqueness of each language teaching situation they enter in order to teach effectively. It would also compel them to engage with their students more intensely in the exploration of the strategies and styles that interest/suit them. The postmethod condition calls for a deeper investment in the local language classrooms from travelling teachers.

Since this approach involves conducting research and teaching in a closely connected, mutually enriching manner, teachers too enjoy the possibility of developing a critical pedagogical practice. Since teachers always have to learn the strategies students adopt and be sensitive to their linguistic and pedagogical consequences, they cannot be sound teachers without active classroom research. This in fact contributes to the pedagogical health of teachers. Giroux emphasizes how such an attitude will help teachers develop a meta-pedagogical and critical awareness: 'By being able to listen critically to the voices of their students, teachers also become border-crossers through their ability both to make different narratives available to themselves and to legitimate difference as a basic condition for understanding the limits of one's own knowledge' (Giroux 1992: 34–5). Letting students' everyday strategies of learning comment on their own teaching, instructors open themselves to a critical interrogation of their educational assumptions and practices in the light of the multiple cultural, social, and pedagogical borders that they have to traverse with their students in order to ensure a valuable learning experience in the post-modern world.

Conclusion

To return to the laudable attempts of centre applied linguists to work out democratic pedagogical relations globally, it is a postmethod pedagogical practice that realizes another of Holliday's well motivated desires – a 'becoming-appropriate methodology'. He articulates a position (unfortunately not realized by his model) where the negotiation for a suitable teaching approach will go on progressively as contexts and purposes change. Since he is stuck with a pre-packaged 'method', it becomes difficult to adopt an ongoing reflective/explorative pedagogical practice. But along with postmethod pedagogical practice, this negotiation between teachers and students will continue creatively. As students continue to become aware of their strategy use, their mature needs and competencies will call for newer strategies. This process solves a crucial problem for the postmethod movement itself. If it begins to rely on a rigidly formulated set of pedagogical principles or approaches as the alternative, it will become difficult to prevent these principles from getting formulated into another 'method'. Overzealous teachers can amplify/formalize the axioms put forward by meta-pedagogical approaches to devise a brand new method. This can become the new orthodoxy that gets defined as *the* 'appropriate method' and gets marketed everywhere. However, such a turn of events would be in contradiction to the liberating forces unleashed by the postmethod paradigm. The notion of negotiating learning strategies as a postmethod pedagogical practice ensures that language acquisition doesn't get reduced to another method, but evolves to form an ongoing teaching/learning agenda.

9 The global coursebook in English Language Teaching

John Gray

Bill Gates is the richest private citizen in the world. There is nothing he can't afford. Every morning, when his alarm clock goes off, the software tycoon is $20 million richer than when he went to bed. His wealth is based on his company, Microsoft, of which he owns 39% of the shares. He has a personal fortune estimated at £18 billion, which is more than the annual economic output of over a hundred countries.

(Soars and Soars, *New Headway/Upper-Intermediate*, 1998: 59)

I think in English, in English books, there is a lot of, a lot of, erm, like the icons of the culture are like very much very present, I think. And sometimes, erm, I don't know if they are very critical of it, I don't think they are . . . for example in relation (to) this, here in, in the new Headway there is a, a text about Bill Gates . . . 'The man who could buy anything' . . . 'The richest private citizen in the world' . . . 'He has a personal fortune which is more than the annual economic output of over a hundred countries'. And I think this like, I mean there is something to be said about this, you know. I mean, obviously I'm not saying that the book, I mean it's there, you can do what you want with it, . . . but . . . they do this a lot, they, they take people, maybe Americans more . . . and then they kind of glorify it a bit, and they are not very critical.

(Catalan teacher of English)[1]

Throughout the 1990s a wave of books, written from Marxist (Phillipson 1992; Holborow 1999), postmodernist, or poststructuralist perspectives (Pennycook 1994, 1998; Canagarajah 1999a), were instrumental in stimulating a considerable degree of soul searching within the English language teaching (ELT) profession. What these books had in common was a belief that the global spread of English was inherently problematic, inextricably linked to wider political issues, and that ELT practices were neither value free, nor always culturally appropriate. This chapter is part of that same critical endeavour and seeks to problematize in particular the phenomenon of the global coursebook – that genre of English language textbook which is produced in English-speaking countries and is designed for use as the core text in language classrooms around the world.[2] Although coursebooks are designed explicitly for the teaching of English language they are also highly wrought cultural constructs and carriers of cultural messages. Here I focus on the ways in which these texts, against a background of increasing globalization, represent the English-speaking world for pedagogic and commercial purposes.

Globalization: dystopia or utopia?

A cluster of factors are associated with globalization. These include the rise of transnational corporations and the concomitant challenge to the autonomy of the nation-state, increasing interconnectedness which transcends national boundaries, technological developments which compress time and space and make global communication instantaneous, and increasing cultural hybridization. However, these factors combine to generate very disparate visions of the present and the future. Two such visions are provided by John Berger (1998/99) and Howard Perlmutter (1991) – one a dystopia of apocalyptic proportions, the other a picture of humanity at the dawn of a new age of civilization.

Berger begins with a meditation on Bosch's fifteenth-century Millennium Triptych. The right panel, which depicts a horizon-less hell where the hordes of the damned are subjected to graphic acts of torture and abuse, provides him with a metaphor for the effects of globalization and neoliberal economic policies.

> The culture in which we live is perhaps the most claustrophobic that has ever existed; in the culture of globalization, as in Bosch's hell, there is no glimpse of an *elsewhere* or an *otherwise*.
>
> (Berger 1998/99: 3)

Like the Zapatistas, whom he cites throughout his paper, Berger equates globalization exclusively with neoliberalism – that set of economic policies which favours unrestricted free trade, the privatization of state assets, and the dismantling or scaling down of institutions associated with welfare statism. The governments of nation-states, he argues, have in effect lost their sovereignty and been reduced to protecting the interests of global capital and policing the unemployed. He concludes his paper, in an echo of Marcuse, with a call for:

> a refusal of the world-picture implanted in our minds and all the false promises used everywhere to justify and idealize the delinquent and insatiable need to sell.
>
> (1998/99: 4)

Howard Perlmutter (1991: 902), on the other hand, has no such problems with globalization. It will, he believes, usher in a brave new world where the previous highpoints of collective human achievement will be revealed as little more than 'subcivilizations of the first global civilization'. The values of this new global civilization are based on what is termed 'global dynamic syncretization' (1991: 911) whereby 'nations and cultures become more open to influence each other . . . there is recognition of the identities and diversities of peoples in various groups, and ethnic and religious pluralism . . . peoples of different ideologies and values both cooperate and compete but no ideology prevails over all the others . . . where the global civilization becomes unique in a holistic sense while still being pluralist . . . where increasingly these values are perceived as shared despite varying interpretations (1991: 898). He mentions the economic dimension of globalization only in passing, and then it is to point out that the 'convenience and material well being' (1991: 903) of the world's consumers are already being catered for by transnational corporations.

Between the opposing visions of Berger and Perlmutter other, less polarized, pictures of globalization emerge. Nederveen Pieterse (1995) suggests that, given the plurality of factors involved, it would be more accurate to talk of globalizations (e.g. economic, political, cultural, religious, etc). Scholte (2000) too subscribes to a plural view, and has argued that because globalization is the result of human activity it can therefore be humanized. However, he hints that this will be an uphill struggle, given the currently pervasive neoliberal orthodoxy. He urges the abandonment of neoliberal economics and active global management of change. What is new and positive about globalization for Scholte is the growth of 'supraterritorial spaces' (2000: 8), by which he means 'a reconfiguration of geography, so that social space is no longer wholly mapped in terms of territorial places, territorial distances and territorial borders' (2000: 16). He cites the emergence of non-territorial communities along gender, racial, religious and political lines – instancing, among a host of other events and developments, the rise of NGOs with global membership, the emergence of lesbian and gay groups which see themselves as part of a global community, and the growth of the women's movement globally.

Clearly it is beyond the scope of this chapter to evaluate the merits of these various positions. My intention has rather been to suggest the diversity of responses to globalization. These responses generate conflicting visions of the present and the future, and global ELT coursebooks, as we shall see, also offer their own particular vision.

Globalization and English

Before turning to coursebooks I want to look at the three main ways in which I think globalization and English are connected. In the first place, the rise of transnational corporations does much to promote the spread of English. Typically these organizations have headquarters located in Europe, North America or Japan, and geographically dispersed (yet flexible) centres of production, all of which are connected electronically. Graddol (1997) explains how English is usually adopted as a lingua franca when transnational corporations enter into joint ventures with local companies in non-English-speaking countries. This can imply business and legal documentation being produced in English, oral and written communication skills training in English for staff, possible spinoffs for the local hotel and tourist industries, and more English being taught in local schools.

Secondly, the increase in the number of world organizations, many of which are themselves implicated in globalized networks, means that English continues to be in demand globally. For example, English functions as the working language of many international bodies and conferences, scientific and many other forms of academic publishing, international banking, international tourism, third level education, international law and human rights, information technology, and Internet communication (see Graddol 1997 for a more extensive list).

The third area is linked specifically to the Internet. English currently predominates on the Internet (although it has been argued that this situation could change). However, the Internet does suggest the possibility of English emerging as the language of global resistance to global exploitation and injustice (see Wallace, Chapter 6 this volume). Berger's (1998/99) paper led me to the Internet where I found that Zapatista statements are regularly posted in Spanish *and* in English. *The First Declaration of La Realidad for Humanity and against Neoliberalism* (Acción Zapatista/La Jornada 1996) is addressed to 'the people of the world'[3] and begins:

> During the last year, the power of money has presented a new mask over its criminal face. Above borders, no matter race or color, the power of money humiliates dignities, insults honesties and assassinates hopes. Re-named as 'Neoliberalism', the historic crime in the concentration of privileges, wealth and impunities, democratizes misery and hopelessness . . . By the name of 'globalization' they call this modern war which assassinates and forgets.
>
> (1996)

Such use of the Internet serves to call into question Berger's uncompromisingly apocalyptic view of the globalizing world. Although the connection is made again between globalization and neoliberalism the very fact that the Zapatistas are using this particular medium to publicize their cause means that the Internet – surely the technological tool of globalization *par excellence* – can also be used as a weapon to combat its current economic manifestations.

The recent campaigns against Nike and Gap in the USA which were aimed at bringing about better conditions for their developing world workers were organized on the Internet. One group called Global Exchange provided an 'online anti-Gap campus-organizing kit' (*The Economist* 23/9/2000: 126) complete with letters for downloading which could be sent to the company, along with anti-Gap flyers, and slogans to chant. Similarly the anti-globalization demonstrations which now regularly accompany World Bank/IMF meetings are organized by a variety of international groups – many of them making extensive use of English and the Internet. Clearly, it would be naive to suggest that access to the Internet is evenly distributed around the world. English predominates on the Internet precisely because the majority of computers with connections are located in English-speaking countries. However, things are changing. The China–Britain Business Council, which conducts and disseminates market research, has estimated that there will be in the region of sixty-six million Chinese Internet users by the end of 2003 (see website at www.cbbc.org). This represents a rise of almost 500 per cent in use from April 2000. Not surprisingly the Chinese authorities have already expressed concern about the possible implications of such a tool in the hands of so many.

Against this background students around the world continue to learn English. Increasingly, however, those of us involved in the provision of ELT services have begun to turn a more critical eye on what it is we do and the tools we use to do it.

The commerce of the global coursebook

ELT publishing is a growing and highly competitive industry. However, accurate figures for coursebook sales are difficult to come by. Pennycook (1994) speculated on annual sales of between £70 and £170 million for British ELT coursebooks (although he did not say how this estimate was arrived at). Littlejohn (1992), himself a coursebook writer, reckoned that a successful coursebook could sell over a hundred thousand copies a year. This figure has been confirmed by one publisher I spoke to as still being valid, although it is widely understood that some well-known series of coursebooks sell in considerably vaster quantities.

The importance of this industry is recognized beyond the world of ELT. In 1990, as the contours of the so-called new world order were becoming apparent, *The Economist* Intelligence Unit produced a report entitled 'English in Eastern Europe'. The report outlined the political and economic developments in seven countries. It paid particular attention to English language teaching policies in the state school sector, the size of the private language school sector and its potential for development, the extent of the penetration of British ELT publishing, and the involvement of British examination boards.

The report pointed out that the demand for English had already created a 'considerable industry' (1990: 2) worldwide, and that the 'principle players in the sector are the private language schools and the English language textbook publishers'. It was noted as an encouraging sign that the state education sector in many eastern bloc countries would be unable to deal with the demand for English and that this represented an opportunity for private business. The conclusion to the report highlighted the importance of coursebooks in paving the way for further business ventures.

↓ Cambridge   CAE

The appeal of the situation to British industry overall, and particularly to companies which are already operating in Eastern Europe or considering starting up there, results from the fact that the scale of demand for English in these countries and the problems they have in meeting this demand would represent an important marketing opportunity. By helping to provide or sponsor desperately needed language learning items such as English course textbooks, the companies could create considerable goodwill and use the sponsorship as a cost effective means of promoting their name and products across key youth and occupational groups in up to seven East European countries.

(1990: 96)

Although not quoted by Phillipson (1992) the report highlights precisely the type of attitude which led him to suggest that the promotion of British ELT was an enterprise with an economic and ideological agenda aimed ultimately at boosting commerce and the dissemination of ideas and language. *The Economist*'s report, though it did not originate within British ELT, was essentially about ELT's potential, as a desirable commodity in the newly independent east, to produce a kind of domino effect for British trade.

The report was indeed followed by the opening up of the East European market in the 1990s. The penetration of British ELT into one East European country has been well documented by Thomas (1999). In his case study of educational change in Slovakia, while careful to absolve British ELT of the kind of imperialism postulated by Phillipson (1992), he does show that ELT publishers were quick to establish themselves. Communist coursebooks, with none of the allure or high tech production values of their western equivalents, were rapidly replaced by coursebooks which were often methodologically (and culturally) at odds with local educational values and practices. The publishers were, he concluded:

instrumental in restricting the freedom of choice which Slovak teachers aspire to, by using their power and influence with the Ministry of Education to ensure that teachers will be persuaded to use their titles. Commercial interests have also meant that, very often, particular coursebooks have been aggressively marketed, not because of their degree of appropriacy for the local market, but because these titles are not achieving the desired turnover elsewhere.

(1999: 247–8)

Such practices are perhaps not all that surprising. As demand for English grows, more providers of ELT services appear and competition becomes fiercer. Some European and Asian countries, which until recently were in receipt of British ELT, are now exporting materials or offering their own English language teaching programmes to the rest of the world.

Coursebook content

It would be inaccurate and simplistic to suppose that ELT publishers and the course-books they produce are solely in the business of making money, or preparing the ground for larger commercial interests waiting in the wings. Clearly coursebooks *are* commodities to be traded, but what they contain is the result of the interplay between, at times, contradictory commercial, pedagogic and ethical interests. ELT publishers may be said to present a vision of the world in the texts they produce, and it is the nature of this vision which I now wish to address.

One of the most notable things about the current crop of global coursebooks is the way in which they have been subtly deterritorialized. The innovative *Strategies* series (Abbs *et al.*), which was launched in 1975, begins by welcoming the students to the course and to London where the book is set. The first unit is preceded by a two-page map of the city showing key locations and the characters from the story-line which runs throughout the book. A modern coursebook like *New Headway/Intermediate* (1996), while still a very British book, is much less exclusively *located* in Britain. In many coursebooks a shift to international settings reflects, no doubt, a growing sense on the part of the publishers of English as an increasingly global language. Students today are welcomed into a much larger world than that (literally) mapped in the opening pages of *Strategies*.

More significant though is the way modern coursebooks now resemble each other, not only in terms of glossy design but also in terms of content. This is partly because all ELT publishers provide their coursebook writers with sets of guidelines with regard to content. These guidelines tend to cover two areas: *inclusivity* and *inappropriacy*. The first refers to the need for a non-sexist approach to the way in which men and women are represented throughout the coursebook, while the second refers to those topics which writers are advised to avoid so as not to offend the perceived sensibilities of potential buyers and readers.

Inclusivity

Early surveys (Hill 1980; Porreca 1984) concluded that women were under-represented, trivialized and stereotyped in a wide selection of British and North American coursebooks. Even the most cursory look at a selection of modern global coursebooks produced in the UK shows that this is no longer the case. Such a state of affairs is largely the result of efforts made by groups like Women in TEFL and Women in EFL Materials. Sunderland (1994) reproduces a set of guidelines pro-duced by the latter group – *On Balance: Guidelines for Representation of Women and Men in English Language Teaching Materials* – which has been accepted by the British ELT Publishers' Association. The in-house documents to which I have had access, drawn up by four leading British publishers, confirm that this is the case. In many instances the wording in these documents is identical to that in the *On Balance* guidelines. The rationale for the guidelines reflects two issues: the extent to which the negative representation of women may adversely affect women students (causing them, it is suggested, to learn less effectively), and the fact that recent language change in English reflects a move away from gender bias. The document makes it clear that fairness and balance should also apply to representations of age, class, ethnic origin and disability.

In the main, however, the concern is with women, the ways in which they are represented, and gender issues in the use of language. Under the heading 'Images of women' the guidelines state the number of women in the coursebook should reflect the fact that they make up over half the population, and that this should apply throughout the course components – to artwork in the students' book, names in grammar practice exercises, voices on tapes, and characters in any accompanying videos. One publisher makes the point that balance is not achieved by having photos of men and line drawings of women.

The guidelines point out that 54 per cent of British women work outside the home, 42 per cent of mothers with young children go out to work, and that 20 per cent of working women are the sole earners for their families. This reality, the writers say, needs to be reflected in materials if women are not to be misrepresented.

A considerable amount of space is devoted to stereotyping and the ways in which this can be avoided. A checklist is provided so that ELT authors can make sure their materials show women being assertive, using their initiative, demonstrating self-control, and men being vulnerable, displaying emotion, and needing reassurance. However, the move towards the use of so-called authentic texts (extracts from newspapers, magazines, advertisements) in coursebooks has meant that sexism cannot always be avoided. Recommendations for dealing with this include confronting the issue by making it available for discussion in the classroom, or making it clear to students that the views expressed are not those of the coursebook author(s). Stereotypes can also be confronted by including examples of real women who have somehow broken with traditional female roles.

Under the heading 'Women in language' the writers refer to research which shows that native English speakers do not think of men *and* women when 'man' is used generically – rather the majority think of men only. To prevent students falling into this Whorfian trap and to ensure coursebooks reflect current language change lists of alternatives to false generic uses of 'man' are provided. For example, instead of 'mankind' coursebooks authors are offered the more acceptable 'people, humans, humanity'. Suggestions are also given for avoiding 'he' and 'his' in rubrics so as not to imply that the student is always male. The writers also recommend avoiding feminine diminutives of job titles, the use of the word 'girl' when 'young woman' would be more appropriate, and the preferability of such modern written forms of address as 'Dear Sir or Madam' or 'Dear Madam or Sir' over the more old-fashioned and sexist 'Dear Sir/s'. One ELT publisher's in-house list runs to over thirty terms to avoid.

The decision to incorporate language change (rather than seek to combat it, for example) is indicative of a stance being taken on a political issue. Teaching language change therefore must mean promoting language change. However, the authors of the *On Balance* guidelines and some of the publishers, as reflected in the in-house documents I have seen, are reluctant to admit having such an explicit agenda. They tend, somewhat disingenuously, to duck the issue by saying that their policies on such matters *reflect* – rather than promote – language change.

A look through the *New Headway/Intermediate* (1996) coursebook reveals close adherence to the guidelines. Women are highly visible and are shown in a variety of roles – as journalist, high-earning graphic designer, artist, writer, intrepid nun and TV presenter, happy unmarried and middle-aged aunt, businesswoman, judge, and film director. Men too are shown in a variety of jobs and in situations where they wear aprons, prepare meals for their female partners, and talk knowledgeably about housework.

Inappropriacy

Running parallel with the inclusivity strand is a set of topics which coursebook writers are usually advised to avoid. Some publishers provide lists of proscribed topics, while others rely informally on the acronym PARSNIP (politics, alcohol, religion, sex, narcotics, isms, and pork) as a rule of thumb. One publisher's list I saw contained some thirty items to be avoided or handled only with extreme care. These included alcohol, anarchy, Aids, Israel and six pointed stars, politics, religion, racism, sex, science when it involves altering nature, e.g. genetic engineering, terrorism, and violence.[4]

Guidelines for inappropriacy are different from guidelines for inclusive language and the representation of women and men. While the latter have the stated aim of improving the learning opportunities for women students and reflecting language change, guidelines for inappropriacy are based on customers' perceived sensitivities. Put simply, foreign buyers may reject material which is seen as culturally offensive. This has a number of consequences. As Ariew (1982) has suggested elsewhere, it means that coursebooks begin to look very much alike, and that target culture(s), having been stripped of some of their distinctive (or inappropriate) characteristics, may be misrepresented. But in addition it means that content can become very bland. The 'one size fits all' philosophy underlying the global coursebook means that safe topics recur again and again – foreign travel being one of the most common. In the first edition of *Headway/Intermediate* (1986) holidays, travel, and tourism were mentioned in ten out of a total of fourteen units.

So while coursebooks can be seen as *feminized* for ethical reasons they are also *sanitized* for commercial purposes. The politically correct (and I use the term positively) inclusivity is undermined by a commercially motivated exclusivity which neutralizes the material and often prevents linguistic engagement with

Movies help?

certain topics. Take the example of *Headway/Pre-Intermediate* (1991) which includes several black characters. Considerable space is devoted to a reading exercise about a non-fictional successful black teenager who started his own computer business – an approach clearly in line with the guidelines referred to above. However, in a subsequent unit there is a listening exercise in which a woman and a man talk about their experience of being mixed race. They explain that as children they were taunted for looking different, but then go on to make it clear that such incidents are nowadays things of the past. The comprehension questions which accompany the listening exercise avoid the issue of racism, and in the follow-up activity, where students *could* discuss the implications of the listening exercise, they are asked instead to invent a new mixed race identity for themselves – as though race were a straightforward matter of mix-and-match. This, along with a plethora of globetrotting characters, could be seen as the coursebook equivalent of crossover celebration so typical of the Perlmutter (1991) vision of globalization.

It is hardly surprising then that coursebooks have come in for criticism in this area. Thornbury (1999) argues that, while the kind of overt sexism revealed by Porreca (1984) has been redressed, there is still room for improvement. Lesbian and gay characters remain excluded from global materials. Thornbury makes the case for widening the scope of inclusivity. Rather than demanding the kind of upfront approach to gayness sometimes found in North American ESL materials, he suggests the inclusion of covert references – a smattering of same-sex flatmates, a few unmarried uncles, and holiday postcards from gay destinations such as Lesbos or Sitges.[5] The rationale behind such an approach, apart from including lesbians and gays as members of humanity, is that it would allow those teachers and students who are not afraid of the topic to address it in the classroom – should they wish to.[6]

But exclusion is not simply a matter of topics and characters (although the disabled, the old, and the poor are all conspicuous by their absence) – it is also a matter of language. The English available in coursebooks has been labelled 'cosmopolitan' by Brown (1990: 13). It is, she suggests, a variety which:

> assumes a materialistic set of values in which international travel, not being bored, positively being entertained, having leisure, and above all spending money casually and without consideration of the sum involved in the pursuit of these ends, are the norm.

Good examples of what Brown is talking about can be found in any number of the practice dialogues in *New Headway/Intermediate* (1996). In the first unit, for example, students are encouraged to invent conversations based on the following set of exchanges:

A What a fantastic coat! Was it expensive?

B It cost an absolute fortune. But the material's beautiful, and it's got a silk lining.

A Where did you get it?

B I saw it in the window of that new shop in town, you know, it's called 'Chic'.

A Yes, I know it. They have some lovely stuff, don't they?

(1996: 14)

The publishers I spoke to use the term 'aspirational' to refer to content of this type. One editor defined this for me as 'something which [students] aspire to and therefore interests them and motivates them'. While it is undeniable that students need scripts it could also be argued that they need exposure to a much wider range than those available in most coursebooks. Students in many learning situations may have problems with visas, need part-time jobs, or have difficulties renting accommodation as well as wanting to know how to enthuse over each other's clothes. Homing in on this variety Rinvolucri (1999) and Wajnryb (1996) have been particularly critical. Rinvolucri attacks 'UK EFLese' (1999: 12) which he sees as characterized by a focus on a very narrow range of functions. Wajnryb (1996) rigorously dissects two coursebooks widely used in Australia: *Headway/Intermediate* (1986) and *The Australian English Course* (Nunan and Lockwood 1991). Her conclusion is that they offer a 'very, very thin slice of a clean, affluent social environment' where daily life is simplified and dialogue is scripted into sets of adjacency pairs that ill-prepare students for the rough and tumble of the real world – where the preferred response may not always be so forthcoming.

What of teachers though? What do they think of the coursebooks which have been designed (partly) for their benefit? Given that coursebooks are written primarily with teachers in mind (something the publishers I spoke to accepted) their views are surely an important element in any discussion about coursebook content.

Teachers' voices

As part of an exploratory study of the way teachers construe cultural content in ELT global materials I conducted twenty-two in-depth interviews with teachers of EFL to adults in a number of schools in the Barcelona area.[7] The interviews were task-based – the informants carried out ranking activities, responded to pieces of material I showed them, talked me through materials they brought to the interview, and responded to a set of true/false type statements about culture, language teaching, and ELT materials. All teachers had between seven and twenty years of teaching experience. Ten spoke Catalan or Spanish as their first language (although all were highly proficient speakers of English and spoke in English during their interview), and twelve spoke English as their first language. Thirteen were women, nine were men. These interviews produced a considerable quantity of data and here I draw on two interviews as they relate to some of the issues outlined above. Pere, a man, and Eulàlia, a woman, are both Catalan teachers and their interviews are symptomatic of the data in that they address issues which recurred in ways which seemed to crystalize a point or articulate an area of general concern to all the informants.

Inclusivity

All the teachers I spoke to were aware of the inclusivity aspect of global course-books. Inclusivity was seen as a positive element although some teachers felt it did not always go far enough – echoing, in several cases, the concerns raised by Thornbury (1999). Eulàlia, who I quoted at the beginning of this chapter, men-tioned the representation of women and men as an aspect of coursebook content she approved of. She was typical in that she thought it was important for coursebooks to challenge stereotypical representations of women. Here she tells me why she liked some artwork from *Headway/Pre-Intermediate* (1991) which showed a man in an apron saying goodbye to his female partner who was leaving for work.

> Eulàlia: I think it's a very different image from what we normally see . . . I think it's good, yeah, it breaks with the, the stereotype of, of him going away and her with the apron. So erm I think that's good . . .
> Interviewer: OK. Can I ask you a question about that? Why is it good to break with male/female stereotypes in your opinion?
> Eulàlia: Erm well I think because it's like the stereotype, because it's a stereo-type, yeah, because I think it doesn't respond to reality, and I think that to have images like more, more varied, of women doing different things and men doing different things, I think it's, it's good as well, yeah. Not always with the, with the same things. So that's why I think it, this one's, like an image I liked.

The extract suggests that this teacher thinks breaking stereotypes is good because they do not reflect reality – an interpretation which is reinforced when she explains her approval of the way black characters feature in the *Headway* course.

> I think it's good because it's more, it's, first more real yes, and second it breaks with the idea that all, everything in English culture is, is white, you know or, or there is like a, a predominance of, of, of men or male activities. So in this book, I mean, I like this yeah, and as well it is true that in England and in the States, I mean there are a lot of black people, so, and they do things as well, so.

An accurate picture of reality, and specifically target language reality in the case of the second quotation, is something this teacher clearly values in coursebook material.

Pere was also concerned with the representation of reality in coursebooks. However, he was the only teacher in the study who felt the inclusivity aspect was overdone, particularly at the artwork level. Although adopting what could be called a fashionably anti-PC stance this teacher emerges in the following extract as someone primarily concerned with empowering his students, but also critical of an inclusivity with regard to black people which he sees as mere tokenism.

> I think really the one area where you're failing to reflect the diversity of, of erm English and the Anglo-Saxon culture is, particularly the area of erm what people sound like, yeah. We know what they look like, we've seen it on television and that, dubbed or whatever, but it's what they sound like that could pose problems, for a lot of my students, you know, through lack of exposure to those accents in class, and erm not only that but a, a kind of, you know in a way you're kind of negating their existence and this is where you're really doing them a disservice I think. This is where you're being racist if you like, by, by not allowing them to be present where it really matters to be present, not so much in the picture on page ninety-one, but really on the recording, because my students, a lot of them they couldn't care less whether the picture on page ninety-one is of a blonde lady or a black lady, they couldn't care less. What they do care about is whether they understand the lady on the, on the cassette or not, yeah. That's when, when they do care, 'cause that's, you know, the meat of it so to speak.

It was the only criticism of this type in the data. Yet I include it here because I feel it makes an important point about teachers' *general* subscription to inclusivity (although in a different way to the other informants). This teacher clearly subscribes to the belief that in language teaching material an inclusivity which does not include language, and the way that language sounds, is tantamount to window-dressing and may in fact belie a deeper and more pernicious exclusivity.

Inappropriacy

Again the teachers in the study showed that they were aware that coursebook content was partly determined by the publishers' need to maximize sales. Pere put it thus:

> I think a lot of publishers erm put together coursebooks that they'll think will sell internationally. OK, so let's write this coursebook and we can sell it in the whole of western Europe and the whole of Europe maybe. As a result of that, the choice of topics tends to be fairly bland topics, erm topics that are not going to annoy many people if at all possible.

And the consequence of this, he felt, was often a lack of student engagement. Eulalia felt that publishers relied too heavily on 'icons' (Bill Gates, Paul Newman, Madonna, Mickey Mouse, Coca-Cola) of what she called the 'dominant culture' which she felt were uncritically included in coursebooks and sat uncomfortably alongside the inclusivity strand. Her interview suggests that the avoidance of more serious topics means that new problems are created for teachers as they have to decide whether or not to adopt a critical stance in the face of so much aspirational content, which this teacher saw as 'glorified' Anglo-American popular culture.

But both agreed, and again this is something which runs throughout the data, that the absence of the *local* was a problematic aspect of global coursebooks. Pere, who argued that good materials were those which promoted student engagement, put it thus:

> but I really think what we need is locally produced coursebooks that really tap on the here and now of the learners locally and that will engage them.

He explained how he often supplemented coursebooks by downloading material on the local area from the Internet. Seeing their Catalan world in English meant that his students responded with real interest. On further prompting about what kind of content he wanted to see in a coursebook he said:

> So erm in, in this kind of setting yeah more controversial topics, more local topics and how those topics might relate to the Anglo-Saxon world, or the English speaking world, yeah, so for example 'Why do British tourists enjoy holidays in Salou?' You know, this is an account of Tom and his wife Julie who spent a fortnight in a hotel in Salou, this is what they liked, this is what they disliked . . . Because it's a kind of bridge isn't it? Erm it's not quite talking about us, it's not quite talking about them, it's talking about how they relate to us and we relate to them, it's closer to home.

The idea of the coursebook or the topic of the lesson as a bridge was one of many metaphors teachers produced in the course of the interviews. It was perhaps the most telling in that it summed up what so many of the informants talked around – the need for something to connect the world of English with the world of the students. The metaphor of the bridge neatly suggests the possibility of two-way traffic, of cultural exchange, of the place for the local in the global.

One area of ELT publishing where the local is of paramount importance is the young learner/secondary school market. The stipulations of Ministries of Education mean that this is a market where one size does not fit all. With a view to finding out what greater consideration of the local involves I spoke to two senior editors and two publishing managers at one major UK ELT publishing house.

Accommodating the local

A summary of the interviews reveals essentially two approaches to producing coursebooks for local markets. Some countries, such as Spain and Italy, have courses written specifically for them. The size of these markets means that publishers can afford to produce materials which are tailor-made and take into consideration the number of hours students are expected to devote to English, the methodologies to be used, and the themes which have to be addressed. A second approach is based around agglomerating countries and involves the production of a core text which is sold in several countries. This is aimed at what the publishers call a 'lead country' and is accompanied by differentiated supplementary materials for satellite countries. These supplements are often written by local authors with specific local knowledge. The stated aim in both approaches is to give the teachers 'a better fit' (a metaphor used repeatedly by the publishers I spoke to).

It is this response to the local (in terms of curriculum and syllabus) and, in the case of some markets, the inclusion of the local (in terms of characters, place names, and references), along with a balance of aspirational and educational topics which set these materials apart from the global coursebooks under discussion.

The publishers and editors I spoke to agreed that the future would involve even greater localization of materials in their sector. Printed core materials, it was felt, would survive, but the demand for 'a better fit' meant that the variety of add-ons would grow, and as technology developed and became more available these supplements would be increasingly available online.

This is also the view taken by some global coursebook writers. Two possible scenarios envisaged by Ingrid Freebairn (2000: 5) are a 'skeleton coursebook' available on CD-ROM which is 'supplemented by up-to-the-minute topical material, local mother-tongue supplements, and alternative activities for mixed-level classes' which can be downloaded from the Internet, and a kind of DIY online coursebook which students and teachers could assemble together depending on level and interests.

It is a much commented on paradox of globalization that high-tech production processes make it possible to tailor products to smaller and smaller market segments. National newspapers in Britain are increasingly 'editionized' – a process whereby editorial comment and advertising are customized for local audiences. Thus it could be argued that globalization has the potential to increase rather than threaten diversity. However, ELT publishers have yet to seriously engage with editionizing global coursebooks. From time to time a North American version of a very successful series is produced but while sales of the 'one size fits all' version remain healthy an attitude of 'if it ain't broke, don't fix it' seems to prevail.

Conclusion

Publishers and the global coursebooks they produce have received a lot of criticism from the ELT profession. In this chapter I have argued that there is a socially progressive and ethical dimension to the work publishers do. This is reflected in the guidelines for inclusivity, although perhaps more so in the guidelines than in the actual coursebooks themselves. However, these coursebooks are also commodities which have to be sold globally to a variety of very different markets. Unlike the coursebooks which are produced for the young learner/secondary school market the underlying philosophy of 'one size fits all' means that the progressive and ethical dimension is all too often undermined by the perceived need to sanitize content. This means that content is limited to a narrow range of bland topics and is predominantly aspirational. But 'one size fits all' also means the exclusion of the local. However, the way in which coursebooks are produced for the young learner/secondary school market may represent one way forward for the development of the global coursebook. Here at least – however imperfectly – an attempt is being made to link the global with the local.

One view of globalization (Robertson 1995) holds that the local is always imbricated in the global and for this reason a more accurate description of the process would be *glocalization*, a neologism which attempts to capture something of the complexity inherent in globalization by conflating the terms global and local. It is certainly the case that the teachers I spoke to about global materials clearly felt the need for what might be called a *glocal* coursebook – something which would give them 'a better fit' and simultaneously connect the world of their students with the world of English.

Notes

1   In this chapter I draw on research interviews in which twenty-two English language teachers working in Barcelona, two senior editors and two publishing managers in a major British publishing house discussed coursebook content. I also draw on the guidelines for content which ELT publishers produce for their authors. I would like to take this opportunity to thank all those who participated for their cooperation and frankness. They have been given pseudonyms to protect their privacy.

2   I focus exclusively on British coursebooks produced for the adult market. Their EFL (English as a Foreign Language) orientation means that they are more widely disseminated globally than North American coursebooks, which tend to have an ESL (English as a Second Language) orientation.

3   The address also lists many non-territorial communities. These include indigenous peoples, workers, ecologists, lesbians, homosexuals, feminists and pacifists.

4   In certain markets these strands could contradict each other. Florent and Walter (1989: 184) from Women in TEFL are on record as saying that 'there will be some places where sexism is, regrettably, unavoidable – for good pedagogical reasons'.

5   *Choice Readings* (1996) by Clarke *et al.* has a reading about a gay male couple and their adopted son. Follow-up exercises draw attention to the diversity of families in the USA today.

6 Burke (2000) goes further and argues that lesbian and gay invisibility in British coursebooks is a form of discrimination and out of line with European Union legislation.
7 My choice of Barcelona was partly determined by the fact that I had worked there as a teacher for many years and because the Spanish market for British global materials is known to be sizeable. In addition, as teachers of EFL to adults in private language schools in a major urban centre, the informants represent a significant group of global coursebook users worldwide.

Bibliography

Abbs, B., Ayton, A. and Freebairn, I. (1975) *Strategies*, London: Longman.

Abercrombie, N and Warde, A. with R. Deem, S. Penna, K. Soothill, J. Urry, A. Sayer and S. Walby (2000) *Contemporary British Society* 3rd edn, Oxford: Polity.

Abraham, R. G and Vann, R. J. (1987) 'Strategies of two language learners: a case study', in A. Wenden and R. Rubin (eds) *Learner Strategies in Language Learning*, Englewood Cliffs: Prentice-Hall.

Acción Zapatista/La Jornada (1996) 'The first declaration of La Realidad for humanity and against neoliberalism'. Online. Available HTTP:<http://www.utexas.edu/students/nave/>(24 October 2000).

Ahlberg, A. and Jaques, F. (1981) *Mr Buzz the Beeman*, Middlesex: Penguin Books.

Albrow, M. (1996) *The Global Age: State and Society Beyond Modernity*, Cambridge: Polity.

Amin, N. (1999) 'Minority women teachers of ESL: Negotiating white English', in G. Braine (ed.) *Non-native Educators in English Language Teaching*, Mahwah, NJ: Lawrence Erlbaum.

Anderson, B. (1983) *Imagined Communities: Reflections on the Origin and Spread of Nationalism*. London: Verso.

Appadurai, A. (1990) 'Disjuncture and difference in the global cultural economy', in M. Featherstone (ed.) *Global Culture: Nationalism, Globalization and Modernity*, London: Sage.

Ariew, R. (1982) 'The textbook as curriculum', in T. Higgs (ed.) *Curriculum, Competence and the Foreign Language Teacher*, Lincolnwood, IL: National Textbook Co.

Aston, G. (1986) 'Trouble-shooting in interaction with learners: the more the merrier', *Applied Linguistics* 7, 2: 128–43.

—— (1993) 'Notes on the interlanguage of comity', in G. Kasper and S. Blum-Kulka (eds) *Interlanguage Pragmatics*, Oxford: Oxford University Press.

Audit Commission (2000) *Money Matters: School Funding and Resource Management*, London: Audit Office. http://www.audit-commission.gov.uk

Auerbach, E. (1993) 'Reexamining English only in the ESL classroom', *TESOL Quarterly* 27, 1: 9–32.

Back, L. (1996) *New Ethnicities and Urban Culture*, London: UCL Press.

Bailey, K. (1983) 'Competitiveness and anxiety in adult language second language acquisition: looking at and through diary studies', in L. Seliger and M. Long (eds) *Classroom Oriented Research in Second Language Acquisition*, Rowley, MA: Newbury House.

Baker, P. and Eversley, J. (2000) *Multilingual Capital: The Languages of London's Schoolchildren and their Relevance to Economic, Social and Educational Policies*, London: Battlebridge Publications.

Bakhtin, M. (1986) *Speech Genres and Other Late Essays*, C. Emerson and M. Holquist (eds), trans. V. W. McGee, Austin: University of Texas Press.

Barber, B. (1995) *Jihad versus McWorld*, New York: Random House.

Barber, M. (1997) *A Reading Revolution: How We can Teach Every Child to Read Well,* London: Institute of Education.

Barton D. (1994) *Literacy: An Introduction to the Ecology of Written Language*, Cambridge: Blackwell.

Barton, D. and Hamilton, M. (1998) *Local Literacies*, London: Routledge.

Basso, K. H. (1972) '"To give up on words": Silence in Western Apache culture', in P. Giglioli (ed.) *Language and Social Context*, Harmondsworth: Penguin.

Bauman, Z. (1992) *Intimations of Postmodernity*, London: Routledge.

—— (1998) *Globalization: The Human Consequences*, Oxford: Polity.

Bauman, R. and Sherzer, J. (eds) (1974) *Exploration in the Ethnography of Speaking*, Cambridge: Cambridge University Press.

Baynham, M. (1995) *Literacy Practices*, London: Longman.

Beauvois, M. H. (1998) 'Write to speak: the effects of electronic communication on the oral achievement of fourth semester French students', in J.A. Muyskens (ed.) *New Ways of Learning and Teaching: Focus on Technology and Foreign Language Education*, Boston: Heinle and Heinle.

Beck, U. (1992) *Risk Society: Towards a New Modernity*, London: Sage.

—— (2000) *What Is Globalization?*, Cambridge: Polity Press.

Berger, J. (1998/99) 'Against the great defeat of the world', *Race and Class* 40, 2/3: 1–4.

Bernstein, B. (1996) *Pedagogy Symbolic Control and Identity*, London: Taylor & Francis.

—— (1999) 'Official knowledge and pedagogic identities', in F. Christie (ed.) *Pedagogy and the Shaping of Consciousness,* London: Continuum.

Billig, M. (1995) *Banal Nationalism*, London: Sage.

Bisong, J. (1995) 'Language choice and imperialism: a Nigerian perspective', *ELT Journal* 49, 2: 122–32.

Block, D. (1999) 'Problem framing and metaphoric accounts of the SLA research process: Who framed SLA research?', in L. Cameron and G. Low (eds) *Researching and Applying Metaphor*, Cambridge: Cambridge University Press.

—— (in preparation) *The Future of SLA*, Edinburgh: Edinburgh University Press.

Blum-Kulka, S. (1997) *Dinner Talk. Cultural Patterns of Sociability and Socialization in Family Discourse*, Mahwah, NJ: Lawrence Erlbaum.

Blyth, C. (1998) *Untangling the Web: St Martin's Guide to Language and Culture on the Internet,* New York: St Martin's Press.

Bourdieu, P. (1984) *Distinction: A Social Critique of the Judgement of Taste*, trans. R. Nice, London: Routledge & Kegan Paul.

—— (1991) *Language and Symbolic Power,* introduced by J. B. Thompson (ed.) trans. G. Raymond and M. Adamson, Cambridge, MA: Harvard University Press.

Brah, A. (1996) *Cartographies of Diaspora,* London: Routledge.

Breen, M. and Candlin, C. (1980) 'The essentials of a communicative curriculum in language teaching', *Applied Linguistics* 1, 1: 89–112.

Breton, R. (1984) 'The production and allocation of symbolic resources: an analysis of the linguistic and ethnocultural fields in Canada', *Canadian Review of Sociology and Anthropology* 21,2: 123–44.

Brown, G. (1990) 'Cultural values: the interpretation of discourse', *ELT Journal* 44,1: 11–17.

Brown, P. and Levinson, S. (1987) *Politeness: Some Universals in Language Use*, Cambridge: Cambridge University Press.

Bruce, B., Peyton, J. K., and Batson, T. (eds) (1993) *Network-Based Classrooms,* Cambridge: Cambridge University Press.

Brumfit, C. (ed.) (1995) *Language Education in the National Curriculum,* Oxford: Blackwell.

Budach, G., Roy, S. and Heller, M. (2000) 'Community and commodity in French Ontario', paper presented at the International Pragmatics Conference, Budapest, July 2000.

Burke, H. (2000) 'Cultural diversity: Managing same-sex orientation in the classroom. Available HTTP: http: //www.developingteachers.com/articles_tchtraining/cultural-diversity_henny.htm (11 June 2000).

Cajolet-Laganière, H. and Martel, P. (1995) *La qualité de la langue au Québec,* Québec: Institut québécois de recherche sur la culture.

Cameron, D. (1995) *Verbal Hygiene*, London: Routledge.

—— (1996) 'The language-gender interface: challenging co-optation', in V. Bergvall, J. Bing, and A. Freed (eds) *Rethinking Language and Gender Research,* London: Longman.

—— (2000) *Good to talk? Living and Working in a Communication Culture,* London: Sage.

Canagarajah, A. S. (1996) 'Non-discursive requirements in academic publishing, material resources of periphery scholars, and the politics of knowledge production', *Written Communication* 13, 4: 435–72.

—— (1997) 'Safe houses in the Contact Zone: Coping Strategies of African American Students in the Academy', *College Composition and Communication* 48/2: 173–96.

—— (1999a) *Resisting Linguistic Imperialism in English Teaching*, Oxford: Oxford University Press.

—— (1999b) 'Interrogating the "native speaker fallacy": Non-linguistic roots, non-pedagogical results', in G. Braine (ed.) *Non-native Educators in English Language Teaching*, Mahwah, NJ: Lawrence Erlbaum.

—— (forthcoming) *The Geopolitics of Academic Literacy and Knowledge Production*, Pittsburgh: University of Pittsburgh Press.

Canale, M. and Swain, M. (1980) 'Theoretical bases of communicative approaches to second language teaching and testing', *Applied Linguistics* 1, 1: 1–47.

Carey, J. W. (1988) *Communication as Culture. Essays on Media and Society,* Boston: Unwin & Hyman.

Casey, D. J. (1968) 'The effectiveness of teaching English as a foreign language to some Finnish secondary schools', unpublished report, University of Helsinki.

Castells, M. (1996) *The Rise of the Networked Society,* Oxford, UK: Blackwell.

Chamot, A. U and O'Malley, J. M. (1994) *The CALLA Handbook: Implementing the Cognitive Academic Language Learning Approach*, Reading, MA: Addison-Wesley.

Chew P. G. (1999) 'Linguistic imperialism, globalism and the English language', in D. Graddol and U. Meinhof (eds) *English in a Changing World*, Guildford: AILA.

Clarke, M., Dobson, B. K. and Silberstein, S. (1996) *Choice Readings*, Ann Arbor: The University of Michigan Press.

Clegg J. (1992) 'The cognitive value of literate talk in small-group classroom discourse', *Thames Valley Working Papers* 1: 1–22.

—— (ed.) (1996) *Introduction in Mainstreaming ESL*: *Case studies in Integrating ESL Students into the Mainstream Curriculum*, Clevedon: Multilingual Matters.

Cohen, R. (1997) *Global Diasporas*: *An Introduction*, London: UCL Press.

Confederation of British Industry (CBI), Press Release 27 November 2000: 'Government gets CBI praise for measures to cut red tape'.

Cononelos, T. and Oliva, M. (1993) 'Using computer networks to enhance foreign language/culture education', *Foreign Language Annals* 26: 525–34.

Contrepois, S. (1999*) Vie de banlieue*: *Jeunes a Ivry*, Mouans-Sartoux, 06 France: PEMF.

Cook, G. (2000) *Language Play, Language Learning*, Oxford: Oxford University Press.

Cooke, M. (2000) 'Wasted opportunities: a case study of two ESOL programmes in a Further Education College in central London', unpublished MA dissertation, Insitutute of Education, University of London.

Cope B. and Kalantzis, M (1993) *Cultures of Schooling*: *Pedagogies of Cultural Difference and Social Access,* Basingstoke: Falmer Press.

—— (eds) (2000) *Multiliteracies*: *Literacy Learning and the Design of Social Futures,* London: Routledge.

Cox, B. (1995) *Cox on the Battle for the English Curriculum,* London: Hodder & Stoughton.

Cox, R. (1996) 'A perspective on globalization', in J. M. Mittelman (ed.) *Globalization*: *Critical Reflections*, London: Lynne Rienner.

Crowley, T. (1996) *Language in History*: *Theories and Texts,* London: Routledge.

Cummins, J. and Swain, M. (1986) *Bilingualism in Education*, London: Longman.

Dalby, A. (1998) *Dictionary of Languages*, London: Bloomsbury.

Dale, P. (1986) *The Myth of Japanese Uniqueness,* London: Croom Helm.

Day, M. and Batson, T. (1995) *The Network-based Writing Classroom*: *The ENFI Idea. Computer Mediated Communication and the On-line Classroom* Vol. 2, Cresskill, NJ: Hampton Press.

Delpit, L. (1995) *Other People's Children*: *Cultural Conflict in the Classroom*, New York: New Press.

Department for Education (DFE). (1995) *English in the National Curriculum,* London: HMSO.

Department for Education and Employment (DfEE) (1999) *Minority Ethnic Pupils in Maintained Schools by Local Education Authority Area in England* – January 1999 (Provisional). DfEE Statistical First Release (SFR 15/1999), _ HYPERLINK<http://www.dfee.gov.uk>. Government Statistical Service.

—— (1997) *Excellence in Schools,* London: HMSO.

—— (1998) *The National Literacy Strategy*: *Framework for Teaching,* London: DfEE.

Department for Education and Science (DES) (1985) *Education for All*: *The Report of the Committee of Inquiry into the Education of Children from Ethnic Minority Groups* - (Chair: Lord Swann), London: HMSO.

Doi, T. (1971) *Amae no kôzô* [Anatomy of dependence], Tokyo: Kôbundô.

Dumont, F. (1993) *La genèse de la société québécoise*, Montréal: Boréal.

Eco, U. (1995) *The Search for the Perfect Language*, trans. J. Fentress. Oxford: Blackwell.

Ellis, R. (1997) *SLA Research and Language Teaching*, Oxford: Oxford University Press.

Ellis, R. (2000) 'Task-based research and language pedagogy', *Language Teaching Research* 4, 2: 193–220.

Emeneau, M. B. (1955) 'India and linguistics', *Journal of the American Oriental Society* 75: 143–53.

Faigley, L. (1992) *Fragments of Rationality: Postmodernity and the Subject of Composition,* Pittsburgh: University of Pittsburgh Press.

Fairclough, N. (1992) *Discourse and Social Change*, Cambridge: Polity Press.

—— (1995) *Critical Discourse Analysis,* London: Longman.

Ferrara, K., Brunner, H., and Whittemore, G. (1991). 'Interactive written discourse as an emergent register', *Written Communication* 8, 1: 8–34.

Feyarabend, P. (1975) *Against Method*, London: Verso.

Fiddick, J. (1999) 'Immigration and Asylum', Research Paper 99/16, London: House of Commons Library.

Firth, A. and Wagner, J. (1997) 'On discourse, communication, and (some) fundamental concepts in SLA research', *Modern Language Journal* 81, 3: 286–300.

Florent, J. and Walter, C. (1989) 'A better role for women in TEFL', *ELT Journal* 43, 3: 180–4.

Foster, P. (1998) 'A classroom perspective on the negotiation of meaning', *Applied Linguistics* 19, 1: 1–23.

Foster, P., Tonkyn, A. and Wigglesworth, G. (2000) 'Measuring spoken language: a unit for all reasons', *Applied Linguistics* 21, 3: 354–75.

Foucault, Michel (1971) L'ordre du discours. Paris: Gallimard, Engl. trsl. in M. Shapiro (ed.) *Language and Politics*, New York: NY Press, 1984.

Fraser, M. (1987) *Quebec Inc.: French-Canadian Entrepreneurs and the New Business Elite,* Toronto: Key Porter Books.

Freebairn, I. (2000) 'The coursebook – future continuous or past?', *English Teaching Professional Issue* 15: 3–5.

Freire P. (1972) *The Pedagogy of the Oppressed*, London: Penguin.

Friedman, J. (1994) *Cultural Identity and Global Process*, London: Sage.

Fujiwara, T. (1995) 'Gaikokujin rôdôsha mondai kara gaikokujin mondai e' [From issues of foreign workers to issues of foreigners], in T. Fujiwara (eds) *Gaikokujin rôdôsha mondai to tabunka kyôiku* [Issues of foreign workers and multicultural education], Tokyo: Akashi shoten.

Gass, S. (1997) *Input, Interaction, and the Second Language Learner*, Mahwah, NJ: Lawrence Erlbaum.

—— (1998) 'Apples and oranges: or why apples are not oranges and don't need to be. A response to Firth and Wagner', *Modern Language Journal* 82, 1: 83–90.

Gee J. (1990) *Social Linguistics and Literacies: Ideology in Discourses*, Basingstoke: Falmer Press.

Gee, J. P., Hull, G. and Lankshear, C. (1996) *The New Work Order: Behind the Language of the New Capitalism*, Boulder, CO: Westview Press.

Giddens, A. (1990) *The Consequences of Modernity*, Cambridge: Polity Press.

—— (1991) *Modernity and Self-Identity: Self and Society in the Late Modern Age*, Cambridge: Polity.

—— (2000). *Runaway World: How Globalization is Reshaping Our Lives*, London: Routledge.

Gillborn, D. (1997) 'Ethnicity and educational performance in the United Kingdom: Racism, ethnicity, and variability in achievement', *Anthropology and Education Quarterly* 28, 3: 375–93.

Gillborn, D. and Gipps, C. (1996) *Recent Research on the Achievement of Ethnic Minority Pupils,* London: Office for Standards in Education.

Gilroy, P. (1987/1991) *There Ain't No Black in the Union Jack*, London: Routledge.

—— (1993) *The Black Atlantic: Modernity and Double Consciousness*, London: Verso.

Giroux, H. (1983) 'Theory of reproduction and resistance in the new sociology of education: a critical analysis', *Harvard Educational Review* 3, 53: 257–93.

—— (1992) *Border Crossings: Cultural Workers and the Politics of Education*, New York: Routledge.

Giroux, H. and McLaren, P. (eds) (1994) *Between Borders: Pedagogy and the Politics of Cultural Studies*, New York: Routledge.

Gleitzman, M. (1992) *Blabbermouth*, London: Macmillan.

Goffman, E. (1959) *The Presentation of Self in Everyday Life*, Garden City, NY: Doubleday.

Grabiner, Lord (2000) *The Informal Economy*, London: HMSO.

Graddol, D. (1997) *The Future of English?*, London: The British Council.

—— (1999) 'The decline of the native speaker', in D. Graddol and U. Meinhof (eds) *English in a Changing World*, Guildford: AILA.

Graddol, D. and Meinhof, U. (eds) (1999) *English in a Changing World*, Guildford: AILA.

Granville, S., Janks, H., Mphahlele, M., Reed, Y., Watson P., Joseph M. and Ramani, E., (1998) 'English with or without g(u)ilt: a position paper on Language in Education Policy for South Africa', *Language and Educational Development* 12, 4: 254–72.

Gray, J. (1992) *Men are from Mars, Women are from Venus*, New York: HarperCollins.

Gray, J. (1998) *False Dawn*, London: Granta Books.

Gregory, E. and Williams, A. (2000) *City Literacies: Learning to Read Across Generations and Cultures*, London: Routledge.

Green, J.M and Oxford, R. (1995) 'A closer look at learner strategies, L2 proficiency, and gender', *TESOL Quarterly* 29, 2: 261–98.

Grossberg, L. (1994) 'Introduction: Bringin' it All Back Home – Pedagogy and Cultural Studies', in Henry Giroux and Peter McLaren (eds) *Between Borders: Pedagogy and the Politics of Cultural Studies*, New York: Routledge.

Habermas, J. (1970) 'Towards a theory of communicative competence', *Inquiry* 13: 360–75.

—— (1979) *Communication and the Evolution of Society*, London: Heinemann.

Hall, S. (1988/1992) 'New ethnicities', in A. Rattansi, and J. Donald (eds), *'Race', Culture and Difference*, London: Sage/The Open University.

—— (1990) 'Cultural identity and diaspora', in J. Rutherford (ed) *Identity: Community, Culture, Difference*, London: Lawrence & Wishart.

Halliday M. A. K. (1996) 'Literacy and linguistics: a functional perspective', in R. Hasan and G. Williams (eds) *Literacy in Society*, London: Longman.

Hanks, William (2000) *Intertexts. Writings on Language, Utterance and Context*, Lanham, MD: Rowman &Littlefield.

Hannerz, U. (1996) *Transnational Connections*, London: Routledge.

Harris, R. (1997) 'Romantic bilingualism: Time for a change?', in C. Leung and C. Cable (eds) *English as an Additional Language: Changing Perspectives*, Watford: NALDIC.

—— (1999) 'Rethinking the bilingual learner', in A. Tosi and C. Leung (eds) *Rethinking Language Education*, London: CILT.

Hart, D., Lapkin, S. and Swain, M. (1990) 'Prospects for immersion graduates: Bilingualism in the private sector', Final report submitted to the Ontario Ministry of Education, Toronto, Ontario.

Harvey, D. (2000) *Spaces of Hope*, Berkeley, CA: University of California Press.

Hatch, E. (1978) 'Discourse analysis and second language acquisition', in Hatch, E. (ed.) *Second Language Acquisition: A book of readings*, Rowley, MA: Newbury House.

Hawisher, G. (1994) 'Blinding Insights: Classification schemes and software for literacy instruction', in C. Selfe and S. Hilligoss (eds) *Literacy and Computers: The Complications of Teaching and Learning with Technology*, New York: MLA.

Hawisher, G. and Selfe, C. (eds) (2000) *Global Literacies and the World-Wide Web*, London: Routledge.

Heath S. B. (1983) *Ways with Words*, Cambridge: Cambridge University Press.

Held, D., McGrew, A., Goldblatt, D. and Perraton, J. (1999) *Global Transformations: Politics, Economics and Culture*, Cambridge: Polity.

Heller, M. (1994) *Crosswords: Language, Education and Ethnicity in French Ontario*, Berlin: Mouton de Gruyter.

—— (1999a) *Linguistic Minorities and Modernity: A Sociolinguistic Ethnography*, London: Longman.

—— (1999b) 'Heated language in a cold climate', in J. Blommaert (ed.) *Language Ideological Debates*, Berlin: Mouton de Gruyter.

—— (In preparation) *Éléments d'une sociolinguistique critique*, Paris: Hatier.

Heller, M. and Budach, G. (1999) 'Prise de parole: la mondialisation et la transformation des discours identitaires chez une minorité linguistique', *Bulletin suisse de linguistique appliquée*, 69, 2: 155–66.

Heller, M., Henry, M., Lingard, B., Rizvi, F. and Taylor, S. (1999) 'Working with/against globalization in education' *Journal of Education Policy* 14, 1: 85–97.

Herring, S. (1996) 'Two variants of an electronic message schema', in S. Herring (ed.), *Computer-mediated Communication: Linguistic, Social and Cross-cultural Perspectives*, Philadelphia: John Benjamins.

—— (1999) 'Interactional coherence in CMC', *Proceedings of the Thirty-Second Annual Hawaii International Conference on Systems Sciences* (CD-ROM), Los Alamitos, CA: IEEE Computer Society.

Hewitt, R. (1986) *White Talk, Black Talk*, Cambridge: Cambridge University Press.

Higuchi, T. (ed.) (1997) *Shôgakkô kara no gaikokugo kyôiku* [Foreign language education from the elementary school], Tokyo: Kenkyûsha.

Hill, P. (1980) 'Women in the World of ELT Textbooks', *EFL Gazette*, June/July.

Hinkel, E. (ed.) (1999) *Culture in Second Language Teaching and Learning*, Cambridge: Cambridge University Press.

Hirst, P. and Thompson, G. (1996/99) *Globalization in Question*, Cambridge: Polity.

Hobsbaum, E. (1994) *The Age of Extremes*, London: Abacus.

Hobsbawm, E. and Ranger, T. (eds) (1983) *The Invention of Tradition*, Cambridge: Cambridge University Press.

Holliday, A. (1994) *Appropriate Methodology and Social Context*, Cambridge: Cambridge University Press.

Hoffman, E. (1989) *Lost in Translation*, London: Longman.

Holborow, M. (1999) *The Politics of English*, London: Sage Publications.

Holmes, D. and Russell, G. (1999) 'Adolescent CIT use: Paradigm shifts for educational and cultural practices?' *British Journal of the Sociology of Education* 20, 1: 69–78.

Horibe, H. (1995) 'Eigo teikoku shugi hihan o dô uketomeru ka: Aru rekishiteki pâsu-pekutibu kara' [How do we understand criticisms of English linguistic imperialism?: From a historical perspective], *Gendai Eigo Kyôiku* [Modern English Language Education], December: 26–9.

Horibe, H. (1998) Kokusai rikai kyôiku, ibunka rikai kyôiku e no iron [A critique of teaching international understanding and intercultural understanding]. *Gendai Eigo Kyôiku* [Modern English Language Education], *December*, 22–5.

Hornberger, N. (1994) 'Ethnography', *TESOL Quarterly* 28, 4: 688–90.

Hymes, D. (1987) 'Communicative competence', in U. Ammon, N. Dittmar and K. Mattheier (eds) *Sociolinguistics/Soziolinguistik*, Berlin: Walter de Gruyter.

Jameson, F. (2000) 'Globalization and political strategy', *New Left Review* 4, July/August: 49–68.

Jameson, F. and Miyoshi, M. (1999) *The Cultures of Globalization*, Durham, NC: Duke University Press.

Japanese Society for History Textbook Reform (1998) *The Restoration of a National History: Why was the Japanese Society for History Textbook Reform Established, and What are its Goals?*, Tokyo: Japanese Society for History Textbook Reform.

Jones, S. G. (ed.) (1995) *Cybersociety. Computer-mediated Communication and Community*, London: Sage.

Juppé, R. Jr (1995) 'An incomplete *Perestroika*: Communicative Language Teaching in Japan', *Gendai Eigo Kyôiku* [Modern English Language Education], June: 18–19.

Kachru, B. B. (1997) 'Past imperfect: The other side of English in Asia', in L. E. Smith and M. L. Foxman (eds), *World Englishes 2000*, Honolulu: University of Hawaii Press.

Kanpol, B. (1994) *Critical Pedagogy: An Introduction*, London: Bergin and Garvey.

Kaplan, R. B. (1966) 'Cultural thought patterns in inter-cultural education', *Language Learning* 16, 1: 1–20.

Kawakami, I. (1999) '"Nihon jijô" kyôiku ni okeru bunka no mondai' [Issues of culture in teaching "Japanese culture"], *21 seiki no "nihon jijô": Nihongo kyôiku kara bunka riterashî e* ["Japanese culture" in the 21st century: From Japanese language education to cultural literary], 16–26.

Kennedy, C. (1987) 'Innovation for a change: Teacher development and innovation', *English Language Teaching Journal* 41, 4: 164–70.

Kern, R. G. (1995) 'Restructuring classroom interaction with networked computers: effects on quantity and characteristics of language production', *Modern Language Journal* 79, 4: 457–76.

—— (1998) 'Technology, social interaction, and FL literacy', in J. A. Muyskens (ed.) *New Ways of Learning and Teaching: Focus on Technology and Foreign Language Education*, Boston: Heinle and Heinle.

—— (2000) *Literacy and Language Teaching*, Oxford: Oxford University Press.

Kilminster, R. (1997) 'Globalization as an emergent concept', in A. Scott, (ed.) *The Limits of Globalization: Cases and Arguments*, London: Routledge.

Kincheloe, J. L. and Steinberg, S. R. (1997) *Changing Multiculturalism*, Buckingham: Open University Press.

Kotoh, K. (1992) *Janru-betsu eibun dokkai izen: Kiso chishiki Jyûjitsu hen* [Foundations of English reading comprehension by genre: Building basic knowledge], Tokyo: Kenkyûsha.

Kramsch, C. (1993) *Context and Culture in Language Teaching*, Oxford: Oxford University Press.
—— (1995) 'The applied linguist and the foreign language teacher: can they talk to each other?', in G. Cook and B. Seidlhofer (eds) *Principle and Practice in Applied Linguistics*, Oxford: Oxford University Press.
—— (1997) 'The privilege of the non-native speaker', *PMLA* May: 359–69.
—— (1998) *Language and Culture*, Oxford: Oxford University Press.
Kramsch, C., Van Ness, F. and Lam, E. W. S. (2000) 'Authenticity and authorship in the computer-mediated acquisition of L2 literacy', *Language Learning and Technology* 4, 2: 78–104. Online. Available<http://llt.msu.edu>
Kubota, R. (1997) 'A reevaluation of the uniqueness of Japanese written discourse: Implications to contrastive rhetoric', *Written Communication* 14, 4: 460–80.
—— (1998a) 'Ideologies of English in Japan', *World Englishes* 17: 295–306.
—— (1998b) 'An investigation of Japanese and English L1 essay organization: Differences and similarities', *The Canadian Modern Language Review* 54: 475–507.
—— (1999) 'Japanese culture constructed by discourses: Implications for applied linguistic research and English language teaching', *TESOL Quarterly* 33, 1: 9–35.
—— (in press) 'Japanese identities in written communication: Politics and discourses', in R. T. Donahue (ed.) *Japanese Enactments of Culture and Consciousness*, Norwood, NJ: Ablex.
Kumaravadivelu, B. (1994) 'The postmethod condition: (E)merging strategies for second/foreign language teaching', *TESOL Quarterly* 28, 1: 27–48.
Labov, W. (1972) 'The logic of non-standard English', in P. P. Giglioli (ed.) *Language and Social Context*, Harmondsworth: Penguin.
Labrie, N., Bélanger, N., Lozon, R. and Roy, S. (2000) 'Mondialisation et exploitation des ressources linguistiques: les défis des communautés francophones de l'Ontario', *Canadian Modern Language Review/ Revue canadienne des langues vivantes* 57, 1: 88–117.
Landry, R. (1982) 'Le bilinguisme additif chez les francophones minoritaires du Canada', *Revue des sciences de l'éducation* 8, 2: 223–44.
Lanham, R. A. (1994) *The Electronic Word: Democracy, Technology and the Arts*, Chicago: University of Chicago Press.
Lankshear C., Gee, J.P., Knobel, M. and Searle, C. (1997) *Changing Literacies*, Buckingham: Open University Press.
Lantolf, J. P. (ed.) (2000) *Sociocultural Theory and Second Language Learning*, Oxford: Oxford University Press.
Latouche, S. (1996) *The Westernizing of the World*, Cambridge: Polity Press.
Latour, B. (1999) *Pandora's Hope. Essays on the Reality of Science Studies*, Cambridge, MA: Harvard University Press.
Lee, L. (1998) 'Going beyond classroom learning: Acquiring cultural knowledge via on-line newspaper and intercultural exchanges via on-line chatrooms', *CALICO Journal* 16, 2: 101–20.
Leki, I. (1995) 'Coping strategies of ESL students in writing tasks across the curriculum', *TESOL Quarterly* 29, 2: 235–60.
Leung, C. and Cable, C. (eds) (1997) *English as an Additional Language: Changing Perspectives*, Watford: NALDIC.
Leung, C., Harris, R. and Rampton, B. (1997) 'The idealised native speaker, reified ethnicities and classroom realities', *TESOL Quarterly* 31, 3: 543–60.

Levin, L. (1972) *Comparative Studies in Foreign Language Teaching*, Stockholm: Almquist & Wiksell.

Littlejohn A. (1992) 'Why are ELT materials the way they are?', unpublished PhD thesis, Lancaster: Lancaster University.

Liu, D. (1995) '"Alternative to" or "addition to" method?' *TESOL Quarterly* 29, 1: 174–7.

Long, M. (1996) 'The role of linguistic environment in second language acquisition', in W. Ritchie and T. Bhatia (eds) *Approaches to Second Language Acquisition*, London: Academic Press.

Long, M. (1997) 'Construct validity in SLA research: a response to Firth and Wagner', *Modern Language Journal* 81, 3: 318–23.

Long, M. (1998) 'SLA: Breaking the siege', *University of Hawai'i Working Papers in ESL* 17: 79–129.

Love, J. F. (1986) *McDonald's: Behind the Arches*, New York: Bantam Books.

Luke, C. (2000) 'Cyber schooling and technological change: Multiliteracies for new times', in B. Cope and M. Kalantzis (ed.) *Multiliteracies*, London: Routledge.

Lummis, D. (1976). *Ideorogî to shite no eikaiwa* [English conversation as ideology], Tokyo: Shôbunsha.

Lutz, C. and Abu-Lughod, L. (eds) (1980) *Language and the Politics of Emotion*, Cambridge: Cambridge University Press.

McCarthy, C. (1998) *The Uses of Culture*: *Education and the Limits of Ethnic Affiliation*, London: Routledge.

MacIntyre, P. D. (1994) 'Toward a social psychological model of strategy use', *Foreign Language Annals* 27: 185–95.

McConnell, D. L. (2000). *Importing diversity*: *Inside Japan's JET Program,* Berkeley, CA: University of California Press.

McDonald's Japan (2000) 'Fujita Den Goroku' [Quotes of Den Fujita], Online. Available <http://www.mcdonalds.co.jp/messe/denroom/2001.html> (11 February 2001).

Marginson, S. (1999) 'After globalization: emerging politics of education', *Journal of Education Policy* 14, 1: 19–31.

Martin-Jones, M. and Bhatt, A. (1998) 'Literacies in the lives of young Gujerati speakers in Leicester', in A. Durgunoglu and L. Verhoeven (eds) *Literacy Development in a Multilingual Context*: *Cross-cultural Perspectives*, Mahwah, NJ: Lawrence Erlbaum.

Marx, L. (1962) *The Machine in the Garden. The Pastoral Ideal in America*, Cambridge, MA: MIT Press.

Mathews, G. (2000) *Global Culture/Individual Identity*: *Searching for a Home in the Cultural Supermarket*, London: Routledge.

Matsuda, A. (2000) 'Japanese attitudes towards English: a case study of high school students', unpublished PhD thesis, Purdue University.

Matsui, Y. (1991) *Nihonjin no kangae kata: "Nihonron" e no annai* [Japanese people's ways of thinking: A guide to the theory of Japan], Urawa: The Japan Foundation Japanese Language Institute.

Matsui, Y. Abe, Y. and Masuda, S. (1994). *Nihongo kyôshi yôsei kôza tekisuto: Nihon jijô* [Text for Japanese teacher training course: Japanese culture], Tokyo: Human Academy.

Mercer, K. (1988) 'Diaspora culture and the dialogic imagination', in M. Cham and C. Watkins (eds) *Blackframes: Critical Perspectives on Black Independent Cinema*, Cambridge, MA: MIT Press.

Mercer N. (1996) 'Language and the guided construction of knowledge', in G. Blue and R. Mitchell (eds) *Language and Education*, Clevedon: Multilingual Matters/BAAL.

Miller, L. (forthcoming) 'Men's beauty work in Japan', in J. Roberson and N. Suzuki (eds) *Men and Masculinities in Contemporary Japan: Beyond the Urban Salaryman Model*, London: Routledge.

Miller, T. and Emel, L. (1988) 'Modern methodology or cultural imperialism', paper presented at TESOL convention, Chicago.

Milroy, J. and Milroy, L. (1998) *Authority in Language*, 3rd edn, London: Routledge.

Ministry of Education (1998) 'Yôchien, shôgakkô, chûgakkô, kôtôgakkô, môgakkô, rôgakkô, oyobi yôgogakkô no kyôiku katei no kijun no kaizen ni tsuite' [On the revisions of the curriculum guidelines for kindergartens, elementary schools, junior high schools, senior high schools, schools for the blind, schools for the deaf, and schools for the mentally/physically handicapped], Online. Available <http://www.mext.go.jp/b_menu/shingi/12/kyouiku/toushin/980703.htm> (11 February 2001).

—— (1999a) 'Heisei 10 nendo kôtôgakkô ni okeru kokusai kôryû no jôkyô' [Current state of international exchange activities in high schools in 1998–9], Monbushô shotô chûtô kyôikukyoku kôtô kyôikuka [Ministry of Education, Elementary and Secondary Education Bureau, High School Education Division].

—— (1999b). 'Gakushû shidô yôryô' [Course of Study], Online. Available <http://www.monbu.go.jp/printing/sidou/00000007/> (11 February 2001).

Ministry of Education, Culture, Sports, Science and Technology (2001) 'Gakkô kihon chôsa [Basic school survey], Online. Available <http://www.mext.go.jp/b_menu/toukei/kyouiku/kihon/hyou/tk0100.gif> (11 February 2001).

Ministry of Justice (2000a) 'Heisei 11 nen ni okeru gaikokujin oyobi nihonjin no shutsu-nyûkokusha tôkei ni tsuite' [Statistics of Japanese and non-Japanese nationals leaving and entering Japan in 1999], Online. Available http://www.moj.go.jp/PRESS/000321–1/000321–1.html (11 February 2001).

—— (2000b) 'Heisei 11 nen matsu genzai ni okeru gaikokujin tôrokusha tôkei ni tusite' [Statistics of registered foreign residents at the end of 1999], Online. Available <http://www.moj.go.jp/PRESS/000530–1/000530–1.html> (11 February 2001).

Mohan, B., Leung, C. and Davison, C. (2001) *English as a Second Language in the Mainstream: Teaching, Learning and Identity*, London: Longman.

Morita, T. (1988) *Rinkyôshin to nihonjin, nihonbunkaron* [The Ad-Hoc Committee for Education Reform and the studies on the Japanese people and culture], Tokyo: Shin Nihon Shuppansha.

Morley, D. and D. Robins (1995) *Spaces of Identity: Global Media, Electronic Landscapes and Cultural Boundaries*, London: Routledge.

Morson, G. S. and Emerson, C. (1990) *Mikhail Bakhtin, Creation of a Prosaics*, Stanford: Stanford University Press.

Muchiri, M. N., Mulamba, N.G., Myers, G. and Ndoloi, D.B. (1995) 'Importing composition: Teaching and researching academic writing beyond North America', *College Composition and Communication* 46, 2: 175–98.

Mukherjee, T. S. (1986) 'ESL: An imported new empire?', *Journal of Moral Education* 15, 1: 43–9.

Nakamura, K. (1989) *Eigo wa donna gengo ka* [What is the English language?], Tokyo: Sanseido.

—— (1999) 'Gengo, neishon, gurôbarizêshon' [Language, nation, and globalization], *Kigôgaku Kenkyû* [Studies in Semiotics] 19: 65–84.

Nakane, C. (1967) *Tate shakai no ningen kankei* [Human relations in vertical society], Tokyo: Kôdansha.

Nakata, M. (2000) 'History, cultural diversity and English language teaching', in B. Cope and M. Kalantzis (eds) *Multiliteracies: Literacy Learning and the Design of Social Futures*, London: Routledge, pp. 106–20.

Nash, K. (2000) *Contemporary Political Sociology: Globalization, Politics and Power*, Oxford: Blackwell.

NCMTT (National Council for Mother Tongue Teaching) (1985) 'The Swann Report: Education for All?', *Journal of Multilingual and Multicultural Development* 6, 6: 497–508.

Noblitt, J. (1995) 'The electronic language learning environment', in C. Kramsch (ed.) *Redefining the Boundaries of Language Sudy*, Boston: Heinle and Heinle.

Noguchi, M. G. and Fotos, S. (eds) (2001) *Studies in Japanese Bilignualism*, Clevedon, UK: Multilingual Matters.

Norton, B. (2000) *Identity and Language Learning*, London: Longman.

Nunan, D. and Lockwood, J. (1991) *The Australian English Course. Book 1*, Cambridge: Cambridge University Press.

Oda, M. (1999) 'English only or English plus?: The language(s) of EFL organization', in G. Braine (ed.) *Non-native Educators in English Language Teaching*, Mahwah, NJ: Lawrence Erlbaum.

Ohmae, K. (1990) *The Borderless World*, London: Collins.

—— (1995) *The End of the Nation State*, New York: Free Press.

Oishi, S. (1990) *"Eigo" ideorogî o tou: Seiô seishin to no kakutô* [Questioning the ideology of "English": Struggle with the Western mind], Tokyo: Kaibunsha Shuppan.

—— (1993) '"Eigo shihai" shûen ni mukete no kojin teki sônen' [Personal thoughts on the termination of "English domination"], in Y. Tsuda (ed.) *Eigo shihai e no iron* [Oppositions to English domination], Tokyo: Daisan Shokan.

Okamoto, S. (1997) 'Social context, linguistic ideology, and indexical expressions in Japanese', *Journal of Pragmatics* 28: 795–817.

—— (1999) 'Situated politeness: manipulating honorific and non-honorific expressions in Japanese conversations', *Pragmatics* 9, 1: 51–74.

Ortega, L. (1997) 'Processes and outcomes in networked classroom interaction: Defining the research agenda for L2 computer-assisted classroom discussion', *Language Learning and Technology* 1, 1: 82–93.

—— (1999) 'Planning and focus on form in L2 oral performance', *Studies in Second Language Acquisition* 21: 109–45.

Oseki, K. (1999) 'Chikyû jidai no aidentiti: Gurôbaru kyôiku kara no teigen' [Identity for the age of globalism: Suggestions from global education], *Kyôiku* November: 55–62.

Oxford, R. (1990) *Language Learning Strategies: What Every Teacher Should Know*, New York: Newbury House.

Papastergiadis, N. (2000) *The Turbulence of Migration: Globalization, Deterritorialization and Hybridity*, Cambridge: Polity Press.

Parmenter, L. and Tomita, Y. (2000a) 'Nihon de wa naze gaikokugo wa eigo dake na no?' [Why is a foreign language only English in Japan?], *Eigo Kyôiku* [The English Teachers' Magazine] 49, 1: 40–1.

Parmenter, L. and Tomita, Y. (2000b) 'Naze eigo kyôiku o okonau no ka? Part 1: Seito no hattatsu no tame no eigo kyôiku' [Why do we teach English? Part 1: English language teaching for student development], *Eigo Kyôiku* [The English Teachers' Magazine], 49, 2: 40–1.

Pavlenko, A. and Lantolf, J. P. (2000) 'Second language learning as participation and the (re)construction of selves', in J. P. Lantolf (ed.) *Sociocultural Theory and Second Language Learning*, Oxford: Oxford University Press.

Peach, C. (1996) 'Introduction', in C. Peach (ed.) *Ethnicity in the 1991 Census*, Volume Two, London: HMSO.

Pennington, M. (1995) 'The teacher change cycle', *TESOL Quarterly* 29, 4: 705–32.

Pennycook, A. (1989) 'The concept of "method", interested knowledge, and the politics of language teaching', *TESOL Quarterly* 23, 4: 589–618.

—— (1994) *The Cultural Politics of English as an International Language*, London: Longman.

—— (1998) *English and the Discourses of Colonialism*, London: Routledge.

Perlmutter, H. V. (1991) 'On the rocky road to the first global civilization', *Human Relations* 44, 9: 897–920.

Péronnet, L. and Kasparian, S. (1998) 'Le français standard acadien: analyse des traits morphosyntaxiques' in A. Boudreau and L. Dubois (eds) *Le français, langue maternelle*, Moncton: Éditions d'Acadie.

Phillips, A. (1998) *Communication: A Key Skill for Education*, London: BT Forum.

Phillipson, R. (1992). *Linguistic Imperialism*, Oxford: Oxford University Press.

Phillipson, R. and Skuttnab-Kangas, T. (1999) 'Englishisation: one dimension of globalisation', in D. Graddol and U. Meinhof (eds) *English in a Changing World*, Guildford: AILA.

Pica, T. (1995) 'The textual outcomes of native-speaker-nonnative speaker negotiation: What do they reveal about second language learning?', in C. Kramsch and S. McConnell-Ginet (eds) *Text and Context. Cross-Disciplinary Perspectives on Language Study*, Lexington, MA: D.C. Heath.

Pica, T., Lincoln-Porter, F., Paninos, D. and Linnell, J. (1996) 'Language learners' interaction: How does it address the input, output, and feedback needs of L2 learners?', *TESOL Quarterly* 30, 1: 59–84.

Pierce, B. N. (1989) 'Toward a pedagogy of the possible in the teaching of English internationally: people's English in South Africa', *TESOL Quarterly*, 23, 3: 401–20.

Pieterse, J. N. (1995) 'Globalization as hybridization', in M. Featherstone, S. Lash and R. Robertson (eds) *Global Modernities*, London: Sage.

Porreca, K. L. (1984) 'Sexism in current ESL textbooks', *TESOL Quarterly* 18, 4: 705–24.

Portes, A. (1997) *Globalization from Below: The Rise of Transnational Communities*, Oxford: ESRC Transnational Communities Working Paper WPTC-98–01. Online. Available http://www.transcomm.oxford.ac.uk

Prabhu, N. S. (1990) 'There is no best method – Why?', *TESOL Quarterly* 24, 2: 161–76.

Qualifications and Curriculum Authority (QCA) (2000) *A Language in Common: Assessing English as an Additional Language*, London: QCA.

Quinn, N. (1987) 'Convergent evidence for a cultural model of American marriage', in D. Holland and N. Quinn (eds) *Cultural Models in Language and Thought*, Cambridge: Cambridge University Press.

Rampton, B. (1988) 'A non-educational view of ESL in Britain', *Journal of Multilingual and Multicultural Development* 9, 6: 503–29.

—— (1990) 'Displacing the "native speaker": Expertise, affiliation and inheritance', *ELT Journal* 44, 2: 97–101.

—— (1995) *Crossing: Language and Ethnicity Among Adolescents*, London: Longman.

—— (1997) 'Second language research in late modernity: a response to Firth and Wagner', *Modern Language Journal* 81, 3: 329–33.

—— (1999a) '*Deutsch* in Inner London and the animation of an instructed foreign language', *Journal of Sociolinguistics* 3, 4: 480–504.

—— (1999b) 'Dichotomies, difference, and ritual in second language learning and teaching', *Applied Linguistics* 20, 3: 316–40.

—— (2001) 'Critique in interaction', *Critique of Anthropology* 21/1.

Rampton, B., Leung, C. and Harris, R. (1997) 'Multilingualism in England', *Annual Review of Applied Linguistics* 17: 224–41.

Reay, D. (1998) 'Rethinking social class: Qualitative perspectives on class and gender', *Sociology* 32, 2: 259–75.

Reddy, M. (1979) 'The conduit metaphor – a case of frame conflict in our language about language', in A. Ortony (ed.) *Metaphor and Thought*, New York: Cambridge University Press.

Reich, R. (1992) *The Work of Nations*, New York: Vintage.

Richards, C. (1998) *Teen Spirits: Music and Identity in Media Education*, London: UCL Press.

Richards, J. and Rodgers, T. (1986) *Approaches and Methods in Language Teaching: A Description and Analysis*, Cambridge: Cambridge University Press.

Rinvolucri, M. (1999) 'The UK, EFLese sub-culture and dialect', *Folio* 5, 2: 12–14.

Ritzer, G. (1996) *The McDonaldization of Society*, revised edn, London: Sage.

—— (1998) *The McDonaldization Thesis*, London: Sage.

—— (1999) *Enchanting a Disenchanted World: Revolutionizing the Means of Consumption*, London: Sage.

Robertson, R. (1992) *Globalization: Social Theory and Global Culture*, London: Sage.

—— (1995) 'Glocalization: time–space and homogeniety–heterogenity', in M. Featherstone, S. Lash and R. Robertson (eds) *Global Modernities* (pp. 25–44). London: Sage Publications.

Rose, E. (1969) *Colour and Citizenship: A Report on British Race Relations*, Oxford: Oxford University Press.

Roy, S. (2000) 'La normalisation linguistique dans une entreprise: le mot d'ordre mondial', *Canadian Modern Language Review / Revue canadienne des langues vivantes* 57, 1: 118–43.

Said, E. (1994) *Culture and Imperialism*, London: Vintage.

Sampson, G. P. (1984) 'Exporting language teaching methods from Canada to China', *TESL Canada Journal* 1: 19–31.

Savignon, S. (1972) *Communicative Competence. An Experiment in Foreign Language Teaching*, Philadelphia: Center for Curriculum Development.

—— (1983) *Communicative Competence: Theory and Classroom Practice*, Reading, MA: Addison-Wesley.

Saville-Troike, M. (1989) *The Ethnography of Communication*, 2nd edn, Oxford: Oxford University Press.

Schieffelin, B. and Ochs, E. (1986) *Language Socialization Across Cultures*, Cambridge: Cambridge University Press.

Schiller, H. I. (1985) 'Transnational media and national development', in K. Nordenstreng and H. I. Schiller (eds) *National Sovereignty and International Communication*, Norwood, NJ: Ablex.

Scholte, J. A. (2000) *Globalization*, London: Macmillan.

Schön, D. (1979) 'Generative metaphor: A perspective on problem setting in social policy', in A. Ortony (ed.) *Metaphor and Thought*, New York: Cambridge University Press.

Schön, D. and Rein, M. (1994) *Frame Reflection*, New York: Basic Books.

Schumann, J. (1997) *The Neurobiology of Affect in Language*, Oxford: Blackwell.

Scollon, R. and Scollon, S. (1995) *Intercultural Communication*, Oxford: Blackwell.

Searle, C. (1983) 'A common language', *Race and Class* 25, 2: 65–74.

Sefton-Green, J. (ed.) (1998) *Digital Diversions: Youth Culture in the Age of Multimedia*, London: UCL Press.

Shannon, C. and Weaver, W. (1949) *The Mathematical Theory of Communication*, Urbana, ILL: University of Illinois Press.

Sheen, R. (1994) 'A critical analysis of the advocacy of the Task-Based syllabus', *TESOL Quarterly* 28, 1: 127–53.

Shimizu, K. (1999) *Kyôiku dêta rando 1999–2000* [Education Data, 1999–2000], Tokyo: Jiji Tsûshin Sha.

Siegal, M. and Okamoto, S. (1996) 'Imagined worlds: Language, gender and socio-cultural "norms" in Japanese language textbooks', in N. Warner, J. Ahlers, L. Bilmes, M. Oliver, S. Wertheim and M. Chen (eds) *Gender and Belief Systems: Proceedings for the Fourth Berkeley Women and Language Conference*, Berkeley, CA: Berkeley Women and Language Group, University of California.

Silverstein, M. and Urban, G. (eds) (1996) *Natural Histories of Discourse*, Chicago: University of Chicago Press.

Skehan, P. (1998) *A Cognitive Approach to Language Learning*, Oxford: Oxford University Press.

Smith, P. (1997) *Millennium Dreams*, London: Verso.

Smith, P.D., Jr (1970) 'A comparison of the cognitive and audio-lingual approaches to foreign language instruction', in *The Pennsylvania Foreign Language Project*, Philadelphia: The Center for Curriculum Development.

Soars, J. and Soars, L. (1986) *Headway/Intermediate*, Oxford: Oxford University Press.

—— (1991) *Headway/Pre-Intermediate*, Oxford: Oxford University Press.

—— (1996) *New Headway English Course/Intermediate*, Oxford: Oxford University Press.

—— (1998) *New Headway Course/Upper Intermediate*, Oxford: Oxford University Press.

Street B. (1984) *Literacy in Theory and Practice*, Cambridge: Cambridge University Press.

Street B. and Street, J. (1995) *The Schooling of Literacy in Social Literacies*, Longman: London.

Stubbs, M. (1991) 'Educational language planning in England and Wales: Multicultural rhetoric and assimilationist assumptions', in F. Coulmas (ed.) *Language Policy for the European Community: Prospects and Quandaries*, Berlin: Mouton de Gruyter.

Sugimoto, Y. (1997) *An Introduction to Japanese Society*, Cambridge: Cambridge University Press.

Sunderland, J. (1994) (ed.) *Exploring Gender: Questions and Implications for English Language Education*, Hemel Hempstead: Prentice-Hall.

Suzuki, T. (1999) *Nihonjin wa naze eigo ga dekinai ka* [Why cannot Japanese people function in English?], Tokyo: Iwanami Shoten.

Swales, J. (1990) *Genre Analysis*, Cambridge: Cambridge University Press.

Tai, E. (1999) '*Kokugo* and colonial education in Taiwan', *Positions: East Asia Cultures Critique* 7, 2: 503–40.

Tannen, D. (1984) *Conversational Style. Analyzing Talk Among Friends*, Norwood, NJ: Ablex.

——— (1993) 'The relativity of linguistic strategies: rethinking power and solidarity in gender and dominance', in Tannen, D. (ed.) *Gender and Conversational Interaction*, Oxford: Oxford University Press.

Tarone, E. (1997) 'Analyzing IL in natural settings: a sociolinguistic perspective on second-language acquisition', *Culture and Cognition* 30: 137–49.

Tate, N (1996) 'Cultural values and identity', speech made at SCAA Conference on Curriculum, Culture and Society Conference, 7 February 1996.

Taylor, M. (1981) *Caught Between: A Review of Research into the Education of Pupils of West Indian Origin*, Windsor: NFER-Nelson.

Taylor, M. and Hegarty, S. (1985) *The Best of Both Worlds? A Review of Research into the Education of Pupils of South Asian Origin*, Windsor: NFER-Nelson.

The Economist (2000) 23 September Issue. London: The Economist Newspaper Limited.

The Economist Intelligence Unit (1990) 'English in Eastern Europe', Special Report No. 2075, London: The Economist Intelligence Unit.

Thomas, D. (1999) 'Culture, ideology and educational change: the case of English language teachers in Slovakia', unpublished PhD thesis, Institute of Education, University of London.

Thornbury, S. (1999) 'Window-dressing or cross-dressing in the EFL sub-culture', *Folio* 5, 2: 15–17.

Thorne, S. (1999) 'An activity theoretical analysis of foreign language electronic discourse', unpublished PhD dissertation, University of California, Berkeley, CA.

——— (2000a) 'Second language acquisition theory and the truth(s) about relativity', in J. P. Lantolf (ed.) *Sociocultural Theory and Second Language Learning*, Oxford: Oxford University Press.

——— (2000b) 'Beyond bounded activity systems: heterogeneous cultures in instructional uses of persistent conversation', *Proceedings of the Thirty-Third Annual Hawaii International Conference on System Sciences* (CD-ROM), IEEE Computer Society, Los Alamitos, CA.

Tomlinson, J. (1999) *Globalization and Culture*, Cambridge: Polity.

Tosi, A. and Leung, C. (eds) (1999) *Rethinking Language Education*, London: CILT.

Tsuda, Y. (1990) *Eigo shihai no kôzô* [Structures of English domination], Tokyo: Daisan Shokan.

——— (1998) 'Eigo shihai kenkyû: Sono dôkô to hôkôsei' [Studies on the domination of English: Its past and future directions], in Y. Tsuda (ed.) *Nihonjin to eigo: Eigo-ka suru nihon no gakusai-teki kenkyû* [The Japanese People and English: Japanese academic studies being Anglicized], Kyoto: International Research Center for Japanese Studies.

Turkle, S. (1995) *Life on the Screen: Identity in the Age of the Internet*, New York: Simon & Schuster.

Van Ek, J. A. (1976) *Significance of the Threshold Level in the Early Teaching of Modern Languages*, Strasbourg: The Council of Europe.

van Lier, L. (2000) 'From input to affordance: Social-interactive learning from an ecological perspective', in J. P. Lantolf (ed.) *Sociocultural Theory and Second Language Learning*, Oxford: Oxford University Press

Von Elek, T. and Oskasson, M. (1973) *Teaching Foreign Language Grammar to Adults: A Comparative Study*, Stockholm: Almquist & Wiksell.

Wada, K. (1999) 'Eigo-ka ni okeru kokusai rikai kyôiku' [Teaching international understanding in teaching English], *Eigo Kôiku, Bessatsu* [The English Teachers' Magazine: Special Issue] 48, 3.

Wajnryb, R. (1996) 'Death, taxes, and jeopardy: systematic omissions in EFL texts, or life was never meant to be an adjacency pair', ELICOS plenary delivered in Sydney, Australia.

Wallace, C. (1988) *Learning to Read in a Multicultural Society: the Social Context of Second Language Literacy*, Hemel Hempstead: Prentice-Hall.

—— (1992) 'Critical literacy awareness in the EFL classroom', in N. Fairclough (ed.) *Critical Language Awareness*, London: Longman.

—— (1999) 'Critical language awareness: key principles for a course in critical reading', *Language Awareness* 8, 2: 98–110.

—— (2001) 'Critical literacy in the second language classroom: power and control', in B. Comber and A. Simpson (eds) *Negotiating Critical Literacies in Classrooms*. Mahwah, NJ: Lawrence Erlbaum.

Warschauer, M. (1996) 'Comparing face-to-face and electronic discussion in the second language classroom', *CALICO Journal* 13, 2: 7–26.

—— (1998) 'Online learning in sociocultural context', *Anthropology and Education Quarterly*, 29/1: 68–88.

—— (1999) *Electronic Literacies. Language, Culture, and Power in Online Education*, Mahwah, NJ: Lawrence Erlbaum.

Warschauer, M. and Kern, R. (eds) (2000) *Network-based Language Teaching: Concepts and Practice*, Cambridge: Cambridge University Press.

Watanabe, K. (1995) 'Wagakuni ni okeru gaikokugo (eigo) ka kyôiku no genjô to kadai' [The current status and issues in foreign language (English) education in Japan], *Nihongogaku* [Japanese Language Studies], 14 June: 66–73.

Waters, M. (1995) *Globalization*, London: Routledge.

Watson, M. and McGregor, R. Asylum Statistics United Kingdom (1998) *Home Office Statistical Bulletin* 10/99.

Watson-Gegeo, K. A. (1988) 'Ethnography in ESL: defining the essentials', *TESOL Quarterly* 22, 4: 575–92.

Wells, G. and Chang-Wells, G. L. (1992) *Constructing Knowledge Together: Classrooms as Centers of Inquiry and Literacy*, Portsmouth NH: Heinemann.

Wenden, A. (1991) *Learner Strategies for Learner Autonomy*, New York: Prentice-Hall.

Wickramasuriya, S. (1981) 'James de Alwis and second language teaching in Sri Lanka', *Navasilu* 4, 11–29.

Williams, R. (1983) *Keywords: A Vocabulary of Culture and Society*, London: Fontana.

Willis, J. (1996) *A Framework for Task-based Learning*, London: Longman.

Yoshino, K. (1992) *Cultural Nationalism in Contemporary Japan*, London: Routledge.

—— (1997) *Bunka nashonarizumu no shakai gaku* [Sociology of cultural nationalism], Nagoya: Nagoya Daigaku Shuppan Kai.

—— (1998) 'Gurôbaru-ka to nashonarizumu: Ibunka komyunikêshon o megutte' [Globalism and nationalism: On cross-cultural communication], in Y. Saeki, I, Kurosaki, M. Sato, T. Tanaka, S. Hamada and H. Fujita (eds) *Iwanami kôza gendai no kyôiku: Kiki to Kaikaku 11, Kokusaika jidai no kyôiku* [Iwanami Seminar Series, Contemporary Education: Crisis and reform, 11, Education for the age of internationalization], Tokyo: Iwanami Shoten.

Yule, G. (1997) *Referential Communication Tasks*, Mahwah, NJ: Lawrence Erlbaum.

Index